The Beginner's KetoDiet Cookbook

OVER 100 DELICIOUS
WHOLE FOOD, LOW-CARB RECIPES
FOR GETTING IN
THE KETOGENIC ZONE,
BREAKING YOUR WEIGHT-LOSS
PLATEAU, AND LIVING
KETO FOR LIFE

MARTINA SLAJEROVA

Author of *The KetoDiet Cookbook* and
Quick Keto Meals in 30 Minutes or Less

FAIR WINDS

Brimming with creative inspiration, how-to projects, and useful information to enrich your everyday life, Quarto Knows is a favorite destination for those pursuing their interests and passions. Visit our site and dig deeper with our books into your area of interest: Quarto Creates, Quarto Cooks, Quarto Homes, Quarto Lives, Quarto Drives, Quarto Explores, Quarto Gifts, or Quarto Kids.

© 2018 Quarto Publishing Group USA Inc.
Text © 2018 Martina Slajerova
Photography © 2018 Quarto Publishing Group USA Inc.

First Published in 2018 by Fair Winds Press, an imprint of The Quarto Group,
100 Cummings Center, Suite 265-D, Beverly, MA 01915, USA.
T (978) 282-9590 F (978) 283-2742 QuartoKnows.com

Fair Winds Press titles are also available at discount for retail, wholesale, promotional, and bulk purchase. For details, contact the Special Sales Manager by email at specialsales@quarto.com or by mail at The Quarto Group, Attn: Special Sales Manager, 401 Second Avenue North, Suite 310, Minneapolis, MN 55401, USA.

22 21 20 19 18   3 4 5 6 7

ISBN: 978-1-59233-815-3

Digital edition published in 2018
eISBN: 978-1-63159-568-4

Library of Congress Cataloging-in-Publication Data available

Interior Design and Page Layout: Rita Sowins / Sowins Design
Photography: Martina Slajerova

Printed in Canada

The information in this book is for educational purposes only. It is not intended to replace the advice of a physician or medical practitioner. Please see your health-care provider before beginning any new health program.

To Nikos, my soul mate and the best
partner I could have ever wished for.
You helped me turn my passion
into a job I love. Thank you for always
being there for me!

To my family and friends who have
always believed in me.
They have made the biggest impression
on who I am today.

Finally, I'd like to dedicate this book to
all my amazing readers.
Thank you so much for your continuous
love and support!

Contents

Chapter 1: Escape the Diet Dogma:
The Science Behind the Ketogenic Lifestyle ... 6

Chapter 2: Keto Break-the-Fast Dishes ... 51

Chapter 3: Light Dishes and Appetizers ... 75

Chapter 4: Nourishing Soups and
Refreshing Salads ... 89

Chapter 5: Quick and Easy Lunchbox Dishes ... 113

Chapter 6: Energy-Boosting, Fat-Fueled
Dinners ... 133

Chapter 7: Drinks and Desserts ... 185

References ... 203
About the Author ... 204
Acknowledgments ... 204
Index ... 205

Chapter 1

Escape the Diet Dogma:

The Science Behind the Ketogenic Lifestyle

We Westerners have been harming our health for decades. How? By following dietary recommendations based on bad science. We've been avoiding saturated fat and cholesterol for fear of increasing our risk of heart disease. We've been told that eating five small meals a day is better for you than eating three regular meals. We replaced saturated fats with carbohydrates, and we've started eating breakfast cereals instead of eggs in the mornings. And you know the rest of the story: we ended up with an obesity epidemic, plus an increase in diagnoses of type 2 diabetes, cardiovascular disease, lipid problems, inflammation, and hypertension—all of which are symptoms of what is known as the metabolic syndrome.

But the good news is that times are changing. Up-to-date research, including a review of studies from 2015 published by the *British Medical Journal*, shows that saturated fat and dietary cholesterol are not our enemies. In fact, they actually help maintain healthy cholesterol levels and balanced hormones. Instead, sugar and processed foods that are high in carbohydrates and inflammatory oils are our true adversaries. And I'm not just talking about obviously unhealthy foods, such as white sugar, pizza, and fries. The culprits include all those "good-for-you" cereals, whole-grain granola bars, low-fat yogurts, and even tropical fruits, which are often marketed as "health foods" that will keep your heart fit and your body trim.

The truth is that eating high-sugar foods such as these creates a vicious cycle: if you eat high-sugar foods like these regularly, it's likely that you'll need to eat five times each day because you're always hungry. The more sugar you eat, the higher your blood sugar and insulin become, and the result is inevitably a sugar crash—which makes you crave sugary snacks even more. This can cause chronically high blood sugar levels, which eventually leads to insulin resistance and other health issues.

But what if there were a simple solution to the sugar spiral? Well, there is. By limiting the amount of carbohydrates we consume and replacing them with healthy sources of fat, we can stabilize our blood sugar and manage our cravings. It's time to take control of our diets and start eating real food again!

My Story

I changed the way I ate in 2011, when I was diagnosed with Hashimoto's, an autoimmune disease that affects the thyroid. I had no energy, and I found it more and more difficult to maintain a healthy weight. Even though I was taking prescription medication to help control my condition and I was hitting the gym almost every day, I was gaining weight, not losing it. The irony was that, like so many other people, I used to follow what I believed to be a healthy, balanced diet. I avoided most fatty foods in fear of clogging my arteries and putting on weight. I based my diet around whole grains and vegetables, and I limited my intake of animal products. I did exactly what the general dietary recommendations advised: I exercised more and ate less. Still, nothing worked. Finally, I got tired of dieting all the time, and I was determined to regain my health by following a different approach.

That's when I decided to quit sugar, grains, and processed foods, and I started following a whole foods–based ketogenic approach to food. After we witnessed the incredible benefits of low-carb eating firsthand, my partner and I created KetoDiet, a tracking and planning application with hundreds of low-carb recipes. It is now one of the best-selling apps on the App Store and Google Play. Then, in 2012, I launched my KetoDiet blog, which helps more than two million monthly visitors follow a whole foods–based, low-carb, ketogenic lifestyle.

Switching to a keto lifestyle wasn't easy at first. It took some time for me to get used to eating fat and to give up carbs: after all those years of dieting, it was only natural that I was having trouble eating more fat without worrying about consuming all those calories. And to make things even more complicated, there was too much conflicting information available, and I didn't know if I was doing the right thing. But I figured it out for myself.

When I started to eat keto, my cravings went away after just a few weeks. I didn't feel hungry, and I had loads of energy to devote to my busy lifestyle. Best of all, for the first time in years, I didn't even think about food. It was so liberating! So these days, when people ask me which "diet" I follow, I simply reply, "It's just the way I eat every day." That's because—for me, at least—keto isn't a diet: it's a lifestyle. The word "diet" suggests a pattern of eating that's both temporary and difficult to stick with, and that's definitely not the case for my approach to eating keto.

I hope this book will give you some clarity about what a truly healthy diet is, and that you'll be motivated to keep learning, do your own research, and listen to your body. I truly believe that a whole foods–based keto diet that reflects your individual needs has the potential to help you achieve your goals—whether that's long-term weight loss, dealing with certain health conditions, or simply improving your overall well-being.

What Is the Ketogenic Diet?

To understand what the ketogenic diet is and how it works, we need to understand how our bodies use carbohydrates. All carbohydrates from the foods we eat are broken down into glucose, which, in non-keto-adapted individuals, is the body's primary source of energy. If you eat more carbohydrates than your body can use immediately, it will store the excess glucose in the liver and muscles as muscle glycogen, which can be used for energy. But when your glycogen tank is full, your body stores extra glycogen as body fat.

Wait a minute, though. Don't our bodies need carbs? Not really. It's a common myth that we need carbs in order to produce glycogen. While it's true that a small amount of glucose is still needed for some basic metabolic functions, our bodies prefer using ketones as an energy source, according to Jeff Volek, Ph.D., R.D., and Stephen Phinney, M.D., Ph.D., best-selling authors of *The Art and Science of Low Carbohydrate Living*. Compared to our "glycogen tank," which is limited to about 2,000 calories, the capacity of our "fat tank" is more than 40,000 calories. Once you become keto-adapted, your body will shift from glucose metabolism to fat metabolism, and you will experience improved energy levels, enhanced satiety, and reduced cravings. Besides, our bodies can produce glucose on demand for the basic metabolic functions that require it through a process called gluconeogenesis, and this process is fueled by non-carbohydrate sources, especially protein.

And let's not forget about insulin and its role in fat loss. Here's how it works: when you eat a high-carb meal, your body has to produce more insulin in order to keep up with the increased levels of glucose in your bloodstream. Raised insulin levels "lock" fat in the cells and block fat burning—until your insulin drops again and you use fat for fuel. When you are insulin-sensitive, this process works perfectly well, and allows you to maintain balanced blood sugar levels. But with a consistently high carbohydrate intake, it can eventually lead to insulin resistance, high LDL cholesterol, low HDL cholesterol, higher triglyceride levels, increased inflammation—and, in some cases, type 2 diabetes. One 1989 study named insulin resistance as one of four cardiovascular risk factors: a "deadly quartet" including hypertension, hypertriglyceridemia, and low HDL cholesterol.

All of this means that any carbs you consume raise your insulin level, which normally leads to increased energy levels or to storing fat. But when you eat fewer carbs, your body requires less insulin to regulate your blood sugar levels: as a result, it uses more fat for energy and stores less of it.

Three Phases of a Whole Foods-Based Ketogenic Diet

✳ PHASE 1: INDUCTION PHASE (3 TO 4 WEEKS) ✳

Keto induction refers to the initial phase of the ketogenic diet, which occurs after you significantly reduce your carbohydrate intake to 20 to 25 grams of daily net carbs (that is, your total carbohydrate intake minus fiber), or even less, in order to enter a metabolic state known as ketosis. The exact amount of carbohydrates required to enter ketosis is different for each person, but the presence of ketones in your body, which shows that your body is burning fat for fuel, typically takes 1 to 3 days. A successful induction phase will significantly increase your chances of achieving your goals, so this phase is an especially important one.

TIPS FOR SUCCESS

Switching to keto can be quite challenging, but it'll take just a few weeks for you to become keto-adapted and to enjoy the (many!) benefits of low-carb eating. Here are some tips for a successful keto induction:

1. Keep it simple. It's normal to feel overwhelmed when you start following a keto diet. To minimize failures, you'll want to keep your diet simple. Stick with foods that are naturally low in carbs. Prepare recipes with just a few common ingredients, and avoid getting bogged down in making complicated meals. Once you get used to low-carb eating, you can start experimenting—and having fun!—with more challenging recipes.

2. Be sure to get enough protein and fat. If you don't eat enough protein and fat, you'll end up hungry, and that'll stall your progress. For more on protein intake, see Protein on a Keto Diet (page 16); for more on fat intake, see The Filler Concept (page 18).

3. Avoid foods that may trigger cravings and/or overeating. Before you introduce low-carb sweeteners, your aim is to get your palate used to low-carb eating. You should avoid potential triggers such as low-carb treats (see page 35, Eating Too Much Of . . .). Other foods that may trigger cravings are keto substitutes for breads (page 48, Garlic and Herb Focaccia), crackers (Multiseed Keto Crackers, page 84), and nuts and cheese, especially if you're using them as snacks. High-fat treats such as fat bombs are usually well tolerated, provided you can stop at one piece. Some people may need to avoid nuts and dairy altogether, while others can use them as an ingredient in a main dish. You'll need to experiment to see what works best for you. I've marked the recipes throughout this book that are most suitable for the induction phase of the ketogenic diet.

4. Minimize or avoid snacking. Instead, keep hunger at bay by sticking to three main meals with adequate protein and fat. Needing to snack may be a sign that your last meal wasn't nutritious enough. Also, people with hypoglycemia issues may need to introduce small, high-fat, moderate-protein snacks between meals.

KETOSIS AND MEASURING KETONES

Nutritional ketosis is achieved when your blood ketones clock in between 0.5 and 3.0 mM. There are several ways to measure ketones. If you choose to do so, the most reliable way is to use a blood ketone meter, which measures the level of beta-hydroxybutyrate—the first ketone body produced in the liver during the fasting state—in the bloodstream. You don't necessarily need to measure your ketones if your goal is to lose body fat or maintain a healthy weight, but if you're following a restricted ketogenic diet in order to deal with health conditions such as epilepsy or cancer, measuring ketones is recommended in order to experience the full benefits of the diet.

Or, if you're new to the ketogenic diet, tracking your ketone levels may help you understand how the foods you eat affect you. Because I've been following a low-carb diet since 2011 and I know what to eat and avoid, I rarely measure my ketone levels. Besides, there are other ways to determine whether you're becoming a fat burner. As you get keto-adapted, the symptoms of keto flu—that is, the result of carbohydrate withdrawal, symptoms of which include headaches, muscle cramps, and fatigue—will dissipate. You won't need to snack; you'll stop craving carbs; and eventually you'll find it easy to skip meals (see page 31, Intermittent Fasting). If you exercise, you'll notice an improvement in your performance—even without carb-loading.

If you do decide to measure your ketone levels, keep in mind that they fluctuate throughout the day. (They are typically higher in the evening and lower in the morning.) To ensure comparable results, be sure to measure your ketones consistently at the same time and under the same circumstances (e.g. 2 hours after a meal) each day. Apart from what you last ate, ketone levels can also be affected by the type of physical activity that you do prior to measuring. For women, fluctuations in hormone levels throughout the month will affect ketone readings, too.

DON'T CONFUSE KETOSIS WITH KETOACIDOSIS

While nutritional ketosis is perfectly safe, ketoacidosis is an indicator of serious health issues such as type 2 diabetes and alcoholism. In ketoacidosis, your body's ketone levels are three to five times higher than when you're in ketosis as a result of following a ketogenic diet. Plus, ketoacidosis is accompanied by high glucose levels.

✱ PHASE 2: KETO ADAPTATION (DURATION DEPENDS ON YOUR INDIVIDUAL GOALS) ✱

KETOSIS VS. KETO ADAPTATION

While it takes about 1 to 3 days to enter ketosis, it can take up to 4 weeks for your body to become keto-adapted, because it's a complex process and involves most of the body's systems. The major adaptations occur in the body's tissues, especially the brain, liver, kidneys, and muscles. That's why you may feel tired or have symptoms of "keto flu" (see page 27, Keto Flu and Electrolytes) during the first few weeks of following a ketogenic diet. This is because your body is becoming accustomed to using fatty acids and ketones as its main sources of energy. This switch from glucose to fatty acids and ketones will take at least 3 to 4 weeks—or it may even be months before your body learns how to use ketones effectively. It's worth it, though: once you become keto-adapted, your primary source of energy will shift from glucose toward fat and ketones, and your energy levels will be restored.

INITIAL WEIGHT LOSS

Your hormone levels change during this phase, and as a result of depleted glycogen levels, your body retains less water. So quick weight loss isn't uncommon in the first few days of keto adaptation. Some of this is water weight, because your body loses glycogen during the first few days of the diet. This is because one molecule of glycogen attracts three to four molecules of water, so your body excretes water as it loses glycogen. After you have depleted your glycogen stores, the process of ketosis begins and you'll start to lose body fat.

HOW TO BEAT COMMON KETO-ADAPTATION ISSUES

Keto adaptation is a lengthy process, and you might encounter a few bumps along the road. Here are some tips for beating a few of the most common ones.

1. Keto flu. During the induction phase, your body will need more electrolytes (that is, foods high in sodium, potassium, and magnesium), or you may experience flu-like symptoms. To ease these symptoms, eat foods high in electrolytes (see page 27, Keto Flu and Electrolytes), make some Electrolyte Agua Fresca (page 186), and take magnesium supplements (see page 28).

Avoid Constipation

Eat foods high in both soluble and insoluble fiber, such as nuts and seeds, leafy greens, and avocado. If you eat psyllium, flax, and/or chia—all of which are sources of insoluble fiber—make sure you drink plenty of liquids with them. Try the PB & Jelly Chia Parfaits on page 70. Add medium-chain triglycerides (MCTs) oil to your drinks and smoothies: MCTs have laxative effects. Try my Superfood Smoothies on page 187.

---

2. Digestive issues. When switching to low-carb eating, some people experience digestive issues. Although they are temporary, they can be quite unpleasant. In case of diarrhea or constipation, stay hydrated by drinking plenty of water or herbal tea and increase your electrolyte intake. Supplementing your diet with probiotics (see page 27, Recommended Supplements), and eating probiotic-rich foods such as sauerkraut and kimchi may also help.

Prevent Diarrhea

- Eat foods high in soluble fiber, such as non-starchy vegetables. Limit your consumption of foods high in insoluble fiber, such as nuts and seeds.
- Watch out for foods or supplements that may be causing loose stools, such as magnesium supplements. The upper limit for magnesium supplements is 350 mg per day.
- Consume less than 80 percent of your calories from fat if you experience digestive issues. If you use MCT oil and coconut oil, avoid them altogether until the issues go away, and then reintroduce them in small amounts, such as 1 teaspoon/5 ml per day.
- Avoid coffee and other sources of caffeine for a few days. Caffeine is a stimulant and has a diuretic effect, which will make the symptoms worse.
- Be sure to avoid dairy if you are lactose intolerant.

3. Cravings. First of all, make sure you're getting enough protein (see page 16) and electrolytes (see above): a lack of protein in your diet will make you hungrier. If you're still hungry, a good way to beat cravings is to have a high-fat snack, such as half an avocado, or one fat bomb (try the Halva Stacks on page 200).

4. Hypoglycemia. Follow the same tips for beating cravings, above. Also, try splitting your three daily meals into five smaller meals to keep your blood sugar stable.

5. "Keto breath." Fruity "ketogenic breath" doesn't affect everyone who follows a ketogenic diet, but if it does, drink lots of water and mint tea and make sure you eat plenty of foods rich in electrolytes. Avoid chewing gum and mints, though: they may kick you out of ketosis due to hidden carbs. And remember that keto breath isn't forever: once you get keto-adapted, it'll go away.

6. Insomnia. This side effect is pretty rare, but you may have difficulty falling asleep once you switch to keto. If so, follow the tips for stress and lack of sleep on page 34.

✳ PHASE 3: MAINTENANCE (A LIFELONG WAY OF EATING) ✳

Whether your goal is weight loss, addressing health issues, or improving your overall well-being, once you reach your target, you should transition to a maintenance mode. For most people, this is a natural process of eating to satiety. For others, weight maintenance may require more attention, and it's good to know how much you should be eating in order to maintain a healthy weight: when you're in weight maintenance, more of your daily calories will come from fat than during the keto adaptation phase.

Remember that keto isn't about losing weight at any cost; it's about adopting a healthier lifestyle. And that includes not being stressed out about your diet. So, don't let your diet rule your life! The aim is to follow an approach that works for you in the long term. This is the time to have an occasional treat or an alcoholic drink. Just don't make it an everyday habit. I do this myself: there are a few occasions during which I let myself eat almost anything—even more carbs than usual! This makes the keto approach much easier to stick with in the long term.

Carbohydrates on a Keto Diet

You should aim for no more than 50 grams of total carbohydrates (20 to 30 grams of net carbohydrates) per day, mostly from non-starchy vegetables, avocados, and nuts. Everyone tolerates a slightly different carbohydrate level, and you'll need to experiment to find out what works best for you.

✱ TOTAL CARBS OR NET CARBS? ✱

Net carbohydrates are total carbohydrates minus the fiber, and there are two types of fiber: soluble and insoluble. Insoluble fiber has no calories, as it simply passes through your colon and helps bulk up your stool. Soluble fiber dissolves in water and forms a gel that slows down the movement of food through your digestive tract, which can help you feel full. Even though soluble fiber provides a few calories, it doesn't raise blood glucose levels and won't kick you out of ketosis. In fact, up-to-date research, including a 2012 study published in the *Gut Microbes Journal*, suggests that soluble fiber may actually improve blood sugar regulation.

But you'll need to watch out for low-carb products with hidden carbs from blood sugar–spiking ingredients such as sorbitol or maltitol, and other ingredients such as dextrose and/or maltodextrin. Although their listed net carbs are low, they may kick you out of ketosis. Steer clear of these ingredients, and try to get most of your carbs from whole foods such as non-starchy vegetables, nuts, seeds, avocados, and berries. This way, you won't need to worry about hidden carbs.

While counting net carbs works well for most people who want to lose weight and improve their overall health, counting total carbs may be a better option for managing a disease, such as cancer, epilepsy, or Alzheimer's, in which carbohydrate restriction is more severe in order to maximize results.

SOURCE—VEGETABLES & FRUIT	SERVING SIZE	TOTAL CARBS (grams per serving)	NET CARBS (grams per serving)
Endive	½ small (75 g/2.7 oz)	2.6	0.2
Arugula	2 cups (20 g/0.7 oz)	0.7	0.4
Watercress, chopped	2 cups (68 g/2.4 oz)	0.9	0.5
Onion, spring, scallion	1 medium (15 g/0.5 oz)	1.1	0.7
Spinach, fresh	4 cups (120 g/4.2 oz)	4.3	1.7
Lettuce, romaine, shredded	3 cups (141 g/5 oz)	4.7	1.7
Lettuce, soft green, shredded	3 cups (108 g/3.8 oz)	3.1	1.7
Coconut, fresh	28 g/1 oz	4.3	1.7
Peppers, green bell	½ medium (60 g/2.1 oz)	2.8	1.7
Kale, dark leaf	2½ cups (125 g/4.4 oz)	5.6	1.8
Celery stalk	2 large (128 g/4.5 oz)	3.8	1.8
Onion, red	½ small (30 g/1.1 oz)	2.4	2.0
Bean sprouts	1 cup (50 g/1.8 oz)	3.0	2.0
Shallots	½ small (15 g/0.5 oz)	2.5	2.0
Radishes, sliced	1 cup (116 g/4.1 oz)	3.9	2.1
Lettuce, Little Gem, shredded	2 cups (144 g/5.1 oz)	3.6	2.2
Onion, yellow (brown)	½ small (35 g/1.2 oz)	2.9	2.2
Cucumber	1 small (150 g/5.3 oz)	3.3	2.3
Peppers, red bell	½ medium (60 g/2.1 oz)	3.6	2.3
Artichoke, globe or French, canned	1 cup (84 g/3 oz)	9.6	2.4
Lettuce, iceberg, shredded	2 cups (144 g/5.1 oz)	4.3	2.6
Onion, white	½ small (35 g/1.2 oz)	3.3	2.7
Avocado, California	1 medium (150 g/5.3 oz)	12.9	2.7
Asparagus	1 small bunch (150 g/5.3 oz)	5.9	2.7
Swiss chard, chopped	4 cups (144 g/5.1 oz)	5.3	3.0
Blackberries, fresh	½ cup (72 g/2.5oz)	6.9	3.1
Mushrooms, cremini, sliced	1½ cups (105 g/3.7 oz)	4.2	3.2

SOURCE—VEGETABLES & FRUIT	SERVING SIZE	TOTAL CARBS (grams per serving)	NET CARBS (grams per serving)
Tomatoes	1 medium (123 g/4.3 oz)	4.8	3.3
Raspberries, fresh	½ cup (62 g/2.2 oz)	7.4	3.3
Cabbage, green, shredded	1½ cups (105 g/3.7 oz)	6.0	3.4
Pumpkin, winter squash, diced	½ cup (58 g/2 oz)	3.8	3.5
Cabbage, white, shredded	1½ cups (105 g/3.7 oz)	5.9	3.5
Kohlrabi, diced	1 cup (135 g/4.8 oz)	8.4	3.5
Fennel, sliced	1 cup (87 g/3.1 oz)	6.4	3.7
Zucchini	1 medium (200 g/7.1 oz)	6.2	4.2
Mushrooms, shiitake	2 cups (100 g/3.5 oz)	6.8	4.3
Lettuce, radicchio, shredded	3 cups (120 g/4.2 oz)	5.4	4.3
Strawberries, fresh, halved	½ cup (76 g/2.7 oz)	5.9	4.3
Okra, chopped	1 cup (100 g/3.5 oz)	7.5	4.5
Eggplant	½ medium (150 g/5.3 oz)	8.9	4.5
Kale, curly, chopped	2½ cups (125 g/4.4 oz)	7.0	4.5
Blueberries, fresh	¼ cup (38 g/1.3 oz)	5.5	4.6
Cauliflower, chopped	1½ cups (161 g/5.7 oz)	8.1	4.8
Broccoli, raw, chopped	1½ cups (137 g/4.8 oz)	9.0	5.5
Leeks, raw	½ medium (45 g/1.6 oz)	6.4	5.6
Cabbage, red, shredded	1½ cups (105 g/3.7 oz)	7.8	5.6
Brussels sprouts, halved	1¼ cups (110 g/3.9 oz)	9.9	5.6
Collard greens, chopped	4 cups (144 g/5.1 oz)	7.8	5.8
Celeriac, chopped	½ cup (78 g/2.8 oz)	7.2	5.8
Spaghetti squash, cooked	¾ cup (116 g/4.1 oz)	7.5	5.8
Turnips, diced	1 cup (130 g/4.6 oz)	8.3	6.0
Rutabaga, diced	¾ cup (105/3.7 oz)	9.0	6.6

Protein on a Keto Diet

Like fats, proteins play an important role in a healthy keto diet. You should always buy the best-quality protein sources you can afford. If your budget allows it, opt for organic eggs and grass-fed, humanely-raised meat. Grass-fed beef contains more micronutrients and more omega-3 fatty acids. Plus, pasture-raised and grass-fed animals have a much better quality of life compared to those kept in large industrial facilities.

Avoid farmed fish, too, and opt for wild-caught, locally sourced, sustainable fish that's low in mercury. According to the Seafood Watch Best Choices list, some of the best options are Pacific sardines, Atlantic mackerel, freshwater Coho salmon, Alaskan salmon, canned salmon, Albacore tuna, and sablefish/black cod. To learn more about healthy, sustainable fish, visit seafoodwatch.org and download the free Seafood Watch app.

You can use canned fish, but when you're using canned products of any kind, such as tuna or coconut milk, avoid BPA-lined cans. BPA has been linked to many negative health effects, such as impaired thyroid function and cancer.

✱ WHY IS PROTEIN INTAKE SO IMPORTANT? ✱

Eating sufficient protein is vital, especially if you're trying to lose weight. Remember that protein is the most sating macronutrient; it will help you feel less hungry and you'll consume fewer calories. How much is enough? According to Volek and Phinney, you'll need between 0.6 and 1 gram of protein per pound (1.3 to 2.2 grams per kilogram) of lean body mass. In most cases, this translates to 65 to 80 grams of protein per day, and sometimes even more. The exact amount of protein you need is highly individual: it depends on your gender, lean body mass, and activity level.

That said, don't obsess over your protein intake. Eating slightly more protein won't kick you out of ketosis or impair your progress. Studies in the *Journal of the American Physiological Society* and *The Journal of Clinical Endocrinology & Metabolism* have shown that you'd have to eat huge amounts of protein to cause your body to go into gluconeogenesis (that is, to cause it to convert protein to glucose), so it's not a major concern. That's why it's imperative to eat an adequate amount of protein if your aim is to lose body fat.

Still, this doesn't mean that you should actively overeat protein. It's not a particularly efficient fuel source and too much of it may raise your insulin levels. If you are insulin-resistant or diabetic, be aware that not all protein sources are equal, and some, such as whey protein, will cause greater insulin responses than others. Also, people who suffer from diabetic nephropathy, a type of kidney disease caused by diabetes, will need to eat less protein.

SOURCES OF PROTEIN	SERVING SIZE	PROTEIN (per serving)	FAT (per serving)	TOTAL CARBS (per serving)	NET CARBS (per serving)
Sea bream	142 g/5 oz	34.4	6.7	0.0	0.0
Wild game, elk, raw	142 g/5 oz	31.0	12.5	0.0	0.0
Wild game, venison, raw	142 g/5 oz	30.5	3.8	0.0	0.0
Wild game, buffalo, raw	142 g/5 oz	30.4	1.8	0.0	0.0
Chicken breasts, boneless, raw	142 g/5 oz	30.1	3.7	0.0	0.0
Pork loin, raw	142 g/5 oz	29.1	12.8	0.0	0.0
Liver, calf, raw	142 g/5 oz	29.0	5.1	5.5	5.5
Salmon, king, wild, raw	142 g/5 oz	28.8	16.6	0.0	0.0
Sardines, raw	142 g/5 oz	28.4	9.9	0.0	0.0
Tuna, canned	142 g/5 oz	27.5	1.4	0.0	0.0
Chicken thighs, boneless, raw	142 g/5 oz	27.4	5.8	0.0	0.0
Sea bass	142 g/5 oz	26.8	5.3	0.0	0.0
Beef, rib eye, raw	142 g/5 oz	26.7	28.1	0.0	0.0
Mackerel, raw	142 g/5 oz	26.4	19.7	0.0	0.0
Chicken, whole, skin on, raw	142 g/5 oz	26.4	22.2	0.0	0.0
Mahimahi, white-flesh fish, raw	142 g/5 oz	26.3	1.0	0.0	0.0
Lamb chops, raw	142 g/5 oz	26.0	20.4	0.0	0.0
Herring, raw	142 g/5 oz	25.6	12.8	0.0	0.0
Cod, white-flesh fish, raw	142 g/5 oz	25.3	1.0	0.0	0.0
Turkey, minced	142 g/5 oz	24.0	17.8	0.0	0.0
Liver, chicken, raw	142 g/5 oz	24.0	6.8	1.0	1.0
Crabmeat, cooked	113 g/4 oz	21.5	2.3	0.0	0.0
Mozzarella cheese, fresh	85 g/3 oz	20.7	13.5	2.4	2.4
Monkfish, white-flesh fish, raw	142 g/5 oz	20.6	2.1	0.0	0.0
Prawns, raw	125 g/4.4 oz	18.0	1.0	0.5	0.5
Mozzarella cheese, low moisture, shredded	½ cup (57 g/2 oz)	14.8	11.4	2.2	2.2
Yogurt, plain, 5% fat	½ cup (125 g/4.4 oz)	11.3	6.3	4.8	4.8
Hemp seeds	28 g/1 oz	9.8	14.0	2.8	0.9
Pumpkin seeds	28 g/1 oz	8.5	13.7	3.0	1.3
Cheese, feta, crumbled	⅓ cup (50 g/1.8 oz)	7.1	10.7	2.1	2.1
Cheese, Cheddar	28 g/1 oz	7.0	9.3	0.4	0.4
Ricotta	¼ cup (60 g/2.1 oz)	6.8	7.8	1.8	1.8
Eggs	1 large (50 g/1.8 oz)	6.3	4.8	0.4	0.4

Fats on a Keto Diet

Following a keto diet isn't just about getting the numbers right. It's also about eating high-quality foods and adopting a healthier lifestyle. Fat is the primary nutrient in a ketogenic diet, and you should pay extra attention to it. Unhealthy fats can do as much damage as excessive carbohydrates.

�֍ HEALTHY COOKING FATS ✖

Use oils and fats high in saturated fats (SFA) such as pastured lard, grass-fed beef tallow, chicken fat, duck fat, goose fat, clarified butter or ghee, butter, virgin coconut oil, and sustainably sourced palm kernel oil.

✖ FATS SUITABLE FOR LIGHT COOKING AND COLD USE ✖

Oils high in monounsaturated fats (MUFA), such as extra-virgin olive oil, avocado oil, and macadamia nut oil, are best for cold use, stir-fries, or for adding after cooking.

✖ FATS ONLY SUITABLE FOR COLD USE ✖

Oils high in polyunsaturated fats (PUFA) are only suitable for cold use or for adding after cooking. These oils are best used in salad dressings and mayonnaise (page 42), and they include nut and seed oils such as walnut, flaxseed, sesame seed, and pumpkin seed oils. Almond and hazelnut oils are good sources of both MUFA and PUFA. When you use oils high in omega-6 fatty acids, increase your intake of omega-3 fatty acids, especially from animal sources.

✖ ALWAYS AVOID ✖

Not all fats are suitable for a healthy, low-carb diet and, unfortunately, the most commonly used oils are unhealthy. Avoid vegetable oils and shortening; hydrogenated and partially hydrogenated oils; margarine; and sunflower, canola, safflower, soy, cottonseed, and grapeseed oils. They are highly processed, inflammatory, and prone to oxidation, which promotes free radicals that have the potential to damage cells, muscles, tissue, and organs.

✖ THE "FILLER" CONCEPT ✖

When following a ketogenic diet, you should be eating to satiety. To do this, aim for an adequate protein intake (see page 16, Protein on a Keto Diet) and use fat as a "filler" to sate your appetite while keeping net carbs low, at 20 to 30 grams. Most people who eat to satiety don't need to count calories on the keto diet because they don't feel hungry and are unlikely to overeat. Listen to your body and only eat when you are hungry, even if it's only one meal a day. Don't let others dictate what you eat or how often you should eat it. (If you find that this isn't working for you, see Not Using Fat as Filler on page 33.)

The KetoDiet Food List

✳ EAT ✳

All of the following foods can be part of your ketogenic lifestyle.

PROTEIN
- Choose grass-fed and wild animal sources (outdoor-reared pork, wild-caught fish, and grass-fed beef), and include organ meats (liver, kidneys, and heart).
- If you are not sensitive to dairy, include organic eggs and raw, full-fat dairy (yogurt, cheese, cream, butter, and ghee).

FATS
- Pasture-raised lard, grass-fed beef tallow, chicken fat, duck fat, goose fat, clarified butter/ghee, butter, MCT oil, and virgin coconut oil are high in saturated fats and heat-stable.
- Monounsaturated fats (MUFA), including heart-healthy avocado, macadamia, and extra-virgin olive oils, are ideal for light cooking and cold use. Other sources of MUFA are almond oil and hazelnut oil.
- Choose animal sources of omega-3 fatty acids, especially EPA and DHA (fatty fish and seafood, grass-fed beef).
- Nut and seed oils are for cold use only, and they should be used sparingly (most are high in omega-6 fatty acids).
- Other sources of healthy fats include nuts and seeds (macadamia nuts, pecans, almonds, walnuts, hazelnuts, pine nuts, Brazil nuts, flaxseed, pumpkin seeds, sesame seeds, sunflower seeds, and hemp seeds), nut and seed butters, coconut, avocado, and cacao butter. Beware of cashew nuts and pistachios: they're relatively high in carbs.

NON-STARCHY VEGETABLES
When it comes to leafy greens, the darker the leaves, the better! Include a variety of greens in your diet, such as spinach, arugula, watercress, Swiss chard, kale, collards, bok choy, lettuce, and beet greens.

It's also important to include other low-carb vegetables such as cabbage, cauliflower, Brussels sprouts, zucchini, broccoli, tomatoes, peppers, radishes, daikon, okra, turnips, rutabaga, cucumber, celery, eggplant, asparagus, pumpkin, spaghetti squash, kohlrabi, sea vegetables, and mushrooms.

LOW-CARB FRUITS
Fruit can add sweetness or acidity to your meals. Choose blackberries, raspberries, strawberries, blueberries, lemon, lime, rhubarb, coconut, and avocado.

Wondering when you should buy organic? Not all fruits and vegetables need to be labeled organic to be safe to eat. To find out which ones are worth paying for, check out the Dirty Dozen list (www.ewg.org). If it's on the list, always buy organic.

EXTRAS: CONDIMENTS AND PANTRY STAPLES

- Fermented foods, such as sauerkraut, kimchi, and kombucha, are a good addition to your diet. It's best to make your own if you can.
- Other staples include: unsweetened nut or seed milk (such as almond or cashew); coconut milk and coconut cream; quality protein powder (without additives), gelatin, and collagen.
- A complete pantry may also include: vinegars (apple cider, coconut vinegar, and wine); coconut aminos; fish sauce; sugar-free tomato products (paste, canned tomatoes, tomato sauce); gluten-free baking powder, baking soda, cream of tartar, etc.
- If you prefer additional sweetness, choose healthy, low-carb sweeteners, such as stevia, erythritol, Swerve, monk fruit extract, and yacon syrup (see page 21, Sweeteners).
- To help you stay hydrated, reach for tea and coffee, still and sparkling water, and Electrolyte Agua Fresca (page 186).
- To add flavor and spice, use dark chocolate (minimum 85% cocoa, ideally sugar-free) and raw cacao powder or unsweetened cocoa powder (Dutch process), unsweetened coconut chips, nori seaweed (including nori chips), lemon zest, lime zest, and orange zest, all herbs and spices, and aromatics such as ginger, turmeric, onion, and garlic.
- In addition to store-bought kelp noodles and shirataki noodles, you can also make some of your own keto staples, such as bone broth and chicken stock, pesto, marinara sauce, and mayonnaise (see page 40, The Basics: Keto Staples Plus Two Recipes).
- Other common condiments and snacks are Dijon mustard, sugar-free ketchup, barbecue sauce, harissa paste, curry paste, vanilla extract, Sriracha sauce, pickles, kale chips, beef jerky, and pork rinds, ideally homemade (You can find these and lots more recipes on my blog: https://ketodietapp.com/Blog/category/Recipes.)
- Drink alcohol in moderation (only dry wine and spirits can be consumed in small amounts, but should be avoided for weight loss). Alcohol used for cooking and vanilla extract are acceptable.

✳ AVOID ✳

- Avoid all grains, even whole-grain versions (wheat, rye, oats, corn, barley, millet, bulgur, sorghum, rice, amaranth, buckwheat, and sprouted grains), quinoa, and potatoes. This includes all products made from grains (pasta, bread, pizza, cookies, crackers, etc.).
- Avoid all foods high in carbs and sugar (cakes, cookies, ice cream, agave syrup, honey, tropical fruit and most high-sugar fruit, dried fruit, etc.).
- Avoid all processed, inflammatory fats (margarine, vegetable oil, canola oil, sunflower oil, safflower oil, soy oil, etc.) and processed products containing soy.
- Avoid products labeled "low-fat" and processed products labeled "low-carb" (which often contain hidden carbs in the form of insulin-spiking sugar, sorbitol, maltitol, dextrose, or maltodextrin, and may also contain other undesirable ingredients, like gluten).
- Avoid condiments and foods that include carrageenan, MSG, sulphites, or artificial sweeteners.
- Avoid factory-farmed pork, farmed fish, fish high in mercury, and unsustainable fish (see page 16 to learn which are sustainable).
- Avoid high-carb alcoholic drinks, including beer, sweet wine, and cocktails.
- Avoid dairy milk (high in carbohydrate), soy (hormone-disrupting effects), and gluten.

Sweeteners

When you follow a ketogenic diet, you need to swap your high-carb sweeteners for low-carb options. I always use only natural low-carb sweeteners that have very little to no effect on blood sugar levels. Two hundred years ago, the average person consumed 6 pounds (2.7 kg) of added sugar per year. Fast-forward to the twenty-first century, and we're now eating 110 pounds (50 kg) of added sugar every year! How has this happened? Soft drinks and processed foods became part of our diet, including those seemingly healthy breakfast cereals. These days, we eat more fructose than ever. And the problem with fructose is that it doesn't trigger the signal in your brain that tells you you've had enough. Unlike glucose, which can be metabolized by almost every cell in the body, fructose can only be metabolized in the liver, and it turns into the worst kind of body fat: visceral fat, which forms around your vital organs. Fructose also forms triglycerides, uric acid, and free radicals. And it lowers "good" HDL cholesterol and reduces LDL particle size—all of which are known factors for developing heart disease. Excessive consumption of sugar—especially fructose—is strongly linked to non alcoholic fatty liver disease, obesity, heart disease, and diabetes.

So, it goes without saying that you will need to avoid insulin-spiking sugar, high-fructose corn syrup, honey, maple syrup, coconut palm sugar, agave syrup, and rice malt syrup. Certain sugar alcohols, including maltitol, sorbitol, dextrose, and maltodextrin, should be avoided, too, because they are known to raise blood sugar. (Don't trust brands that exclude these sweeteners from the "net" carb count.)

Artificial sweeteners, such as aspartame and sucralose, may sound like the obvious solution here, but they're not what they seem to be. Studies show that artificial sweeteners are linked to a number of negative health effects, including migraines and increased appetite, resulting in weight gain. Use the following natural low-carb sweeteners.

✳ STEVIA ✳

The extract from the stevia herb has zero effect on blood sugar and contains no calories. Liquid stevia and stevia powder are 200 to 300 times sweeter than sugar; use very small amounts to avoid a bitter aftertaste (3 to 5 drops per serving). There are other types of stevia products on the market, including stevia glycerite (which is about twice as sweet as sugar with a gooey texture), and granulated stevia-and-erythritol blends.

✳ ERYTHRITOL AND OTHER ERYTHRITOL-BASED SWEETENERS ✳

Erythritol is a sugar alcohol found in fruits, vegetables, and fermented foods. It does not affect blood glucose and, like stevia, has zero calories. Ninety percent of erythritol is absorbed by your digestive system before it enters the large intestine and is subsequently excreted in your urine. Unlike xylitol—a sugar alcohol that may cause stomach discomfort—it's usually well tolerated. A good option is a product called Swerve, which is made with a blend of erythritol and prebiotic fibers called fructooligosaccharides.

✴ MONK FRUIT (LUO HAN GUO) ✴

Monk fruit is 300 times sweeter than sugar and should be used in small amounts. It's available in both liquid and powdered form. Just like stevia, it appears in some brand-name sweeteners where it's combined with erythritol.

✴ YACON SYRUP ✴

Yacon syrup is extracted from the South American yacon plant. It has a slightly caramel-like taste that's similar to blackstrap molasses. Although it's low in carbs, it's not a zero-carb sweetener, so you should use small amounts—about 1 to 2 tablespoons (15 to 30 ml) per recipe, or 1 teaspoon per serving.

✴ HOW TO SUBSTITUTE "REGULAR" SWEETENERS WITH LOW-CARB SWEETENERS ✴

The amount of sweetener you'll use depends on your palate. You may prefer foods more sweet or less sweet, so you may need to add or reduce the amount of sweetener used in recipes. Personally, I don't use the equivalent of sugar in most recipes: I use a lot less. As you get used to low-carb eating, you too will use smaller amounts of sweeteners or you may even avoid them altogether. On the other hand, if you're new to a low-carb diet, then you may find that some recipes aren't sweet enough. If so, you can add a few extra drops of stevia or a little more erythritol to suit your palate.

✴ KEEP IN MIND THE FOLLOWING CONVERSIONS ✴

1 CUP (200 G/7.1 OZ) OF GRANULATED STEVIA OR MONK FRUIT BLEND = 1 teaspoon of powdered or liquid stevia or liquid monk fruit

1 TABLESPOON (10 G/0.4 OZ) SUGAR = 6 to 9 drops of liquid or ¼ teaspoon powdered stevia or monk fruit

1 TEASPOON SUGAR = 2 to 4 drops of liquid or a pinch of powdered stevia or monk fruit

1 CUP (200 G/7.1 OZ) GRANULATED SWERVE = 1 cup (200 g/7.1 oz) table sugar

1 CUP (120 G/4.2 OZ) CONFECTIONERS' SWERVE = 1 cup (120 g/4.2 oz) confectioners' sugar

1⅓ CUPS (267 G/9.4 OZ) GRANULATED ERYTHRITOL = 1 cup (267 g/9.4 oz) table sugar

2 TABLESPOONS (40 G/1.4 OZ) YACON SYRUP = 1 tablespoon (20 g/0.7 oz) blackstrap molasses or honey

∽— Nuts and Seeds on a Keto Diet —∽

Nuts and seeds have come under fire for their apparently high carb content. Although some people may have valid reasons for minimizing their consumption (such as allergies or intolerances), nuts and seeds should be part of a well-balanced keto or low-carb diet for most people.

Nuts and seeds are high in vitamin E, B vitamins, zinc, copper, and selenium. They are also high in healthy fats, especially macadamia nuts (which are rich in heart-healthy monounsaturated fats) and flaxseeds (which area high in omega-3 fatty acids). Beware of nuts and seeds high in omega-6 fatty acids: consume these in moderation.

THE TRUTH ABOUT FLAXSEEDS

It's safe to eat flax. Flax has gotten a bad reputation within the low-carb community: it's been said to increase the risk of certain cancers because it is high in phytoestrogens. However, not all phytoestrogens have the same effects. While flavones and other phytoestrogens found in soy may stimulate cancer growth, lignans found in flaxseed may actually reduce the risk of some cancers. Apart from its cancer protective effects, a review of studies published in the journal *Integrative Cancer Therapies* also showed that flax may ease menopausal symptoms, reduce inflammation, and protect heart and digestive health.

SOURCE – NUTS & SEEDS	SERVING SIZE	TOTAL CARBS (grams per serving)	NET CARBS (grams per serving)	MAGNESIUM (% RDA)	POTASSIUM (% EMR)
Flaxseeds	14 g/0.5 oz	4.0	0.2	14%	6%
Chia seeds	14 g/0.5 oz	5.6	0.7	12%	3%
Hemp seeds	28 g/1 oz	2.8	0.9	42%	12%
Pecans	28 g/1 oz	3.9	1.2	8%	6%
Pine nuts	14 g/0.5 oz	1.8	1.3	9%	4%
Pumpkin seeds	28 g/1 oz	3.0	1.3	41%	11%
Brazil nuts	28 g/1 oz	3.4	1.3	26%	9%
Macadamia nuts	28 g/1 oz	3.9	1.5	9%	5%
Hazelnuts	28 g/1 oz	4.7	2.0	11%	10%
Walnuts	28 g/1 oz	3.8	2.0	11%	6%
Almonds	28 g/1 oz	6.1	2.7	19%	10%
Sunflower seeds	28 g/1 oz	5.6	3.2	23%	9%
Sesame seeds and sesame paste (tahini)	28 g/1 oz	6.6	3.2	25%	7%
Pistachios	28 g/1 oz	7.8	4.8	8%	14%
Cashews	28 g/1 oz	8.5	7.5	20%	9%

Nuts and seeds are high in fiber, about 70 to 75 percent of which is insoluble. (To find out why fiber doesn't conflict with ketosis, see Total Carbs or Net Carbs on page 13.) There is a catch, though: if weight loss is your goal, you should minimize your consumption of nuts and seeds. (See Eating Too Much Of . . . on page 35 for details.)

Dairy: Friend or Foe?

Dairy is probably one of the most demonized foods in the keto community. But when I say "dairy," I'm not referring to milk, low-fat products, and processed foods, which must be avoided on a ketogenic diet. I'm talking about raw, full-fat dairy, such as butter, ghee, cream, cheese, and yogurt.

✴ THE ANTI-DAIRY ARGUMENT ✴

Here are the claims being made against dairy—and the truth about each of them.

1. Dairy causes inflammation. Multiple studies, including a 2015 review of fifty-two clinical trials published in the *Critical Reviews in Food Science and Nutrition Journal*, demonstrate that the opposite is true: Dairy was found to have anti-inflammatory effects in these studies.

2. Dairy is linked to cancer. There is conflicting evidence on this from *observational* studies. A 2016 review of studies published in the *Food & Nutrition Research Journal* found that evidence linking dairy to prostate cancer is inconsistent. Some studies have linked dairy to cancer, while other studies have shown that dairy contains properties that *prevent* cancer.

3. Dairy leads to weight gain: its sole purpose is to provide nutrients to allow baby mammals to grow. Although dairy is nutrient-dense and it's high in protein and fat, there's no evidence that consuming full-fat dairy leads to weight gain, unless you're eating more calories than you need. In fact, in 2007 the *American Journal of Clinical Nutrition* published a meta-analysis of human studies that suggests dairy can help you lose fat and maintain a healthy weight due to its high concentration of conjugated linoleic acid (CLA). CLA aids weight loss, especially of visceral fat in the abdominal area.

4. Dairy raises insulin levels. Raised insulin levels will make your body store more fat. But the truth is that while dairy can raise insulin levels, it isn't much different from other sources of protein, at least when it comes to studies conducted on adults. A study from 1997 published in the *American Journal of Clinical Nutrition* shows that, for instance, cheese may be more insulinogenic (insulin-producing) than eggs, but it is less insulinogenic than beef or fish. If dairy spikes your insulin, just cut back on high-protein dairy products such as cheese and yogurt.

Should I Avoid Dairy?

You only need to avoid dairy if you have a milk protein allergy, lactose intolerance, or a hormone-sensitive type of cancer (such as breast cancer or prostate cancer). If your weight loss has been stalling for more than 2 weeks, try cutting back on dairy or eliminating it altogether for a few weeks. (See Eating Too Much Of . . . on page 35.)

Legumes: Are They Keto-Friendly?

Except for peanuts, legumes are high in carbs and should be avoided. Actually, even peanuts aren't ideal for a keto diet. Although they're relatively low in carbs, peanuts contain lectins and phytic acid, both of which make them hard to digest. Peanuts have also been linked to leaky gut syndrome, polycystic ovary syndrome (PCOS), irritable bowel syndrome (IBS), and Hashimoto's. Personally, I avoid peanuts. If you can tolerate them, you can eat peanuts in moderation. Just be sure to soak them first to remove most of the phytic acid. Soak them for 8 hours or overnight, then dehydrate them in the oven at about 120°F (50°C), just like nuts and seeds. See page 42 for more informtion.

Alcohol

In moderation, dry red and white wine are allowed, as are spirits. My favorite drinks are dry wine spritzers and spirits mixed with sparkling water, lemon or lime juice, and ice, plus a few drops of stevia. But if you're trying to lose weight, you should avoid alcohol altogether (see page 36).

Low-Carb Swaps

Pasta > zucchini noodles, shirataki noodles, or kelp noodles (pages 40–41)
Try in Induction Carbonara (page 174) or Salmon Ramen (page 93).

Rice > cauliflower rice or shirataki rice (pages 40–41)
Try in them with Butter Chicken (page 151).

Potatoes > chopped rutabaga, turnips, radishes, or cauliflower
Try them in Nordic Salad (page 108).

Potato mash > cauliflower mash
Try it in Salisbury Steak with Quick Mash (page 166).

Crackers > Multiseed Keto Crackers (page 84); celery sticks, cucumber slices, radishes, or sliced bell peppers; dehydrated vegetables; and beef jerky.

Bread > Garlic & Herb Focaccia (page 48); lettuce leaves
Try the Induction Unwich Two Ways (page 114).

Tortillas > lettuce leaves or keto tortilla dough
Try the Carne Asada Salad (page 100) or Mexican Pockets (page 117).

Pizza > Pizza Dutch Baby (page 56)
You'll also find several other keto-friendly pizza recipes on my blog at ketodietapp.com/blog.

Bulgur and quinoa > cauliflower rice (page 40) or hulled hemp seeds
Try in Chicken Satay with Superfood Tabbouleh (page 164).

Oats and cereals > chia seeds, unsweetened almond and coconut flakes, hulled hemp seeds
Try chia seeds in PB & Jelly Chia Parfaits (page 70).

Treats made with wheat flour > keto treats made with almond flour and coconut flour
Try the Czech Butter Cake (page 195) or the Chocolate Cupcakes with German Buttercream (page 198).

Keto Flu and Electrolytes: Sodium, Magnesium, and Potassium

Some people experience "keto flu" when they enter the induction phase of a ketogenic diet. This is because you're "starving" your body of carbohydrates in order to enter ketosis. Common symptoms of keto flu vary, and they can include headaches, nausea, fatigue, brain fog, muscle weakness, cramps, and heart palpitations.

Don't let keto flu break your stride! You can easily minimize its symptoms by using the following remedies:

Replenish electrolytes, especially sodium, magnesium, and potassium. Include foods rich in electrolytes in your everyday diet and take food supplements, if needed. Be aware of nutritional guidelines for these minerals. The Recommended Daily Allowance (RDA) of magnesium for healthy adults is 400 mg per day. Although there is no RDA for potassium, the Estimated Minimum Requirement (EMR) is around 2,000 mg per day, and Adequate Intake (AI) is 4,700 mg per day.

Don't be afraid to use salt every day. When your insulin drops, it will cause your sodium levels to drop significantly, too. To compensate for the extra sodium loss, you should eat 3,000 to 5,000 mg of additional sodium. I recommend pink Himalayan salt and sea salt.

Stay hydrated. To help with this, drink plenty of Electrolyte Agua Fresca (page 186) and bone broth (page 42).

Take supplements, especially magnesium (see page 28 for suggestions).

Take it easy when it comes to exercise. If you don't feel well, don't push yourself. Instead, limit your daily exercise to brisk walks and light cardio.

Recommended Supplements

As with any dietary approach—including the ketogenic diet—you may be lacking in vital micronutrients, so you need to pay attention to potential deficiencies. For instance, if you don't eat avocados, or if you follow a vegetarian keto diet, you may be deficient in potassium. Or if you don't like fatty fish, you may be deficient in omega-3s. Whatever your limitations are, identify them, and then consider supplementing your diet to make up for them.

✳ MAGNESIUM ✳

The best options are supplements made with magnesium glycinate, magnesium taurate, and magnesium malate. Natural Calm is a magnesium supplement that is made with magnesium citrate. Although it is usually well tolerated when used as recommended, it can cause stomach issues and loose stools when the recommended dose is exceeded. Avoid commonly available magnesium oxide: it's poorly absorbed.

Consult your doctor before taking magnesium supplements if you have kidney disease or take medications for high blood pressure

SOURCE	SERVING SIZE	MAGNESIUM (% RDA per serving)	NET CARBS (grams per serving)
Hemp seeds	28 g/1 oz	42%	2.8
Pumpkin seeds	28 g/1 oz	41%	3.0
Swiss chard, chopped	4 cups (144 g/5.1 oz)	29%	5.3
Kale, dark leaf	2½ cups (125 g/4.5 oz)	28%	5.6
Mackerel, raw	142 g/5 oz	27%	0.0
Brazil nuts	28 g/1 oz	26%	3.4
Sesame seeds and sesame paste (tahini)	28 g/1 oz	25%	6.6
Spinach, fresh	4 cups (120 g/4.2 oz)	24%	4.3
Sunflower seeds	28 g/1 oz	23%	5.6
Cashews	28 g/1 oz	20%	8.5
Almonds	28 g/1 oz	19%	6.1
Crabmeat, cooked	113 g/4 oz	18%	0.0
Dark chocolate, 85% cacao	28 g/1 oz	16%	7.7
Okra, chopped	1 cup (100 g/3.5 oz)	14%	7.5
Flaxseed	14 g/0.5 oz	14%	4.0
Sea bream	142 g/5 oz	13%	0.0
Coconut milk	½ cup (120 ml)	13%	3.2
Cacao powder	2 tablespoons (10 g/0.4 oz)	12%	5.8
Sardines, raw	142 g/5 oz	12%	0.0
Chia seeds	14 g/0.5 oz	12%	5.6

✶ POTASSIUM ✶

If you eat keto foods that are high in potassium, you won't need to take potassium supplements. However, they can help you get through the initial phase of the ketogenic diet, and are especially useful for beating keto flu. Apart from regular potassium supplements and multivitamin blends, you can use potassium chloride (available in most online health stores) to make Electrolyte Agua Fresca (page 186).

Too much potassium can be toxic: always consult your doctor before taking supplements.

SOURCE	SERVING SIZE	POTASSIUM (% EMR per serving)	NET CARBS (grams per servings)
Avocado, California	1 medium (150 g/5.3 oz)	38%	2.7
Spinach, fresh	4 cups (120 g/4.2 oz)	33%	1.7
Sea bream	142 g/5 oz	32%	0.0
Kale, dark leaf	2½ cups (125 g/4.5 oz)	31%	1.8
Mahimahi, white-flesh fish, raw	142 g/5 oz	30%	0.0
Cod, white-flesh fish, raw	142 g/5 oz	29%	0.0
Monkfish, white-flesh fish, raw	142 g/5 oz	28%	0.0
Swiss chard, chopped	4 cups (144 g/5.1 oz)	27%	3.0
Chicken breasts, boneless, raw	142 g/5 oz	26%	0.0
Salmon, king, wild, raw	142 g/5 oz	26%	0.0
Zucchini	1 medium (200 g/7.1 oz)	26%	4.2
Pork loin, raw	142 g/5 oz	26%	0.0
Beef, rib eye, raw	142 g/5 oz	25%	0.0
Sea bass	142 g/5 oz	25%	0.0
Wild game, buffalo, raw	142 g/5 oz	25%	0.0
Sardines, raw	142 g/5 oz	24%	0.0
Cauliflower, chopped	1½ cups (161 g/5.7 oz)	24%	4.8
Kohlrabi, diced	1 cup (135 g/4.8 oz)	24%	3.5
Mushrooms, cremini, sliced	1½ cups (105 g/3.7 oz)	24%	3.2
Herring, raw	142 g/5 oz	23%	0.0

✳ FERMENTED COD LIVER OIL ✳

Fermented cod liver oil provides healthy omega-3 fatty acids and vitamin D, both of which are deficient in modern diets. Adequate intake of quality omega-3s from animal sources can help reduce inflammation and improve other symptoms of metabolic syndrome. Meanwhile, vitamin D improves calcium absorption, which is essential for bone health, and maintains adequate calcium levels in your blood, which is essential for many of the body's vital functions. Consider taking vitamin K supplements, too: vitamin K works in synergy with vitamin D.

✳ MCT OIL ✳

Medium-chain triglycerides (MCTs) are saturated fats that our bodies can easily digest. MCTs are passed directly to the liver to be used as an immediate form of energy. I use pure MCT oil in smoothies, salad dressings, and pre-workout snacks. Look for products high in caprylic acid (C8), which provides a quick source of energy, encourages ketone production, and provides maximum cognitive benefits. If you are new to MCT oil, make sure you start with a small amount (such as a teaspoon) and gradually add more as you learn to tolerate it in order to avoid digestive discomfort.

✳ GRASS-FED COLLAGEN AND GELATIN ✳

Just like gelatin, collagen is beneficial for our health: it improves immunity, hormone balance, and leaky gut, and helps maintain healthy skin, hair, and joints. Unlike gelatin, though, collagen doesn't gel, so it's great for making smoothies and recipes in which you want to avoid a thick texture.

✳ MELATONIN ✳

Melatonin is a hormone produced by the body, and it's primarily associated with regulation of the sleep/wake cycles (also known as circadian rhythms). It's a potent antioxidant that defends against free radicals and helps reduce stress levels. Because stress is one of the many factors that can inhibit successful weight loss, melatonin supplements may help you shed unwanted pounds.

✳ PROBIOTICS ✳

Along with fermented foods, probiotic supplements will help your digestion, restore the proper balance of bacteria in your gut, and improve overall immunity.

✳ MULTIVITAMINS AND OTHER SUPPLEMENTS ✳

Depending on your individual needs, you may want to consider taking other dietary supplements. For example, if you have a thyroid disease like I do, think about taking magnesium, zinc, selenium, vitamin D, and B vitamins—or eat foods high in these nutrients. For instance, I eat a Brazil nut every day (just one Brazil nut provides more than 100 percent of your RDA of selenium!). But, on the other hand, because my thyroid issue is autoimmune, I avoid iodine supplements.

✳ PROTEIN POWDER ✳

An increased amount of protein is generally recommended for physically active individuals, elderly people, and people recovering from injuries. Also, if you avoid all or most animal foods, you're probably not getting enough protein, so supplementing is a good option. You can use whey protein powder or egg white protein powder, hydrolyzed gelatin (collagen), or even plant-based versions, such as pea protein powder. Look for quality ingredients that are free of artificial sweeteners and colors, hormones, preservatives, soy, and gluten.

I use protein powders in smoothies (page 187, Superfood Smoothies) and hot drinks (page 35, "Butter" Coffee). If you exercise, add them to post-workout snacks, fat bombs, and travel-friendly bars (such as the Keto Power Bars on page 129, or the Halva Stacks on page 200). They work wonderfully in baked goods as a replacement for gluten; the Czech Butter Cake on page 195 is a good example. Finally, I use it to make a quick frozen treat when I'm craving something cold and creamy: blend ¼ cup (25 g/0.9 oz) quality protein powder with ½ cup (75 g/2.7 oz) frozen berries and ¼ cup (60 ml) coconut milk or almond milk to make a quick keto "ice cream" in less than five minutes!

⁓ Intermittent Fasting ⁓

Fasting goes hand in hand with the ketogenic lifestyle. Here's why: Healthy low-carb eating is great for appetite control and keeps you fuller for longer. And as your body gets used to using fat and ketones as its main energy sources, you will naturally eat less, and eat less frequently. That's the best time to try intermittent fasting (IF).

Fasting has a number of benefits:

- It may help slow the aging process.
- It may increase longevity by altering the body's levels of insulin growth factor-1 (IGF-1), glucose, insulin, and human growth factor.
- It may promote fat loss.
- It may reduce your risk of developing type 2 diabetes.
- It may offer a promising therapeutic potential for multiple sclerosis.
- It may switch on specific repair genes within the body (known as autophagy).
- It may offer protection from certain cancers and help mitigate the side effects of standard cancer treatment.

✳ FOUR WAYS TO TRY INTERMITTENT FASTING ✳

There are several ways to practice intermittent fasting:

1. Skip meals (fast for 16 hours, eat for 8 hours). This is my favorite way to do IF, and I practice this four or five times a week, usually by skipping breakfast.

2. Break a 24-hour period into two segments (e.g., 18/6 or 20/4), then fast (drinking only water or tea) for 18 hours, followed by a 6-hour period of calorie intake.

3. Alternate days of calorie restriction with days of unrestricted eating. Reduce your calorie intake by 20 to 30 percent on day one, followed by unrestricted eating on day two.

4. Alternate days of fasting with days of unrestricted eating. This approach may be too extreme for most people. I wouldn't recommend following it unless you've tried one of the above methods first. You can do this by including one or two fasting days a week.

(I've tagged higher-calorie, nutrient-dense recipes that are suitable for intermittent fasting throughout this book.)

✳ TIPS FOR SUCCESSFUL FASTING ✳

Keep these tips in mind if you're thinking about trying IF:

Start slow. Avoid IF during the induction phase of the ketogenic diet (see page 9). This is very important, as your body should be fully utilizing ketones instead of glucose for energy: if you are glucose-dependent, you will find it hard to fast.

Don't force yourself. There's no need to deprive yourself unnecessarily. Once you become fat-adapted, you will naturally feel less hungry, and fasting will be easier. Start by avoiding snacking between meals. Then, try skipping "regular" meals—but only do so if you don't feel hungry. IF is not about starving!

Who should avoid fasting? People suffering from anorexia nervosa, bulimia nervosa, and type 1 diabetes should avoid fasting completely. If you have type 2 diabetes, or are pregnant or breastfeeding, you should consult your doctor before implementing IF. And if you have thyroid or adrenal issues, you should avoid fasting or limit it to skipping meals only.

Have You Hit a Weight-Loss Plateau?

It's happened to most of us: After weeks of successful dieting, you reach a weight-loss plateau and your progress stalls. And by "weight-loss plateau," I don't mean a short-term fluctuation, but a long-lasting stall. If this happens, sometimes focusing on other aspects of your life—such as emotional or psychological issues that may be affecting your progress—may help you figure out what went wrong. We are all different, and we have different dietary requirements, which is why you should always listen to your body's signals. To reduce the likelihood of hitting a plateau, avoid these common mistakes:

✳ NOT KNOWING YOUR MACRONUTRIENTS ✳

In an ideal world, when you eat nutritious foods low in carbs, moderate in protein, and high in fat, you will naturally eat less. For this reason, most people won't need to count calories as they get used to this style of eating.

Why should you worry about "macros"? Well, when you're new to the ketogenic diet, what you eat and how much you eat will change dramatically, so relying purely on your body's signals may not be enough. I've met so many people who either aren't eating enough because they are afraid of fat, or are overeating because they can't control their cravings. And weight loss always gets more difficult as you approach your goal weight.

So, when you reach a weight-loss plateau, it's easier to eliminate the obvious potential factor: your macros. Maybe you're not getting enough protein, which would make you hungrier. Or maybe you're not estimating your daily carbs correctly, and are exceeding the limit that allows you to use fat for fuel. For these reasons, tracking your diet—especially if you are new to the keto diet—is an absolute necessity.

✳ NOT USING FAT AS A FILLER ✳

On a typical ketogenic diet, 75 percent of calories come from fat, 20 percent come from protein, and 5 percent come from carbs. Although this gives you a good general idea of the diet's composition, your personal needs may be very different, depending on your goals.

On a ketogenic diet, fat is the filler. This means that it supplies the extra calories your body needs (in place of carbohydrates). So, if you want to lose body fat, you need to stay in a calorie deficit. That may happen naturally, through the appetite-suppressing effects of the ketogenic diet, or from intentionally limiting your calorie intake. Some people will need to get 40 to 60 percent of their calories from fat (typically during weight loss), while others will need to get as much as 80 percent of their calories from fat (typically during weight maintenance). To calculate your ideal calorie intake, visit my blog at ketodietapp.com/Blog/page/KetoDiet-Buddy.

✳ OBSESSING OVER YOUR KETONE LEVELS ✳

People often ask me the same question: "I have high blood ketone readings, so why am I not losing weight?" It's a myth that high ketone levels will guarantee fat loss. Ketone levels vary among individuals, especially when we take keto adaptation into account. Ketone levels will show you how much "fuel" you have in your "tank," but not how much fuel your body is using for energy. Compared to someone who's just started following a ketogenic diet, keto-adapted individuals are more likely to have lower ketone levels, simply because their bodies can use them more effectively than non-keto-adapted individuals.

Nutritional ketosis is achieved when your blood ketones are between 0.5 and 3.0 mM, and there is no scientific evidence that higher values will lead to enhanced fat loss. Besides, weight loss isn't even a goal for many people who follow a keto approach. People who follow the ketogenic diet for thera-peutic purposes, such as managing epilepsy or cancer, may want to maintain—or even gain—weight. Same goes for athletes who stick to a keto diet to promote top-level performance. Severe carbohy-drate restriction (below 20 grams of total carbs daily) is not sustainable in the long term, and will not enhance weight loss. On the contrary, vegetables and other high-fiber foods can help you stabilize your blood sugar and help you lose weight.

✳ SUFFERING FROM STRESS AND LACK OF SLEEP ✳

Stress is a major factor when it comes to weight loss. When you are stressed, your body produces more of the stress hormone cortisol. This raises blood sugar and lowers your ketone levels. In order to cope with chronically elevated blood sugar, your body will produce more insulin and you won't be able to follow a keto approach to its full potential.

Lack of sleep or a circadian rhythm disorder may be one of the factors that is causing you to plateau. With less energy, it will be more difficult to lose weight: sleep-deprived individuals produce less growth hormone, have impaired glucose metabolism, and show a decreased level of leptin—the hormone that signals satiety. Lack of sleep also leads to an increased level of ghrelin, which is the hormone that tells your brain when you are hungry.

Here's how to minimize stress and promote healthy sleep patterns:

1. Meditate, take a walk, or make time for an activity that helps you relax. Avoid activities that stress you out.

2. Take it easy at the gym. Too much exercise, especially heavy cardio workouts, increases cortisol, which is linked to increased fat storage (especially the unhealthy visceral fat around your belly). Replace some of your cardio sessions with strength training and yoga. And don't exercise 3 to 4 hours before bed.

3. Try supplements such as melatonin, magnesium (ideally magnesium glycinate), and B-complex. These will help reduce your stress levels and improve your circadian rhythms (see page 27, Recom-mended Supplements).

4. Don't eat heavy meals before bed. Your body needs to rest, so it shouldn't have to spend the whole night digesting your dinner.

5. Don't use your computer before bed, and try blue light blockers. Don't keep your laptop, tablet, or phone in the bedroom. Sleep in complete darkness, and try to get 7 to 9 hours of sleep each night.

Dairy and nuts One of the common mistakes people make is overeating nuts and dairy. Both are high in calories and are very easy to overeat. Having too many coffees with cream can add up to half of your daily fat intake! To avoid overdoing it on nuts, only use them for sprinkling over salads, adding to yogurt, or in occasional keto treats and fat bombs (like the ones in chapter 7, Drinks and Desserts).

Low-carb treats Traditional sweeteners are off-limits on the ketogenic diet, and even low-carb sweeteners should be used with caution, especially if you just started eating keto and need to conquer your sugar addiction. That's because keto treats and low-carb sweeteners can increase cravings, stimulate appetite, and stall your progress. You should minimize or even avoid them completely when you're trying to lose weight. If you have a sweet tooth and high-fat foods don't curb your cravings, have a piece of dark chocolate or a fat bomb (page 200, Halva Stacks and page 192, Paradise Squares).

Eating products labeled "low-carb" Simply put: eat real food. Avoid prepared meals, which are full of additives and may feature deceptive labeling. A common practice is to exclude all sugar alcohols and other insulin-spiking sweeteners from the carb count on the package. That said, there are a few decent products you can use even on a keto diet—just be sure to read the labels!

Drinking your calories As a rule, you should get your calories from real, nutritious foods that also supply protein, vitamins, and minerals.

"Butter" coffee In case you're not familiar with it, butter coffee is a blend of coffee, MCT oil, and butter or coconut oil. It seems to suppress hunger in some people, and it may be a good addition to your diet. However, others who have experienced weight stalling have started losing weight again once they ditch their morning dose of butter coffee. I make my own "keto coffee," into which I put 2 to 3 raw egg yolks and a tablespoon each of (15 ml) coconut milk and (7 g) collagen. You can add a pinch of cinnamon, vanilla powder, and/or stevia, if you like. Unlike traditional butter coffee, it provides enough energy and nutrients to be used as a meal replacement.

Alcohol Avoid alcohol if you want to lose weight. Even if your alcoholic drink is sugar-free, your body can't store alcohol as fat: it has to metabolize it. This means that your body will utilize alcohol instead of body fat, which will slow down weight loss. (Also, keep in mind that your alcohol tolerance will decrease when you switch to keto.) Plus, alcohol increases appetite and dehydration and suppresses self-control—none of which are good for weight loss. However, dry wine used for cooking and alcohol in food extracts are acceptable: most of the alcohol will evaporate during cooking, leaving the amazing flavor intact.

Snacking If you follow a nutritious low-carb or ketogenic diet, you shouldn't need to snack. Unless you have hypoglycemia issues, three main meals a day (or even fewer) should be enough to keep you sated. Here are a few simple rules on snacking:

- Don't eat unless you are hungry, even if it means skipping a meal. In fact, once you get keto-adapted, you will find intermittent fasting easy.
- If you feel hungry and need to snack, it's likely that your meals weren't nutritious enough, and you should increase your portion size. A lack of protein will keep you hungry, so make sure you eat enough of it.
- Eat real food in order to stay fuller for longer: eggs, meat, fatty fish, non-starchy vegetables, fermented foods, and some raw dairy.

Not exercising effectively Not exercising at all or exercising too much are both counterproductive for weight loss on a keto diet. Here's how to find the right balance:

- Don't exercise just to burn calories. This approach simply doesn't work in the long run. Studies show that excessive exercise leads to increased appetite, and you will end up eating more.
- Choose the type of exercise that's right for you, depending on your goal. Light cardio has great health benefits, especially for the heart and brain. Weight training and high-intensity intermittent training (HIIT) promote muscle growth and long-term weight loss. (Post-workout carb-ups in the form of paleo-friendly carbs—such as potatoes, sweet potatoes, parsnips, and banana—can be added to your diet if you engage in HIIT.)
- Know that your protein requirements will increase when you exercise. (Use our macronutrient calculator at ketodietapp.com/blog.)

Cheat meals There is a difference between carb-ups and cheat meals. You can have a meal higher in carbs after HIIT (see above)—but a cheat meal is completely different, as it usually refers to eating anything from the "banned" foods list. Having regular cheat meals is counterproductive for your diet (and your goals).

✳ HEALTH CONDITIONS ✳

If you're certain that you're doing everything right and still the scales aren't moving, you may have a health issue you're not aware of. Here are a few potential issues:

- Hypothyroidism or adrenal dysfunction. It only takes a blood test or a saliva test to find out whether you have a thyroid or an adrenal issue. Increasing your carbs may help: I have Hashimoto's syndrome, and I generally don't go below 25–30 grams of net carbs daily. Also, cruciferous vegetables, such as cauliflower, cabbage, broccoli, arugula, Brussels sprouts, watercress, collards, horseradish, radishes, rutabaga, turnips, bok choy, and kohlrabi, are known as goitrogens. If eaten on a regular basis, goitrogens may disrupt the production of thyroid hormones by interfering with iodine uptake in the thyroid gland. Luckily, these veggies are only goitrogenic in their raw state. Cooking, light steaming, or even fermenting deactivates and diminishes their goitrogenic activity.
- Sex hormones can affect your weight. Polycystic ovarian syndrome (PCOS) can be the culprit for women; men experience a decreased level of testosterone as they age.
- Certain medications, such as insulin injections, other diabetes medications, and cortisone, are known to cause weight gain. Consult your doctor for possible alternatives.
- If you suffer from chronic pain, your cortisol levels are likely to be high. This will impair your weight loss. Consult your doctor on ways to mitigate this effect and try to find ways to reduce stress (see page 34, Suffering from Stress and Lack of Sleep).

✳ LACK OF MOTIVATION ✳

Online community support and accountability are the most powerful tools and will help you boost your motivation, because they connect you with like-minded people. And with social media, you can do that no matter where you live. For instance, my KetoDiet Blog Support Group on Facebook has more than fifty thousand members and is completely free to join.

Need even more motivation? Join my KetoDiet Challenge (www.ketodietapp.com/Challenges) to share your experiences, ask questions, and get inspired by reading success stories and learning from others. Follow me on Instagram and use the #KetoDietChallenge or #KetoDietApp when sharing your progress!

How to Use This Book

✳ USE NATURAL INGREDIENTS ✳

When you're sourcing ingredients, go for organic and additive-free. Buy organic eggs; organic unwaxed lemons; pastured beef and butter; outdoor-reared pork; wild-caught fish; and extra-virgin olive oil.

✳ REMEMBER ✳

Nutrition values for each recipe in this book are per serving unless stated otherwise. The nutrition data are derived from the USDA National Nutrient Database (ndb.nal.usda.gov).

Nutrition facts are calculated from edible parts. For example, if one large avocado is listed as 200 g/7.1 oz, this value represents its edible parts (pit and peel removed) unless otherwise specified. Optional ingredients and suggested sides and toppings are not included in the nutrition information. You can use raw cacao powder and unsweetened cocoa powder (Dutch process) interchangeably. Ingredients such as cream cheese, ricotta, or Halloumi cheese are all full-fat unless otherwise specified.

All ingredients should be sugar-free, unless you use dark 85% to 90% chocolate, which contains a small and acceptable amount of sugar.

All recipes are tagged with the following icons, as needed.

- dairy-free
- nut-free
- egg free
- nightshade-free
- vegetarian
- ideal for intermittent fasting
- high in electrolytes
- induction-friendly

The induction-friendly icon indicates which recipes are most suitable for the initial phase of the ketogenic diet.

✳ OPTIONAL INGREDIENTS ✳

Optional ingredients, suggested sides, and suggested alternatives and toppings are not included in the nutrition information.

If options are included, such recipes are tagged 🥛, 🥜, etc. For example, Green Skillet Eggs (page 60) call for ghee or duck fat, and are therefore optionally dairy-free and carry the gray dairy-free icon, 🥛.

1 CUP (240 ML) HEAVY WHIPPING CREAM = 1 cup (240 ml) coconut milk for recipes that require liquid cream, or 1 cup (240 ml) coconut cream (see page 73) where whipped cream is required

1 CUP (240 G/8.5 OZ) MASCARPONE CHEESE = 1 cup (240 g/8.5 oz) coconut cream (see page 73)

1 CUP (100 G/3.5 OZ) ALMOND FLOUR = ⅓ cup (40 g/1.4 oz) coconut flour, plus increased liquids (1 to 2 extra eggs, or ¼ to ½ cup [60 to 120 ml] more nut milk, cream, etc.)

1 LARGE EGG = 1 tablespoon (7 g/0.2 oz) ground flaxseed or 1 tablespoon (8 g/0.3 oz) ground chia seeds or 1 tablespoon (7 g/0.2 oz) gelatin powder, mixed with 3 tablespoons (45 ml) water (although this swap has limited use, as it won't work for mayonnaise, hollandaise, or Garlic & Herb Focaccia, page 48)

1 CUP (250 G/8.8 OZ) ALMOND BUTTER = 1 cup (250 g/8.8 oz) coconut butter or any seed butter

1 TABLESPOON (15 G/0.5 OZ) GHEE OR BUTTER = 1 tablespoon (15 g/0.5 oz) lard, tallow, duck fat, goose fat, or virgin coconut oil

✳ AN IMPORTANT NOTE ABOUT MEASUREMENTS ✳

If you are following a ketogenic diet for specific health reasons, you should be aware that accuracy is vital in order for this diet to work. Always use a kitchen scale to measure ingredients: using measurements like cups or tablespoons can lead to inaccuracies that may affect the macronutrient composition of your meal. And all it takes to shift your body out of ketosis is a few extra grams of carbohydrates. Plus, cups and tablespoons for dried products (flax meal, etc.) may vary depending on the brand.

The Basics:
Keto Staples Plus Two Recipes

At least a quarter of my fridge space is reserved for homemade basics. (And I have a big fridge!) There are good reasons for making most condiments and basic ingredients instead of buying them. They are easy to prepare, budget-friendly, and taste so much better than store-bought versions. Most importantly, this way you'll have complete control over what you eat, and you won't have to worry about added gluten, sugar, and other unwanted ingredients.

This chapter lists plenty of recipes for keto-friendly condiments and basic ingredients that'll help you keep your diet squeaky clean. Can't find mayo made with healthy oils? Make your own in just a few minutes! Not sure what to serve with your curry? Swap starchy sides for low-carb vegetables by serving your mains with quick-prep zucchini noodles, cauliflower rice, or shirataki noodles.

For even more homemade basics, such as ketchup, barbecue sauce, salsa verde, harissa paste, Thai curry paste, sauerkraut, pickles, and keto cheese sauce, visit my website at ketodietapp.com/blog and use the filtering tool to see all "homemade basics."

✶ KETO STAPLES TO HELP YOU GET STARTED ✶

New to keto eating? You'll be returning to these staples again and again as you get used to the keto approach.

ZUCCHINI NOODLES

Use a julienne peeler or a spiralizer to turn the zucchini into thin or wide "noodles." Chop the soft cores and add them to the noodles. Sprinkle the noodles with salt and let them sit for 10 minutes. Use a paper towel to pat them dry. Set aside, then pan-fry them with a little ghee or other cooking fat for 2 to 5 minutes.

RECOMMENDED SERVING SIZE: 1 small (150 g/5.3 oz) to medium (200 g/7.1 oz) zucchini

CARBS PER 1 SMALL ZUCCHINI: 3.2 g net carbs, 4.7 g total carbs

CARBS PER 1 MEDIUM ZUCCHINI: 4.2 g net carbs, 6.2 g total carbs

CAULIFLOWER RICE

Wash the cauliflower thoroughly and dry well. Grate with a hand grater, or place the florets in a food processor with a grating blade and pulse until it looks like rice. A grating blade will make it look more like real rice. Don't overdo it. It only takes a few extra seconds to make purée out of your cauli-rice! Place in an airtight container and store in the fridge for up to 4 days. Use any of these methods for cooking your cauli-rice:

STEAMING: Place in a steamer and cook for 5 to 7 minutes.

MICROWAVING: Place the cauli-rice in a microwave-safe bowl and cook on medium-high for 5 to 7 minutes (no water necessary).

PAN ROASTING: You can briefly cook the cauli-rice in a pan greased with butter or ghee, or add it directly to the pot with the meat or sauce you plan to serve it with. This method adds lots of extra flavor to your cauli-rice!

BAKING: Preheat the oven to 400°F (200°C, or gas mark 6). Spread the grated cauli-rice over a baking sheet lined with parchment paper. Cook for 12 to 15 minutes, flipping with a spatula two to three times during cooking. This method is great when you want the rice to be as dry as possible.

RECOMMENDED SERVING SIZE: 1 to 1½ cups (120 to 180 g/4.2 to 6.4 oz)

CARBS PER 1 CUP (120 G): 3.6 g net carbs, 6 g total carbs

CARBS PER 1½ CUPS (180 G): 5.4 g net carbs, 9 g total carbs

SHIRATAKI NOODLES/RICE

Wash the shirataki noodles thoroughly and boil them for 2 to 3 minutes. Drain well. Place the noodles in a hot dry pan. Fry over medium-high heat for about 10 minutes. Using tongs, toss the noodles as they cook. Add the fried noodles directly to a meal, or place in an airtight container and refrigerate for up to 3 days.

RECOMMENDED SERVING SIZE: 3.5 to 5.3 oz (100 to 150 g)

CARBS PER 3.5 OZ (100 G): 1.5 g net carbs, 2.9 g total carbs

CARBS PER 5.3 OZ (150 G): 2.3 g net carbs, 4.4 g total carbs

KELP NOODLES (SEAWEED NOODLES)

Wash the kelp noodles thoroughly and drain. Add to your meal in the last 1 to 2 minutes of the cooking process (as a side or in soups), or eat raw (in a salad).

RECOMMENDED SERVING SIZE: 3.5 to 5.3 oz (100 to 150 g)

CARBS PER 3.5 OZ (100 G): 0 g net carbs, 0.9 g total carbs

CARBS PER 5.3 OZ (150 G): 0 g net carbs, 1.3 g total carbs

TWO WAYS TO MAKE CRISPY BACON

Oven baking (best for larger quantities): Preheat the oven to 325°F (160°C, or gas mark 3). Line a baking tray with parchment paper. Lay the bacon strips out flat in a single layer, or lay on a wire rack set on top of the parchment. Place the tray in the oven and cook for 25 to 30 minutes. Remove the tray from the oven and let cool for 5 minutes. Strain the bacon grease into a small jar. Let the bacon slices cool completely and store them in an airtight container in the fridge. Use within 1 week or freeze for up to 3 months.

Pan roasting (best for smaller quantities): Place the bacon strips in a large pan and add ½ cup (120 ml) water. Cook over medium-high heat until the water starts to boil. Reduce the heat to medium, and cook until the water evaporates and the bacon fat is rendered. Reduce the heat to low, and cook until the bacon is lightly browned and crispy. Let it cool slightly and cut it into pieces.

EGGS

Boiled eggs: Fresh eggs don't peel well. It's better to use eggs that you bought 7 to 10 days before cooking. Place the eggs in a pot, and cover them with water by an inch (2.5 cm). Bring to a boil over high heat. Turn off the heat and cover. Remove from the burner and keep the eggs covered in the pot (10 to 12 minutes for medium-size eggs; 13 to 14 minutes for large; 15 to 16 minutes for extra large; 17 to 18 minutes for jumbo and duck eggs). Transfer to a bowl filled with ice water and let the eggs sit for 5 minutes. To peel, remove the eggs from the water and knock each egg several times against the countertop or work surface to crack the shells. Gently peel off the shells. Store cooled, unpeeled eggs in the fridge for up to a week. To soft-boil the eggs, leave them covered in hot water for 5 to 7 minutes.

Poached eggs: Fill a medium saucepan with water and a dash of vinegar. Bring to a boil over high heat. Crack each egg individually into a ramekin or a cup. Using a spoon, create a gentle whirlpool in the water; this will help the egg white wrap around the egg yolk. Slowly lower the egg into the water in the center of the whirlpool. Turn off the heat and cook for 3 to 4 minutes. Use a slotted spoon to remove the egg from the water and place it on a plate. Repeat for all remaining eggs. Once cool, place all the eggs in an airtight container filled with cold water and keep refrigerated for up to 5 days. To reheat the eggs, place them in a mug filled with hot tap water for a couple of minutes. This will be enough to warm them up without overcooking.

ACTIVATED NUTS AND SEEDS

Activated nuts and seeds are more easily digested, and their nutrients are better absorbed. Place the nuts or seeds in a bowl filled with water or salted water. Leave at room temperature overnight. Drain and spread on a parchment-lined baking sheet. Place in the oven and dry at the lowest possible temperature, or use a dehydrator and dry the nuts for 12 to 24 hours, turning occasionally, until completely dry. Store in an airtight container.

BONE BROTH (MAKES 9 TO 10 CUPS/ABOUT 2 L)

Place all the ingredients in a slow cooker: 3 to 4 pounds (1.4 kg) assorted bones and cartilages (such as oxtail, chicken feet, marrowbones, or leftover bones from any roasts); 1 large (150 g/3.5 oz) halved yellow onion with skin on; 2 medium (120 g/4.2 oz) carrots, peeled and cut into thirds; 2 large (128 g/4.5 oz) celery stalks; 4 halved cloves garlic; 3 bay leaves; 1 to 2 teaspoons sea salt; 1 teaspoon whole black peppercorns; and 2.6 quarts (2.5 L) water. If you're using meaty parts, remove them from the slow cooker and shred the meat off after 4 to 5 hours of cooking on high, or 6 to 8 hours of cooking on low. Return the bones to the slow cooker and continue cooking for at least 12 or up to 48 hours. Discard the bones and vegetables and let cool. Refrigerate overnight. Once chilled, a fatty layer will appear on top of the broth: simply scrape it off and discard, or use it for cooking just like lard.

GOOD-FOR-YOUR GUT MAYONNAISE (MAKES ABOUT 2 CUPS/480 G)

Use a wide-mouth Mason jar that barely fits the head of your immersion blender. This is vital for the recipe to work. Place 2 large egg yolks, 2 teaspoons Dijon mustard (or nightshade-free yellow mustard), 2 tablespoons (30 ml) apple cider vinegar, 2 tablespoons (30 ml) fresh lemon juice,

½ teaspoon fine sea salt, and ¼ teaspoon ground black pepper into the jar. Pour 1½ cups (360 ml) walnut oil (or macadamia oil, avocado oil, or light olive oil) on top, and let it settle for 20 seconds. Place the head of the immersion blender at the bottom of the jar and turn it on high speed. (Do not pulse.) As the mayonnaise starts to thicken, gently tilt and move the head of the immersion blender until the mayonnaise is thick. Add 2 tablespoons (30 ml/1 oz) whey (the liquid part on top of raw full-fat yogurt), or powder from 1 to 2 probiotic capsules. Cover the jar loosely with a lid or a cloth, and let it sit on the kitchen counter for 8 hours. This is essential in order to activate the enzymes that will keep your mayo fresh. Refrigerate after 8 hours, and use within the next 3 months.

Note: When using raw eggs, prevent any health risks by using eggs with pasteurized shells. To pasteurize eggs at home, simply pour enough water into a saucepan to cover the eggs. Heat to about 140°F (60°C). Using a spoon, slowly place the eggs in the saucepan. Keep the eggs in the water for about 3 minutes. This should be enough to pasteurize the eggs and kill any potential bacteria. Let cool, then store in the fridge for 6 to 8 weeks.

Convert your mayo into basic aioli or pesto aioli dip! Here's how:

To make aioli, mix ½ cup (110 g/3.9 oz) mayonnaise with 1 clove crushed garlic. Optionally, add freshly chopped herbs of your choice.

To make pesto aioli, mix ½ cup (110 g/3.9 oz) mayonnaise with 1 tablespoon (15 ml) lemon juice and 3 tablespoons (45 g/1.4 oz) pesto (below). Refrigerate for up to 5 days.

PESTO TWO WAYS
Basil Pesto (makes about 240 ml/1 cup)
Place all the ingredients in a blender: 2 cups (30 g/1.1 oz) fresh basil; ⅓ cup (45 g/1.6 oz) macadamia nuts or sunflower seeds; 2 tablespoons (15 g/0.5 oz) pine nuts or more sunflower seeds; 4 cloves minced garlic; 1 teaspoon fresh lemon zest; 1 tablespoon (15 ml) fresh lemon juice; and ½ cup (120 ml) extra-virgin olive oil. Optionally, add ⅓ cup (30 g/1.1 oz) grated Parmesan cheese. Process until smooth, then season with sea salt and black pepper to taste.

Mint-Walnut Pesto (makes about 160 ml/⅔ cup)
Place all the ingredients in a blender: 1 cup (15 g/0.5 oz) loosely packed mint leaves; 1 cup (15 g/0.5 oz) loosely packed parsley or cilantro; 2 cloves minced garlic; 1 tablespoon (15 ml) fresh lemon juice; 1 teaspoon fresh lemon zest; ⅓ cup (80 ml) extra-virgin olive oil; and ⅓ cup (33 g/1.2 oz) walnuts or sunflower seeds. Process until smooth, then season with sea salt and black pepper to taste.

You can keep your pesto in the fridge for up to 1 to 2 weeks. Whenever you use the pesto, always remember to add a thin layer of olive oil on top before you place it back in the fridge. To preserve pesto for longer, spoon it into an ice cube tray and place in the freezer. Once frozen, empty the ice cube tray into a resealable plastic bag. Keep your frozen pesto cubes for up to 6 months.

MARINARA SAUCE (MAKES 300 ML/1¼ CUPS)
Place 1 cup (150 g/5.3 oz) chopped tomatoes, ½ cup (20 g/0.7 oz) fresh basil, 2 cloves garlic, 1 small (30 g/1.1 oz) shallot or white onion, 4 tablespoons (60 g/2.1 oz) tomato paste, ¼ cup (60 ml) extra-virgin olive oil, ¼ teaspoon salt, and black pepper to taste into a blender. Pulse until smooth.

Flavored Butter Twelve Ways

MAKES (EACH RECIPE): 4 to 6 ounces (113 to 168 g) flavored butter
HANDS-ON TIME: 10 minutes
OVERALL TIME: 30 minutes

I reach for flavored butter when I don't have time to get creative in the kitchen, but I don't want to compromise on taste, either. And it's a great way to add healthy fats to just about any meal. If you can't eat butter, swap it for ghee, lard, duck fat, or even virgin coconut oil.

Savory Butters:

½ cup (113 g/4 oz) softened unsalted butter, ghee, lard, duck fat, or virgin coconut oil
¼ to ½ teaspoon sea salt (or less, if other salty ingredients are added)
¼ teaspoon black pepper

Garlic & Herb Butter:

2 tablespoons (30 ml) extra-virgin olive oil
4 cloves garlic, crushed
2 tablespoons (8 g/0.3 oz) chopped parsley or 2 teaspoons dried parsley

Bacon & Cheese Butter:

2 large slices (32 g/1.1 oz) crisp bacon, crumbled
½ cup (28 g/1 oz) grated Cheddar cheese
1 to 2 tablespoons (4 to 8 g/0.2 to 0.3 oz) chopped chives or spring onion

Jalapeño & Lime Butter:

1 (14 g/0.5 oz) jalapeño pepper, seeded and finely chopped
1 tablespoon (15 ml) fresh lime juice
1 to 2 tablespoons (4 to 8 g/0.2 to 0.3 oz) chopped cilantro

Spicy Harissa Butter:

3 tablespoons (45 g/1.6 oz) harissa paste

Thai Curry Butter:

2 tablespoons (30 g/1.1 oz) Thai curry paste

Lemon & Herb Butter:

1 tablespoon (15 ml) fresh lemon juice
2 teaspoons (4 g/0.1 oz) fresh lemon zest
2 cloves garlic, crushed
1 to 2 tablespoons (4 to 8 g/ 0.2 to 0.3 oz) chopped herbs, such as basil, dill, or thyme, or 1 to 2 teaspoons (2 g/0.1 oz) dried herbs

Walnut & Blue Cheese Butter:

⅓ cup (45 g/1.6 oz) crumbled blue cheese
¼ cup (25 g/0.9 oz) chopped walnuts or pecans
1 teaspoon onion powder
1 to 2 tablespoons (4 to 8 g/0.2 to 0.3 oz) chopped parsley

Salty Anchovy Butter:

8 pieces (32 g/1.1 oz) canned anchovies, drained
2 cloves garlic, crushed
¼ teaspoon chili powder

NUTRITION FACTS PER SERVING (AVERAGE PER 14 G/½ OZ):
Total carbs: 0.5 g / Fiber: 0.1 g / Net carbs: 0.4 g / Protein: 0.2 g / Fat: 9.9 g / Calories: 90 kcal
Macronutrient ratio: Calories from carbs (2%), protein (1%), fat (97%)

Sweet Butters:

½ cup (113 g/4 oz) softened
    unsalted butter

Pumpkin Pie Butter:

¼ cup (50 g/1.8 oz) pumpkin
    purée
1 teaspoon pumpkin pie spice
1 tablespoon (10 g/0.4 oz)
    powdered erythritol or Swerve

Maple & Pecan Pie Butter:

⅓ cup pecans, chopped (33 g/
    1.2 oz)
½ teaspoon ground cinnamon
2 tablespoons (20 g/0.7 oz)
    powdered erythritol or Swerve
¼ teaspoon sugar-free maple
    extract

Chocolate & Orange Ganache Butter:

2 tablespoons (10 g/0.4 oz) cacao
    powder
1 teaspoon fresh orange zest
2 tablespoons (20 g/0.7 oz)
    powdered erythritol or Swerve
⅛ teaspoon sea salt

Vanilla & Cinnamon Cream Butter:

½ teaspoon vanilla powder or
    1 tablespoon (15 ml) sugar-free
    vanilla extract
½ teaspoon ground cinnamon
1 tablespoon (10 g/0.4 oz)
    powdered Erythritol or Swerve

In a medium bowl, mix the softened butter and your preferred spices, herbs, and other ingredients. Spoon the butter onto a piece of parchment paper. Wrap the butter tightly and roll it to create a log shape. Twist the ends of the paper in opposite directions to seal. Store the butter in the fridge for up to a week or freeze for up to 6 months. To freeze it, it helps if you slice it into as many servings as needed. Instead of butter, you can also use ghee or virgin coconut oil (both for sweet and savory butter), and lard or duck fat (for savory butter). If you use butter alternatives, pour the mixture into a silicone ice cube tray and refrigerate: it's perfect for portion control!

How to Serve Flavored Butter

Spread on Garlic & Herb Focaccia (page 48), Multiseed Keto Crackers (page 84), Butter-Stuffed Spatchcock Chicken (page 148), Harissa Skillet Chicken (page 152), Mediterranean Chicken Tray Bake (page 154), The Perfect Skirt Steak (page 170), or with pork chops, fish and seafood, roasted or steamed vegetables, cauliflower mash (page 166), or cauliflower rice (page 40). Try sweet butters on top of Crispy Cinnamon Waffles (page 72) or use in "Butter" Coffee (page 35).

Garlic & Herb Focaccia

MAKES: 16 slices
HANDS-ON TIME: 20 minutes
OVERALL TIME: 50 minutes

This flavorful grain-free, nut-free focaccia is based on one of the most popular recipes on my blog. It's ultra-low in net carbs, and makes an ideal addition to your lunchbox!

½ cup (75 g/2.6 oz) flax meal

⅓ cup (40 g/1.4 oz) coconut flour

⅔ cup (80 g/2.8 oz) psyllium husk powder

1 teaspoon sea salt

½ teaspoon black pepper

1 teaspoon baking soda

1 tablespoon (4 g/0.2 oz) chopped thyme, or 1 teaspoon dried thyme

1 tablespoon (4 g/0.2 oz) chopped rosemary, or 1 teaspoon dried rosemary

2 cloves garlic, crushed

½ cup (120 ml) extra-virgin olive oil

8 large egg whites

2 teaspoons (10 ml) cream of tartar or apple cider vinegar

1 cup (240 ml) lukewarm water

Preheat the oven to 350°F (175°C, or gas mark 4). Line a baking tray with heavy-duty parchment paper. In a bowl, combine the flax meal, coconut flour, psyllium powder, salt, pepper, and baking soda. In another bowl, combine the thyme, rosemary, garlic, and olive oil.

In a third bowl, beat the egg whites until they create soft—but not stiff—peaks. Add the cream of tartar while beating (this will help them stay fluffy).

Using an electric mixer, add the lukewarm water and half of the herb-oil mixture to the bowl with the dry ingredients and process well (reserve the remaining herb-oil mixture for topping). Immediately after you pour in the water and herb-oil mixture, add a quarter of the whipped egg whites to make the dough fluffy, mixing well. Then gently mix in the remaining egg whites.

Transfer the dough to the tray lined with parchment paper. Use your hands to flatten it until you create a rectangle, slightly over ½ inch (1 cm) thick. Using your fingers, create small dimples in the dough, then pour over the remaining herb-oil mixture. Bake for 25 to 30 minutes. When done, place on a cooling rack for 5 minutes, then cut into 16 pieces (4 rows by 4 columns). Store at room temperature covered with a kitchen towel for up to 3 days, or freeze for up to 6 months.

NUTRITION FACTS PER SERVING (1 SLICE):
Total carbs: 7 g / Fiber: 5.8 g / Net carbs: 1.2 g / Protein: 3.5 g / Fat: 9.8 g / Calories: 113 kcal
Macronutrient ratio: Calories from carbs (4%), protein (13%), fat (83%)

Chapter 2

Keto Break-the-Fast Dishes

When's breakfast? It's whenever you have your first meal of the day, whether that's in the morning or not. Some people like to eat as soon as they wake up—but if you're like me, you might want to wait until the afternoon to have your first meal. Either way is fine: even if you skip meals like I do, there's no need to miss out on your breakfast favorites whenever you're ready to eat.

This chapter features lots of healthy, sweet and savory breakfast meals that'll provide plenty of fat-fueled energy, helping you stay full for longer. There are plenty of options, even if you have food allergies: if you can't tolerate eggs, make the Easy Breakfast Italian Bake on page 64; or if dairy isn't your friend, try the Abundance Breakfast Bowls on page 69 and the California Crab Cakes on page 67. Don't feel like eating meat in the morning? Make a batch of Green Skillet Eggs (page 60) or Jalapeño & Cheese Muffins (page 65). And if you've got a sweet tooth, you'll love warm Crispy Cinnamon Waffles (page 72) served with your favorite Flavored Butter (page 44). Breakfast is about to become your favorite meal!

Cheesy Spinach Pancakes

MAKES: 12 pancakes
HANDS-ON TIME: 25 minutes
OVERALL TIME: 25 minutes

Simplicity is the key to success when you're new to a healthy, low-carb diet. And these savory pancakes check all the boxes! Plus they're high in micronutrients, low in carbs, and great for batch cooking. Don't limit them to breakfast: add them to your lunchbox for a complete meal on the go.

14.1 ounces (400 g) frozen spinach, drained

8 large eggs

1 cup (90 g/3.2 oz) finely grated Parmesan

¼ cup (37 g/1.3 oz) chopped sun-dried tomatoes

2 tablespoons (16 g/0.6 oz) coconut flour

1 tablespoon (5 g/0.2 oz) dried Italian herbs

½ teaspoon sea salt

¼ teaspoon black pepper

2 tablespoons (30 g/1.1 oz) ghee or duck fat

Optional: sliced avocado, cooked bacon, and Sriracha sauce for serving

Defrost the spinach (in a microwave oven or in the fridge overnight). Squeeze out as much moisture as possible (you will end up with about half of the original weight). Crack the eggs into a large bowl and whisk to combine. Add the drained spinach, Parmesan, sun-dried tomatoes, coconut flour, Italian herbs, salt, and pepper. Mix until well combined.

Heat a large skillet greased with the ghee over medium heat. Once the skillet is hot, use a ⅓-cup measure to make 3 to 4 pancakes at a time. Shape them into small pancakes in the pan using a spatula. Cook for 2 to 3 minutes, or until lightly browned and firm enough to flip onto the other side, and then cook for another 1 to 2 minutes. Repeat for the remaining pancakes. Serve warm, or let cool and store in an airtight container in the fridge for 4 to 5 days. Optionally, serve with avocado, cooked bacon, and Sriracha sauce.

NUTRITION FACTS PER SERVING (2 PANCAKES):
Total carbs: 6.5 g / Fiber: 3 g / Net carbs: 3.5 g / Protein: 17 g / Fat: 16.9 g / Calories: 244 kcal
Macronutrient ratio: Calories from carbs (6%), protein (29%), fat (65%)

Spicy Chorizo Cloud Eggs

MAKES: 2 servings
HANDS-ON TIME: 10 minutes
OVERALL TIME: 15 minutes

"Egg nests," also known as "cloud eggs," are a recent social media phenomenon. Think of them as savory, low-carb meringues. They may look sophisticated, but don't worry: they're actually very easy to make. Here's my take on this fun-to-eat, keto-friendly meal.

2 large eggs

⅛ teaspoon cream of tartar or apple cider vinegar

1 ounce (28 g) Spanish chorizo or pepperoni, chopped

1 (14 g/0.5 oz) jalapeño pepper, finely chopped

⅓ cup (37 g/1.3 oz) grated Cheddar cheese

1 tablespoon (4 g/0.2 oz) chopped chives

Pinch of sea salt and black pepper

1 medium (150 g/5.3 oz) avocado, sliced

1 cup (30 g/1.1 oz) leafy greens, such as spinach, arugula, or watercress

Optional: 2 teaspoons (10 ml) Sriracha sauce

Preheat the oven to 450°F (230°C, or gas mark 8). Separate the egg whites from the egg yolks carefully. Reserve the egg yolks: return them to the broken shells, place them in the egg carton, and set aside.

Using an electric mixer, beat the egg whites with the cream of tartar until stiff peaks form. Add the chorizo, jalapeño, Cheddar, and chives, folding them in gently with a rubber spatula.

Place a piece of heat-resistant parchment paper or a silicone mat on a baking tray. Create 2 mounds on the baking tray from the egg white mixture and create small wells in the center of each so they look like nests. Bake for about 3 minutes. Then carefully add the reserved egg yolks to the center of each nest. Season with salt and pepper, and bake for 3 minutes more. Serve with avocado and leafy greens. Top with Sriracha sauce, if desired.

NUTRITION FACTS PER SERVING:
Total carbs: 8.7 g / Fiber: 5.6 g / Net carbs: 3.1 g / Protein: 16.5 g / Fat: 27.9 g / Calories: 343 kcal
Macronutrient ratio: Calories from carbs (4%), protein (20%), fat (76%)

Breakfast Chili Bowls

MAKES: 6 servings
HANDS-ON TIME: 20 minutes
OVERALL TIME: 50 minutes

Who said you can't have chili for breakfast? Not me! These hearty, nutritious breakfast bowls are packed with sunny flavors—think ancho chiles, cumin, and cilantro—and there's nothing better for warming your tummy on a cold winter's day.

Breakfast Chili:

1 tablespoon (15 g/0.5 oz) ghee or duck fat

1 small (70 g/2.5 oz) yellow onion, chopped

2 cloves garlic, minced

1.1 pounds (500 g) ground beef

1 tablespoon (5 g/0.2 oz) dried oregano

1 tablespoon (7 g/0.2 oz) paprika

1 tablespoon (6 g/0.2 oz) mild chile powder, such as ancho chile

1 tablespoon (5 g/0.2 oz) ground cumin

⅛ to ¼ teaspoon cayenne pepper

1 can (400 g/14.1 oz) tomatoes

1 cup (240 ml) water

1 medium (200 g/7.1 oz) zucchini, diced

1 medium (120 g/4.2 oz) green pepper, diced

1 medium (120 g/4.2 oz) red pepper, diced

1 (14 g/0.5 oz) jalapeño pepper, diced

Sea salt

Toppings (per bowl):

1 large egg, fried or poached (see page 42)

¼ medium (40 g/1.4 oz) avocado, sliced

1 slice (16 g/0.6 oz) crispy bacon, crumbled

Black pepper, fresh cilantro, and lime wedges for garnish

Heat a large skillet greased with ghee. Cook the onion over medium-high heat for 5 to 7 minutes, and then add the garlic and cook for 1 minute more. Add the beef, oregano, paprika, chile powder, cumin, and cayenne pepper. Cook, stirring frequently, until the beef is browned on all sides, about 5 minutes. Add the tomatoes and water. Bring to a boil and cook for about 5 minutes. Finally, add the zucchini, peppers, and jalapeño. Reduce the heat, cover, and cook for about 20 minutes, or until the vegetables are tender.

Remove from the heat, add salt to taste, and serve (about 1 cup/240 g per serving) with fried or poached eggs, avocado, crispy bacon, black pepper, cilantro, and lime wedges. To store the chili, let it cool, then refrigerate for up to 4 days (minus the toppings). Reheat as needed.

NUTRITION FACTS PER SERVING:
Total carbs: 13.2 g / Fiber: 5.8 g / Net carbs: 7.4 g / Protein: 28.2 g / Fat: 32.2 g / Calories: 449 kcal
Macronutrient ratio: Calories from carbs (7%), protein (26%), fat (67%)

Pizza Dutch Baby

MAKES: 2 servings
HANDS-ON TIME: 15 minutes
OVERALL TIME: 25 minutes

Never had a Dutch baby before? It tastes a lot better than it sounds: it's a light and fluffy cross between a pancake and soufflé, and it makes such a satisfying breakfast or brunch. In this low-carb, margherita pizza–inspired version, I've replaced wheat flour with finely grated Parmesan cheese.

4 large eggs

¼ teaspoon cream of tartar

1 tablespoon (15 ml) ghee or duck fat

½ cup (45 g/1.6 oz) grated Parmesan cheese

1 teaspoon Italian seasoning

⅓ cup (80 g/2.8 oz) marinara sauce (page 43)

4 ounces (113 g) fresh mozzarella, sliced

1 tablespoon (4 g/0.2 oz) chopped fresh basil

Salt and pepper to taste

Carefully separate the egg whites from the egg yolks. Reserve the egg yolks and set aside. Add the cream of tartar to the bowl with egg whites. Using an electric mixer, beat the egg white mixture until stiff peaks form.

Preheat the broiler to high. Grease an 8-inch (20-cm) skillet with ghee and place over medium heat. Gently fold the reserved egg yolks, Parmesan, and Italian seasoning into the whipped egg whites. Pour into the hot pan. Cook for 1 minute, then place the pan under the broiler and cook for 5 minutes. Remove the pan from the oven, place it on a cooling rack, and top with the marinara sauce and mozzarella slices. Return the pan to the oven and broil for 5 to 8 minutes more, until the top is golden and the cheese is melted. Serve immediately, topped with fresh basil and seasoned with salt and pepper, or let cool and refrigerate for up to 3 days.

NUTRITION FACTS PER SERVING (½ PANCAKE):
Total carbs: 5.8 g / Fiber: 0.8 g / Net carbs: 5 g / Protein: 34.9 g / Fat: 38.4 g / Calories: 513 kcal
MACRONUTRIENT RATIO: Calories from carbs (4%), protein (28%), fat (68%)

Breakfast Egg Muffins Two Ways

MAKES: 12 muffins
HANDS-ON TIME: 10 minutes
OVERALL TIME: 35 minutes

Keep a batch of these egg muffins on hand so that you'll always have a keto-friendly breakfast to grab as you're running out the door in the morning. The Brie Egg Muffins are perfect for vegetarians, while the dairy-free Sausage-Zucchini version is ideal if you're lactose intolerant.

Brie Egg Muffins:

- 2 tablespoons (30 g/1.1 oz) ghee or duck fat
- 2 cloves garlic, minced
- 2 cups (100 g/3.5 oz) sliced wild mushrooms
- 2 cups (100 g/3.5 oz) chopped kale, spinach, or chard
- 8 large eggs
- ½ cup (120 g/4.2 oz) ricotta cheese
- ½ teaspoon sea salt
- ¼ teaspoon black pepper
- 5 ounces (142 g) Brie cheese, or blue, Swiss, or Cheddar cheese

Sausage-Zucchini Egg Muffins:

- 2 tablespoons (30 g/1.1 oz) ghee or duck fat
- 1 medium (100 g/3.5 oz) onion, finely chopped
- 14.1 ounces (400 g) gluten-free sausages, casings removed
- 8 large eggs
- ½ cup (120 ml) heavy whipping cream or coconut milk
- ½ teaspoon sea salt
- ¼ teaspoon black pepper
- 1 medium (150 g/5.3 oz) zucchini, cut into 12 slices

Preheat the oven to 350°F (175°C, or gas mark 4). Grease a muffin pan with 1 tablespoon (15 g/0.5 oz) of the ghee or duck fat.

TO MAKE THE BRIE EGG MUFFINS: Heat a skillet greased with the remaining 1 tablespoon (15 g/0.5 oz) ghee over medium heat. Add the garlic and cook for 1 minute. Then add the mushrooms and kale and cook for another 5 minutes, stirring occasionally. When the mushrooms are cooked and the kale is wilted, take off the heat and set aside. In a bowl, whisk the eggs with ricotta, salt, and pepper. Distribute the cooked mushroom-kale mixture among 12 muffin tins, top each with an equal portion of the egg mixture, and finish each with a slice of Brie cheese. Season with more black pepper and transfer to the oven. Bake for 20 to 25 minutes, or until the muffins are golden brown and puffed up.

TO MAKE THE SAUSAGE-ZUCCHINI EGG MUFFINS: Heat a skillet greased with the remaining 1 tablespoon (15 g/0.5 oz) ghee over medium-high heat. Add the onion and cook about 5 minutes, until fragrant. Add the sausage meat and cook until browned on all sides, about 5 minutes. Remove from the heat and set aside. In a bowl, whisk the eggs with the cream, salt, and pepper. Distribute the cooked sausage meat between among 12 muffin tins, top each with an equal portion of the egg mixture, and finish each with a slice of zucchini. Season with more black pepper and transfer to the oven. Bake for 20 to 25 minutes, or until the muffins are golden brown and puffed up.

Egg muffins are delicious served warm or cold. Store in the fridge in an airtight container for 4 to 5 days.

NUTRITION FACTS PER MUFFIN (BRIE/SAUSAGE):
Total carbs: 1.5/1.9 g / Fiber: 0.3/0.3 g / Net carbs: 1.2/1.6 g / Protein: 8.1/9.4 g / Fat: 10.3/20 g / Calories: 132/228 kcal / Macronutrient ratio: Calories from carbs (4/3%), protein (25/17%), fat (71/80%)

Cheesy Waffle Stacks

MAKES: 4 servings
HANDS-ON TIME: 20 minutes
OVERALL TIME: 30 minutes

There's no need to say good-bye to waffles just because you're following a keto lifestyle. These savory, quick-prep fat stacks feature cheese and cauliflower rice (page 40) instead of wheat flour. Top them with homemade guacamole and they're sure to keep you full for hours.

Quick Guacamole:

- 2 medium (300 g/10.6 oz) avocados, pitted and peeled
- ½ small (35 g/1.2 oz) yellow onion, chopped
- 3 tablespoons (45 ml) fresh lime juice
- 1 clove garlic, crushed
- ½ cup (75 g/2.5 oz) chopped cherry or regular tomatoes
- Fresh cilantro, sea salt, and black pepper

Waffles:

- 1 tablespoon (15 g/0.5 oz) ghee or duck fat
- ½ medium (35 g/1.2 oz) yellow onion, chopped
- 1½ cups (180 g/6.3 oz) cauliflower rice (page 40)
- 3 large eggs
- ⅓ cup (30 g/1.1 oz) grated Parmesan cheese
- ¼ cup (28 g/1 oz) grated mozzarella
- 2 tablespoons (16 g/0.6 oz) coconut flour
- ½ teaspoon gluten-free baking powder
- ¼ teaspoon sea salt
- ¼ teaspoon black pepper

Fried Eggs:

- 1 tablespoon (15 g/0.5 oz) ghee or duck fat
- 4 large eggs

TO MAKE THE GUACAMOLE: In a bowl, mash the avocados until chunky. Add the onion, lime juice, garlic, and tomatoes, and mix until well combined. Add the cilantro, salt, and pepper to taste, and set aside. To store, keep refrigerated for up to 3 days.

TO MAKE THE WAFFLES: Grease a skillet with the ghee and place over medium-high heat. Add the onion and cook for about 5 minutes, until fragrant and lightly browned. Then add the cauliflower rice and cook for 5 to 7 minutes, stirring frequently. Remove from the heat and set aside to cool.

In a bowl, combine the cooked cauliflower rice, eggs, Parmesan, mozzarella, coconut flour, baking powder, salt, and pepper. Spoon the batter (¼ of the total amount per waffle) into a preheated waffle maker, close, and cook for 1 to 2 minutes, or until crisp and cooked through. Transfer the waffles to a plate and let cool for a few minutes before serving. Store any leftover waffles in an airtight container in the fridge for up to 5 days, or freeze for up to 3 months.

TO MAKE THE FRIED EGGS: Then, fry the eggs. Grease the pan with the ghee and place over medium-high heat. Once the skillet is hot, add the eggs. Cook until the egg whites are opaque and the egg yolks are still runny.

To assemble, place one waffle on a plate and top with the prepared guacamole and fried egg. Serve immediately.

NOTE: Get creative! Instead of waffles, try panfried bacon slices, or small patties made with sausage meat, ground beef, or pork.

NUTRITION FACTS PER SERVING (1 WAFFLE + GUACAMOLE + FRIED EGG):
Total carbs: 14.4 g / Fiber: 7.4 g / Net carbs: 7 g / Protein: 19 g / Fat: 31 g / Calories: 405 kcal
Macronutrient ratio: Calories from carbs (7%), protein (20%), fat (73%)

Green Skillet Eggs

MAKES: 1 serving
HANDS-ON TIME: 10 minutes
OVERALL TIME: 10 minutes

Stuffed with nutrient-dense leafy greens, potassium-packed zucchini, and choline-rich eggs, this ten-minute meal is one of my favorite vegetarian breakfasts, but it makes a great light lunch or dinner in a pinch, too.

1 tablespoon (15 g/0.5 oz) ghee or duck fat

½ small (35 g/1.2 oz) yellow onion, chopped

1 clove garlic, minced

1 cup (124 g/4.4 oz) diced zucchini

2 cups (72 g/2.5 oz) leafy greens such as collards, spinach, or Swiss chard

2 large eggs

Sea salt, black pepper, and (optionally) red pepper flakes

Optional: sliced avocado for serving

Grease a skillet with the ghee, and add the onion and garlic. Cook over medium heat for about 3 minutes, or until fragrant and lightly browned. Add the zucchini and cook for 3 to 5 minutes, or until tender. Add the greens (chopped or whole), and cook until wilted, 1 to 2 minutes.

Using a spatula, create 2 wells in the vegetable mixture and crack in the eggs. Cook over medium heat for 2 to 3 minutes, or until the egg white is almost cooked through. Then cover the skillet with a lid and cook for 1 minute more. (Alternatively, place the skillet under the broiler for 1 minute, or until the egg whites are cooked through and the egg yolks are still runny.) Season with salt, pepper, and red pepper flakes, if you like. Serve immediately—perhaps with some avocado.

NUTRITION FACTS PER SERVING:
Total carbs: 12.4 g / Fiber: 4.8 g / Net carbs: 7.6 g / Protein: 16.8 g / Fat: 25.4 g / Calories: 340 kcal
Macronutrient ratio: Calories from carbs (9%), protein (21%), fat (70%)

Greek Omelet

MAKES: 2 servings
HANDS-ON TIME: 10 minutes
OVERALL TIME: 10 minutes

Versatile, low in carbs, and highly nutritious, omelets are a keto staple! Half of this Mediterranean-style omelet will be enough as a regular breakfast, while a whole omelet will provide you with enough energy if you practice intermittent fasting (see page 31) and need an extra-hearty meal to keep you going until dinner.

2 tablespoons (30 g/1.1 oz) ghee, divided

½ medium (60 g/2.1 oz) green pepper, sliced

1 clove garlic, minced

2 cups (60 g/2.1 oz) fresh spinach

½ teaspoon dried oregano

1 teaspoon chopped fresh mint or ¼ teaspoon dried mint

3 large eggs

Sea salt and black pepper

⅓ cup (50 g/1.8 oz) chopped cherry tomatoes

¼ cup (38 g/1.3 oz) crumbled feta cheese

4 (12 g/0.4 oz) black or green olives, sliced

2 teaspoons (10 ml) extra-virgin olive oil

Grease a skillet with 1 tablespoon (15 g/0.5 oz) of the ghee and add the green pepper. Cook over medium-high for about 5 minutes. Add the garlic, and cook for 1 minute more. Add the spinach and herbs (reserve a pinch of the herbs for topping), and cook until wilted, about 1 minute. Transfer to a bowl and set aside.

Grease the skillet with the remaining 1 tablespoon (15 g/0.5 oz) ghee. In a bowl, beat the eggs with a pinch of salt and pepper. Once the skillet is hot, pour in the eggs. Use a spatula to fold the eggs from the sides of the pan toward the center for the first 30 seconds. Tilt the pan as needed to cover it with the eggs. Lower the heat and cook for 1 minute more. Don't rush it, and don't try to cook it too fast, or the omelet will end up being too crispy and dry. When the top is almost cooked, add the reserved vegetable mixture. Top with the tomatoes, feta, olives, and remaining herbs. Drizzle with the olive oil, fold the omelet in half, cook for another minute to warm up the toppings, and slide onto a serving plate.

NUTRITION FACTS PER SERVING (½ OMELET):
Total carbs: 5.6 g / Fiber: 1.9 g / Net carbs: 3.7 g / Protein: 13.6 g / Fat: 31.8 g / Calories: 362 kcal
Macronutrient ratio: Calories from carbs (4%), protein (15%), fat (81%)

Sausage & Brussels Sprout Hash

MAKES: 4 servings
HANDS-ON TIME: 15 minutes
OVERALL TIME: 20 minutes

This hash makes the perfect weekend breakfast: it's a great way to use up any leftover vegetables that have been lurking in the fridge all week. Don't have Brussels sprouts? No problem: try it with kale, cabbage, or even chard, and serve it topped with fried or poached eggs or sliced avocado.

2 tablespoons (30 g/1.1 oz) ghee or duck fat

4 slices (60 g/2.1 oz) bacon

½ small (35 g/1.2 oz) yellow onion, chopped

10.6 ounces (300 g) gluten-free Italian-style sausages, casing removed

1 tablespoon (15 g/0.5 oz) Dijon mustard

10.6 ounces (300 g) white mushrooms, sliced

14.1 ounces (400 g) Brussels sprouts, sliced

¼ cup (60 ml) water

Sea salt and pepper

4 large eggs, or 1 large (200 g/7.1 oz) avocado, sliced

Heat a large skillet greased with the ghee over medium-high heat. Add the bacon and cook for about 5 minutes, until lightly crispy. Add the onion and cook for another 5 minutes, then add the sausage meat and cook for 3 to 5 minutes more. Add the mustard, mushrooms, and Brussels sprouts. Add the water, mix, and cover with a lid. Reduce the heat to medium-low and cook for 5 to 7 minutes, or until the Brussels sprouts are tender. To serve, use a spatula to create 4 wells in the mixture and crack in the eggs. Cook until the egg whites are opaque and the egg yolks are still runny. Season with salt and pepper. If you're not serving immediately, don't add the eggs; let the meat-vegetable mixture cool and store it in the fridge for up to 4 days. Serve with freshly fried or poached eggs or with sliced avocado.

NUTRITION FACTS PER SERVING:
Total carbs: 13.2 g/ Fiber: 4.8 g / Net carbs: 8.4 g / Protein: 125 g / Fat: 40.5 g / Calories: 511 kcal
Macronutrient ratio: Calories from carbs (7%), protein (20%), fat (73%)

Easy Breakfast Italian Bake

MAKES: 4 servings
HANDS-ON TIME: 10 minutes
OVERALL TIME: 30 minutes

This six-ingredient breakfast bake is a low-carb, dairy-free riff on lasagna—except it calls for sausage and vitamin-rich broccoli in place of unhealthy, high-carb noodles. It couldn't be simpler to make, but its payoff is huge. Prepare it the night before, and you'll have breakfast taken care of for the next few days!

1 tablespoon (15 g/0.5 oz) ghee or duck fat

10.6 ounces (300 g) gluten-free Italian-style sausages, casing removed

⅔ cup (160 g/5.6 oz) marinara sauce (page 43)

1½ cups (170 g/6 oz) shredded mozzarella

7.1 ounces (200 g) broccoli florets or broccolini

4 tablespoons (20 g/0.7 oz) grated Parmesan cheese

Preheat the oven to 360°F (180°C, or gas mark 4). Heat a skillet greased with the ghee over medium-high heat. Add the sausage and cook for 3 to 5 minutes, until browned on all sides. Add about half of the marinara sauce to the skillet and remove from the heat. Distribute the sausage-marinara mixture evenly among 4 mini baking dishes (or use one regular-size dish). Top with half of the mozzarella, the broccoli florets, and the remaining marinara sauce. Top with the remaining mozzarella and sprinkle with the Parmesan. Place in the oven and bake for about 20 minutes. Serve warm, or let cool and refrigerate for up to 4 days.

NUTRITION FACTS PER SERVING:
Total carbs: 7.9 g / Fiber: 1.8 g / Net carbs: 6.1 g / Protein: 25.3 g / Fat: 43.7 g / Calories: 526 kcal
Macronutrient ratio: Calories from carbs (5%), protein (20%), fat (75%)

Jalapeño & Cheese Muffins

MAKES: 12 muffins
HANDS-ON TIME: 10 minutes
OVERALL TIME: 40 minutes

Moist and utterly delicious, these spicy, cheesy muffins are miniature powerhouses. They make a filling breakfast, but they're also yummy additions to lunchboxes, and work well as accompaniments to Salisbury Steak with Quick Mash (page 166) or Mexican Chicken Bowls (page 126).

6 large eggs

⅓ cup (80 ml) extra-virgin olive oil or melted butter

¼ cup (60 ml) water

½ teaspoon sea salt

¼ teaspoon black pepper

1 medium (200 g/7.1 oz) zucchini, grated

1½ cups (170 g/6 oz) grated Cheddar cheese

2 (28 g/1 oz) jalapeño peppers, finely chopped

1 cup (100 g/3.5 oz) almond flour

⅓ cup (40 g/1.4 oz) coconut flour

4 tablespoons (28 g/1 oz) flax meal

2 teaspoons onion powder

½ teaspoon garlic powder

2 teaspoons gluten-free baking powder

Preheat the oven to 350°F (175°C, or gas mark 4). Crack the eggs into a bowl and beat with the olive oil, water, salt, and pepper. Add all the remaining ingredients and mix until well combined. Spoon the mixture into a silicone muffin pan to make 12 muffins (or use a regular muffin pan greased with a small amount of ghee). Place in the oven and bake for about 30 minutes, until the tops are golden brown and the insides are set and fluffy. Remove from the oven and let cool slightly. While the muffins are still warm, remove them from the muffin pan and place on a cooling rack. To store, place in an airtight container and refrigerate for up to 5 days, or freeze for up to 6 months.

NUTRITION FACTS PER SERVING (1 MUFFIN):
Total carbs: 4.8 g / Fiber: 2.4 g / Net carbs: 2.4 g / Protein: 9.7 g / Fat: 19 g / Calories: 226 kcal
Macronutrient ratio: Calories from carbs (4%), protein (18%), fat (78%)

Bubble & Squeak Breakfast Bake

MAKES: 6 servings
HANDS-ON TIME: 15 minutes
OVERALL TIME: 30 minutes

Bubble and squeak is a simple all-day English breakfast dish made with leftover veggies. The traditional recipe uses mashed potatoes, which acts as the "glue" that holds the dish together. To create the same effect and flavor with fewer carbs, I've replaced the mashed potatoes with cauliflower and a few beaten eggs. Serve with pickles, fried eggs, sausages, or avocado.

2 tablespoons (30 ml) duck fat or ghee

8 slices (240 g/8.5 oz) bacon, chopped

1 small (70 g/2.5 oz) yellow onion, chopped

1 clove garlic, minced

1 small (300 g/10.6 oz) cauliflower, chopped

1 small (300 g/10.6 oz) green cabbage, shredded

2 cups (200 g/7.1 oz) shredded Brussels sprouts,

¼ cup (60 ml) water

4 large eggs, lightly beaten

Salt and black pepper

Heat a large deep-dish skillet greased with the duck fat over medium-high heat. Add the bacon and cook for about 5 minutes, until lightly browned and crispy. Add the onion and cook for another 5 minutes, then add the garlic and cook for 1 minute more. Add the cauliflower, reduce the heat to medium, and cover with a lid. Cook for about 5 minutes. Add the cabbage, Brussels sprouts, and water. Cook, covered, for 2 minutes. Then remove the lid and cook for 3 to 4 minutes more. Mix in the eggs and cook until set, about 5 minutes. Alternatively, place the skillet under the broiler and cook for about 5 minutes until lightly golden and set. Season with salt and pepper.

NUTRITION FACTS PER SERVING:
Total carbs: 9.7 g / Fiber: 3.8 g / Net carbs: 5.9 g / Protein: 12.4 g / Fat: 17.8 g / Calories: 240 kcal
Macronutrient ratio: Calories from carbs (10%), protein (21%), fat (69%)

California Crab Cakes

MAKES: 6 servings (12 patties)
HANDS-ON TIME: 30 minutes
OVERALL TIME: 30 minutes

Crab cakes are easy to dress up or down. Served with asparagus, avocado, and my Spicy Hollandaise Sauce, they make an elegant weekend brunch. You can also prepare a batch in advance and pop a couple into your lunchbox for a no-fuss workday lunch.

Crab Cakes:

1 pound (450 g) cooked or canned crabmeat
2 large eggs
¼ cup (30 g/1.1 oz) coconut flour
2 tablespoons (14 g/0.5 oz) flax meal
¼ cup (55 g/1.9 oz) mayonnaise
½ teaspoon salt
¼ teaspoon black pepper
1 teaspoon Dijon mustard
1 teaspoon Sriracha sauce
2 tablespoons (8 g/0.3 oz) chopped fresh parsley
1 tablespoon (15 g/0.5 oz) ghee or duck fat

Spicy Hollandaise Sauce:

3 large egg yolks
3 tablespoons (45 ml) each fresh lemon juice and water
¾ teaspoon Dijon mustard
⅓ cup (80 ml) extra-virgin olive oil
1 tablespoon plus 1 teaspoon (20 g/0.7 oz) Sriracha
Salt and black pepper

Serve with (per serving):

6 to 10 asparagus spears (57 g/2 oz), woody ends removed
Optional: handful of fresh arugula
¼ medium (40 g/1.4 oz) avocado, sliced

TO MAKE THE CRAB CAKES: Place all the ingredients except the ghee in a mixing bowl and combine. Use a ¼-cup measuring cup (about 55 g/1.9 oz) to measure out each patty. The mixture will be wet so you'll need to use your hands to form the patties. Heat a large pan greased with the ghee over medium heat. Once hot, add as many patties as you can fit in a single layer, until you've cooked 12 patties in total. Cook them on each side for 4 to 5 minutes and use a spatula to flip them over. (Do not force the patties out of the pan: if a patty doesn't release when you try to flip it, cook it for a few more seconds until it's crisp and ready to flip.) Set the cooked patties aside.

TO MAKE THE HOLLANDAISE SAUCE: fill a medium saucepan with a cup of water and bring to a boil. Mix the egg yolks with the lemon juice and 3 tablespoons water, plus more if it's too thick, and the Dijon mustard. (Use the leftover egg whites to make focaccia on page 48). Place the bowl over the saucepan filled with water. The water should not touch the bottom of the bowl. Keep mixing until the sauce starts to thicken. Slowly pour the olive oil into the mixture, and stir constantly until the sauce becomes thick and creamy. Stir in the Sriracha sauce, and season to taste. If the sauce is too thick, add a splash of water.

Boil the asparagus in a saucepan filled with salter water for about 2 minutes until crisp-tender. Drain and keep warm.

To serve, place a few asparagus spears, and, optionally arugula, on a plate. Top with crab cakes and avocado, and serve with hollandaise sauce. The crab cakes can be stored in the fridge (minus the toppings) for up to 4 days.

NUTRITION FACTS PER SERVING (2 CRAB CAKES + VEGETABLES + 2 TABLESPOONS/30 ML HOLLANDAISE SAUCE):
Total carbs: 9.7 g / Fiber: 5.6 g / Net carbs: 4.1 g / Protein: 21.5 g / Fat: 35.5 g / Calories: 437 kcal
Macronutrient ratio: Calories from carbs (4%), protein (20%), fat (76%)

Abundance Breakfast Bowls

MAKES: 4 servings
HANDS-ON TIME: 20 minutes
OVERALL TIME: 45 minutes

Breakfast pancakes don't have to be sweet. Here, spicy, savory, zucchini pancakes act as a base for all kinds of filling, low-carb toppings, such as sausage, avocado, kimchi, and egg. These breakfast bowls are nutritious, are good for your gut, and provide enough protein and fat to keep you going for hours.

Curried Zucchini Pancakes:

- 2 medium (400 g/14.1 oz) zucchini, grated
- 1 teaspoon salt
- 2 teaspoons (4 g/0.2 oz) mild curry powder
- 1 teaspoon onion powder
- ½ teaspoon ground turmeric
- ¼ teaspoon black pepper
- 4 large eggs
- 3 tablespoons (24 g/0.8 oz) coconut flour
- 2 tablespoons (8 g/0.3 oz) chopped fresh herbs, such as parsley, cilantro, or mint
- 2 tablespoons (30 ml) duck fat or ghee, divided

Serve with (per serving):

- 2 pieces (134 g/4.7 oz) gluten-free sausages
- 1 cup (30 g/1.1 oz) spinach or other soft leafy greens
- ¼ large (50 g/1.8 oz) avocado, sliced
- ¼ medium (50 g/1.8 oz) cucumber, sliced
- ¼ cup (35 g/1.2 oz) kimchi or sauerkraut, drained
- 1 large egg, soft-boiled, fried, or poached (see page 42)
- 1 teaspoon sesame seeds
- Pinch of salt and red pepper flakes

TO MAKE THE PANCAKES: Combine the zucchini and salt in a large bowl. Let it sit for 20 to 30 minutes, then squeeze out the extra liquid with your hands. Place the drained zucchini into another bowl. After draining, you should end up with about 9.5 ounces (270 g) of zucchini.

Add the remaining ingredients, except the duck fat, to the bowl with the drained zucchini and mix until well combined. Grease a large pan with a tablespoon (15 ml) of the duck fat. Scoop some of the zucchini mixture into a ⅓-cup (80 ml) measuring cup to measure out the pancakes. Place 3 to 4 pancakes at a time in the hot pan, and cook over medium heat for 4 to 5 minutes. Use a spatula to flip them over. Cook for another 2 to 3 minutes until golden brown. Transfer to a plate, and repeat for the remaining mixture until you've make 8 pancakes, greasing with more ghee as needed.

Once the pancakes are cooked, add the sausages. Cook for 5 to 7 minutes, turning occasionally, until golden brown and cooked through.

Serve the pancakes with the cooked sausages, spinach, avocado, cucumber, kimchi, and egg. Sprinkle with sesame seeds and red pepper flakes. Season with salt to taste, and serve immediately.

NUTRITION FACTS PER SERVING (2 PANCAKES + ALL SERVING OPTIONS):
Total carbs: 15 g / Fiber: 7.7 g / Net carbs: 7.3 g / Protein: 38.1 g / Fat: 48.6 g / Calories: 642 kcal
Macronutrient ratio: Calories from carbs (5%), protein (25%), fat (70%)

PB & Jelly Chia Parfaits

MAKES: 4 servings
HANDS-ON TIME: 15 minutes
OVERALL TIME: 30 minutes

Based on everyone's favorite lunchtime treat, these breakfast parfaits are naturally sweetened with black-berries and call for paleo-friendly almond butter instead of peanut butter. Plus, MCT oil adds an extra energy boost and helps keep you full until lunch. Sweeteners are optional—but best avoided during the induction phase—in this guilt-free, low-carb breakfast.

Chia Layer:

1 cup (240 ml) unsweetened almond milk

½ cup (120 ml) coconut milk

2 tablespoons (32 g/1.1 oz) almond butter, preferably roasted almond butter

2 tablespoons (30 ml) MCT oil, or MUFA-based mild-tasting oil (see page 18)

½ teaspoon vanilla bean powder or ground cinnamon

Pinch of sea salt

¼ cup (32 g/1.1 oz) whole chia seeds

Optional: 2 tablespoons (20 g/0.7 oz) powdered erythritol or Swerve, or 5 to 10 drops liquid stevia extract

Jelly Layer:

1 cup (144 g/5 oz) blackberries, fresh or frozen

3 tablespoons (45 ml) water

1 tablespoon (15 ml) fresh lemon juice

1 teaspoon fresh lemon zest

Optional: 1 tablespoon (10 g/0.4 oz) erythritol or Swerve, or a few drops of stevia, to taste

1 tablespoon (8 g/0.3 oz) whole chia seeds

To Assemble:

¼ cup (64 g/2.2 oz) almond butter, preferably roasted almond butter

TO MAKE THE CHIA LAYER: Place all the ingredients, except the chia seeds, into a blender. Pulse until smooth and then pour into a bowl. Add the chia seeds and erythritol or stevia, if using, and set aside for 20 to 30 minutes, or overnight.

TO MAKE THE JELLY LAYER: Place the blackberries, water, lemon juice, lemon zest, and erythritol, if using, into a saucepan. Bring to a boil over medium heat. Cook for 2 to 3 minutes to soften, then remove from the heat. Mix in the chia seeds and set aside for 15 to 20 minutes.

TO ASSEMBLE: Divide the prepared chia layer among 4 jars. Top each with the blackberry jelly, followed by a tablespoon (16 g/0.5 oz) of almond butter each. Serve immediately, or refrigerate for up to 4 days.

NUTRITION FACTS PER SERVING:
Total carbs: 13.5 g / Fiber: 8.6 g / Net carbs: 4.9 g / Protein: 7.9 g / Fat: 28.9 g / Calories: 351 kcal
Macronutrient ratio: Calories from carbs (6%), protein (10%), fat (84%)

Crispy Cinnamon Waffles

MAKES: 8 waffles
HANDS-ON TIME: 15 minutes
OVERALL TIME: 15 minutes

These fragrant cinnamon waffles are just what you need on a Sunday morning. And because they only take fifteen minutes to whip up, you won't have to spend all morning in the kitchen, either. They're especially irresistible when served with your favorite sweet Flavored Butter (page 47).

1½ cups (150 g/5.3 oz) almond flour

1 tablespoon (8 g/0.3 oz) psyllium husk powder

2 teaspoons (4 g/0.2 oz) ground cinnamon

¼ teaspoon vanilla bean powder, or 1 teaspoon sugar-free vanilla extract

2 tablespoons (20 g/0.7 oz) granulated erythritol or Swerve

¼ teaspoon baking soda

½ teaspoon cream of tartar or fresh lemon juice

2 large eggs

¼ cup (60 ml) unsweetened almond or cashew milk

2 tablespoons (30 ml) coconut oil for greasing

Optional per serving: ½ to ¾ ounce (10 to 20 g) of any sweet Flavored Butter (page 47), and few slices of crispy bacon (page 41)

Place all the dry ingredients in a bowl and combine well. Add the eggs and almond milk, and mix well until you create a loose cookie dough–like batter. To make each waffle, spoon about ¼ cup/60 g of the batter into a greased, preheated waffle maker, close, and cook for 1 to 2 minutes, or until crisped up and cooked through. Re-grease as needed until you make 8 waffles. Transfer the waffles to a plate and let cool for a few minutes before serving. Store any leftover waffles in an airtight container in the fridge for up to 5 days, or freeze for up to 3 months.

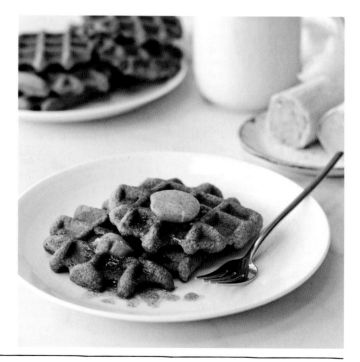

NUTRITION FACTS PER SERVING (2 WAFFLES):
Total carbs: 10.3 g / Fiber: 5.9 g / Net carbs: 4.4 g / Protein: 11.4 g / Fat: 22.3 g / Calories: 265 kcal
Macronutrient ratio: Calories from carbs (7%), protein (17%), fat (76%)

Chocolate Soufflé Pancake with Pumpkin Pie Swirl

MAKES: 2 servings
HANDS-ON TIME: 15 minutes
OVERALL TIME: 20 minutes

Treats like pancakes aren't usually allowed on a keto diet, right? Wrong! You can enjoy this indulgent chocolate soufflé pancake and still stay within your carb limit. And its presentation is so impressive: I've made several variations of these fluffy pancakes, and they're a big hit on social media.

4 large eggs

¼ teaspoon cream of tartar or apple cider vinegar

Pinch of sea salt

¼ cup (40 g/1.4 oz) powdered erythritol or Swerve, divided

2 tablespoons (10 g/0.4 oz) cacao powder

2 tablespoons (30 ml) melted butter, ghee, or virgin coconut oil

½ teaspoon pumpkin pie spice

1 tablespoon (15 ml) ghee or virgin coconut oil

Preheat the oven to 400°F (200°C, or gas mark 6).

Separate the egg whites from the yolks. Mix the yolks with a fork. Add the cream of tartar and salt to the egg whites. Using an electric mixer, beat the egg whites on medium-low speed for about 2 minutes until the whites become foamy. Add 3 tablespoons (30 g/1.1 oz) of the erythritol. Keep beating until stiff peaks form.

Fold 3 egg yolks (keep one egg yolk in the bowl) into the mixture using a silicone spatula. Sift in the cacao powder and gently combine with the egg white mixture without deflating them. To the bowl with the reserved egg yolk, add the melted butter, pumpkin pie spice mix, and the remaining 1 tablespoon (10 g/0.4 oz) erythritol.

Spread the pancake batter in a hot 8- to 9-inch (20- to 23-cm) skillet greased with the ghee. Use the rounded side of a teaspoon to draw a spiral-shaped swirl into the pancake, starting in the middle and ending at the edges. Then use the teaspoon to drizzle the prepared pumpkin pie filling into the swirl. Cook over low heat for about 5 minutes, until the bottom of the pancake starts to brown. Remove from the burner and place under the broiler for about 5 minutes, or until the top is lightly browned. Serve immediately with a dollop of sour cream, whipped cream, or coconut cream.

> **FOR DAIRY-FREE WHIPPED CREAM:**
> Simply place the contents of a 13.5 ounce (400-ml) can of coconut milk in a bowl. Use an electric mixer to slowly whip it up until fluffy, just like dairy whipped cream.

NUTRITION FACTS PER SERVING (½ PANCAKE):
Total carbs: 5.9 g / Fiber: 2.4 g / Net carbs: 3.6 g / Protein: 13.8 g / Fat: 31.8 g / Calories: 354 kcal
Macronutrient ratio: Calories from carbs (4%), protein (16%), fat (80%)

Chapter 3

Light Dishes and Appetizers

When you're following a ketogenic diet, snacking is generally discouraged, because it can stall your progress (to find out why, see page 36). But the fact is that life gets busy, and you might not always have time to make healthy meals when you're running around all day. That's why it makes sense to have some healthy snack options on hand.

The recipes in this chapter are here to help, and they're way better than the high-carb, processed foods we grab without thinking when hunger strikes—like crackers, chips, or a burger from your local fast-food chain. If you're traveling and need a quick on-the-go snack, make a batch of Multiseed Keto Crackers (page 84) and munch on them with a low-carb dip—like the Macadamia Cheese Dip on page 86—or some sliced avocado. Super-portable Deviled Eggs Two Ways (page 77)—a keto classic!—do the trick, too. They're full of protein and good-for-you fats, and they are easy to pop into your bag for a quick, nourishing nibble. And if you're throwing a party, you'll find plenty of keto-friendly crowd-pleasers, here, too: none of your guests will be able to say no to Crispy Ranch Chicken Wings (page 81) or Tomato & Feta Bruschetta (page 82)—and neither will you!

Bacon-Wrapped Jalapeño Poppers Two Ways

MAKES: 6 servings
HANDS-ON TIME: 15 minutes
OVERALL TIME: 30 minutes

In addition to being the ideal keto appetizers (just try to keep your guests away from them at your next party!), these jalapeño poppers are super-portable. They're a handy way to add spice—not to mention low-carb veggies and plenty of healthy fats—to your lunchbox on Monday morning.

Cheese Filling:

½ cup (125 g / 4.4 oz) ricotta cheese
⅓ cup (38g / 1.3 oz) grated Swiss cheese or Cheddar cheese
1 tablespoon (4 g/0.2 oz) chopped fresh cilantro or parsley

Guacamole Filling:

1 large (200 g/7.1 oz) avocado, pitted and peeled
⅔ cup (100 g/3.5 oz) chopped cherry tomatoes
½ small (30 g/1.1 oz) yellow onion, finely chopped
1 teaspoon chopped chile pepper
1 clove garlic, crushed
2 tablespoons (30 ml) fresh lime juice
2 tablespoons (8 g/0.3 oz) chopped fresh cilantro
Sea salt and black pepper

To Assemble:

6 (85 g/3 oz) jalapeño peppers, halved and seeded
12 slices (180 g/6.3 oz) bacon

Preheat the oven to 400°F (200°C, or gas mark 6).

TO MAKE THE CHEESE FILLING: Combine the ricotta, cheese, and cilantro in a bowl. Fill each jalapeño half with a tablespoon (14 g/0.5 oz) of the cheese mixture.

TO MAKE THE GUACAMOLE FILLING: Place half of the avocado in a bowl and mash with a fork. Dice the remaining avocado and add to the bowl with the tomatoes, onion, chile, garlic, lime juice, cilantro, and salt and pepper to taste. Fill each jalapeño half with 2 tablespoons (31 g/1.1 oz) of the guacamole mixture.

TO ASSEMBLE: Wrap each jalapeño half in one bacon slice and place on a baking sheet lined with parchment paper. Bake for 20 to 25 minutes, until golden and crispy. Serve hot, or let them cool and refrigerate for up to 4 days.

NUTRITION FACTS PER SERVING (2 CHEESE/GUACAMOLE POPPERS):
Total carbs: 1.6/5.3 g / Fiber: 0.4/3 g / Net carbs: 1.2/2.3 g / Protein: 8.1/5.2 g / Fat: 12.3/12.6 g
Calories: 149/149 kcal / Macronutrient ratio: Calories from carbs (3/6%), protein (22/14%), fat (75/80%)

Deviled Eggs Two Ways

MAKES: 4 servings
HANDS-ON TIME: 10 minutes
OVERALL TIME: 15 minutes

When it comes to quick and easy keto appetizers and snacks, deviled eggs are an absolute classic. They're beautifully simple to make, but you can really get creative with them. Here's proof! These are two of my favorite versions, but the options are endless.

4 large eggs

Buffalo Deviled Eggs:

2 tablespoons (30 g/1.1 oz) mayonnaise (page 42)

1 tablespoon (12 g/0.4 oz) sour cream

⅓ cup (45 g/1.6 oz) crumbled blue cheese

1 tablespoon (15 g/0.5 oz) Sriracha sauce

1 clove crushed garlic or ¼ teaspoon garlic powder

1 medium (15 g/0.5 oz) spring onion, chopped

1 tablespoon (4 g/0.2 oz) chopped fresh parsley

1 tablespoon (4 g/0.2 oz) chopped fresh dill

Sea salt and pepper

Guacamole Deviled Eggs:

½ medium (75 g/2.6 oz) avocado

1 tablespoon (15 g/0.5 oz) mayonnaise (page 42)

1 tablespoon (15 ml) fresh lime juice

1 to 2 teaspoons finely chopped red or green chile

1 tablespoon (4 g/0.2 oz) chopped fresh cilantro

Sea salt and black pepper

First, hard-boil the eggs by following the instructions on page 42. Cut the eggs in half and carefully—without breaking the egg whites—spoon the egg yolks into a bowl. Set the whites aside.

TO MAKE THE BUFFALO DEVILED EGGS: Combine the cooked egg yolks, mayonnaise, sour cream, blue cheese, Sriracha sauce, garlic, spring onion, parsley, and dill (reserve some herbs or spring onion for topping). Season with salt and pepper.

ALTERNATIVELY, TO MAKE THE GUACAMOLE DEVILED EGGS: Place the avocado, mayonnaise, lime juice, chile, and cilantro into a bowl. Mash with a fork until well combined. Season with salt and pepper to taste.

Use a spoon or a small cookie scoop to fill the egg white halves with the prepared mixture of your choice. Store in an airtight container in the fridge for up to 2 days.

NUTRITION FACTS PER SERVING (2 BUFFALO/GUACAMOLE DEVILED EGGS):
Total carbs: 1.8/2.5 g / Fiber: 0.2/1.3 g / Net carbs: 1.6/1.2 g / Protein: 9.1/6.8 g / Fat: 15.1/10.7 g
Calories: 180/132 kcal / Macronutrient ratio: Calories from carbs (4/4%), protein (20/21%), fat (76/75%)

Parma Ham Roll-Ups Three Ways

MAKES: 12 roll-ups
HANDS-ON TIME: 20 minutes
OVERALL TIME: 20 minutes

Keto-friendly Parma ham takes the place of high-carb tortillas in these fun-to-eat roll-ups. Serve them at your next party: even the pickiest eaters love them!

MCT Balsamic Vinaigrette:

¼ cup (60 ml) extra-virgin olive oil
1 tablespoon (15 ml) MCT oil or MUFA-based oil (see page 18)
1 tablespoon (15 ml) balsamic vinegar
1 tablespoon (15 ml) fresh lemon juice
1 tablespoon (4 g/0.2 oz) chopped fresh herbs, or 1 teaspoon dried herbs of your choice (such as thyme, basil, or parsley)
Sea salt and black pepper

Roll-Ups:

12 slices (160 g/5.6 oz) Parma ham in total (use 4 slices for each variation)

Spinach & Blue Cheese Roll-Ups:

4 ounces (113 g) cream cheese
½ cup (57 g/2 oz) crumbled blue cheese
2 tablespoons (17 g/0.6 oz) drained capers or sliced olives
Handful (20 g/0.7 oz) of fresh spinach or arugula

TO MAKE THE VINAIGRETTE: Place all the ingredients in a sealable jar, close tightly, and shake until well combined. Set aside to allow the flavors to combine. (If not used immediately, the vinaigrette can be stored in the fridge for up to a week.)

While assembling the roll-ups, keep the individual slices of the Parma ham on the plastic separator included in the package to minimize any tearing.

TO MAKE THE SPINACH & BLUE CHEESE ROLL-UPS: Spread 2 tablespoons (28 g/1 oz) of cream cheese on each of the 4 slices of Parma ham. Top with the blue cheese, capers, and greens. Gently roll up starting from the short side.

TO MAKE THE MOZZARELLA ROLL-UPS: Place a piece of mozzarella on each of the 4 slices of Parma ham. Top each one with a piece of sun-dried tomato (whole or chopped), and 2 basil leaves. Gently roll up starting from the short side.

TO MAKE THE HORSERADISH & PICKLE ROLL-UPS: Mix the cream cheese with the horseradish. Spread 2 tablespoons (28 g/1 oz) of the cream cheese mixture on each of the 4 slices of Parma ham. Top with a pickle and gently roll up starting from the short side.

Serve the roll-ups with the prepared vinaigrette (shake well again before serving to combine). The roll-ups can be prepared up to 1 day in advance and stored, covered, in the fridge.

NUTRITION FACTS PER SERVING (1 SPINACH/MOZZARELLA/HORSERADISH ROLL-UP + DIP):
Total carbs: 2/1.8/2.2 g / Fiber: 0.3/0.2/0.4 g / Net carbs: 1.7/1.6/1.8 g / Protein: 8.7/10.5/5.7 g
Fat: 19.2/12.1/15.6 g / Calories: 201/158/157 kcal / Macronutrient ratio: Calories from carbs (3/4/4%), protein (16/27/13%), fat (81/69/83%)

Mozzarella Roll-Ups:

4 ounces (113 g) fresh mozzarella,
  cut into 4 pieces
4 pieces (12 g/0.4 oz) sun-dried
  tomatoes
8 basil leaves

Horseradish & Pickle Roll-Ups:

4 ounces (113 g) cream cheese
1 teaspoon (5 g) grated horseradish,
  or more to taste
4 small (113 g/4 oz) pickles

Crispy Ranch Chicken Wings

MAKES: 6 servings
HANDS-ON TIME: 20 minutes
OVERALL TIME: 1 hour 30 minutes

Even your non-keto guests won't be able to resist these hot, addictively crispy chicken wings—especially when you serve them alongside a bowl of creamy, homemade ranch dressing.

Crispy Chicken Wings:

18 chicken wings (about 1.5 kg/3.3 lbs)

1½ tablespoons (18 g/0.6 oz) gluten-free baking powder (do not replace with baking soda)

¾ teaspoon sea salt

1½ tablespoons (23 ml) ghee or duck fat, melted

Ranch Dressing:

¼ cup (58 g/2 oz) sour cream

¼ cup (60 ml) heavy whipping cream

½ cup (110 g/3.9 oz) mayonnaise (page 42)

2 medium (30 g/1.1 oz) spring onions, sliced

1 clove garlic, minced

2 tablespoons (8 g/0.3 oz) chopped fresh parsley, or 2 teaspoons dried parsley

1 tablespoon (4 g/0.2 oz) chopped fresh dill, or 1 teaspoon dried dill

1 tablespoon (15 ml) apple cider vinegar or fresh lemon juice

¼ teaspoon paprika

Sea salt and black pepper

Preheat the oven to 250°F (120°C, or gas mark ½). Place the oven racks in the lower-middle and upper-middle positions in the oven. Use a baking tray deep enough to gather the fat as the chicken wings bake. Line the tray with baking foil to make it easy to clean. Place a rack on top of the foil.

TO MAKE THE CHICKEN WINGS: Use a sharp knife or meat scissors to cut the wings at the joints: you will end up with three pieces per wing. Pat all the pieces dry using a paper towel. Store the 18 wing tips in the freezer to make bone broth (page 42) or chicken stock. Place the remaining wing pieces (you should have 36 pieces) in a large resealable bag or a bowl. Add the baking powder and salt. Toss to coat on all sides.

Place the wings on the rack skin-side up and spread them in a single layer. Brush each piece with the ghee, then bake the wings on the lower-middle rack for 30 minutes. Then, move the wings to the upper-middle rack, increase the temperature to 425°F (220°C, or gas mark 7), and bake for another 40 to 50 minutes. Rotate the tray halfway to ensure even cooking. When done, remove the tray from the oven and let the wings rest for 5 minutes before serving.

TO MAKE THE DRESSING: While the wings are baking, prepare the ranch dressing by mixing all the ingredients in a bowl. Season with salt and pepper to taste, and serve with the crispy chicken wings.

NOTE: Instead of ranch dressing, try these wings with dairy-free Satay Dip (page 164) or Pesto Aioli (page 43)—or serve with all three!

NUTRITION FACTS PER SERVING (6 CHICKEN PIECES + 3 TABLESPOONS/45 ML RANCH DRESSING):
Total carbs: 2.1 g / Fiber: 0.2 g / Net carbs: 1.9 g / Protein: 23.2 g / Fat: 44.3 g / Calories: 505 kcal
Macronutrient ratio: Calories from carbs (2%), protein (19%), fat (79%)

Tomato & Feta Bruschetta

MAKES: 2 servings
HANDS-ON TIME: 10 minutes
OVERALL TIME: 10 minutes

I love Italian food, especially its wide variety of appetizers and starters, so I've created keto versions of lots of Italian classics. This low-carb bruschetta is just like the one I used to order every time I went to our local Italian restaurant—except it's so much healthier!

2 slices Garlic & Herb Focaccia (page 48), cut widthwise

1 cup (150 g/5.3 oz) chopped cherry or regular tomatoes

2 cups (20 g/0.7 oz) arugula, spinach, or watercress

½ cup (75 g/2.6 oz) crumbled feta

2 tablespoons (8 g/0.3 oz) chopped fresh basil

2 tablespoons (30 ml) extra-virgin olive oil

Sea salt and black pepper

Cut the focaccia widthwise. Preheat the broiler and then crisp up the focaccia for 3 to 5 minutes. When done, transfer to a plate and top with the tomatoes, arugula, feta, and basil. Drizzle with the olive oil, season with salt and pepper, and serve immediately.

NUTRITION FACTS PER SERVING:
Total carbs: 11.3 g / Fiber: 7 g / Net carbs: 4.4 g / Protein: 9.7 g / Fat: 31.6 g / Calories: 348 kcal
Macronutrient ratio: Calories from carbs (5%), protein (11%), fat (84%)

Golden Sardine & Caramelized Onion Dip

MAKES: 9 servings
HANDS-ON TIME: 10 minutes
OVERALL TIME: 30 minutes

This dip is the perfect partner for that batch of Multiseed Keto Crackers (page 84) you just made. And it's ridiculously healthy: sardines provide plenty of omega-3 fatty acids, while the curcumin in turmeric has anti-stress and anti-aging effects and can strengthen your immunity, help relieve muscle pain, and improve digestion. Dig in!

2 tablespoons (30 g/1.1 oz) ghee or
  duck fat
1 medium (150 g/5.3 oz) yellow onion,
  chopped
2 cans (250 g/8.8 oz) drained sardines
2 tablespoons (30 ml) fresh lemon
  juice
1 teaspoon fresh lemon zest
2 tablespoons (30 ml) extra-virgin
  olive oil
2 tablespoons (30 g/1.1 oz)
  mayonnaise (page 42)
½ teaspoon ground turmeric
2 tablespoons (6 g/0.2 oz) chopped
  fresh chives
Sea salt and black pepper
Multiseed Keto Crackers
  (page 84), freshly sliced cucumbers
  or peppers, or Garlic & Herb
  Focaccia (page 48) for serving

Heat a skillet greased with the ghee over medium-high heat. Add the onion and cook for about 5 minutes, then reduce the heat to medium and cook for 12 to 15 minutes, until softened and caramelized. When done, set aside for 5 minutes.

Place the sardines and all the remaining ingredients in a blender and process until smooth. (If you prefer a chunkier texture, use a fork and mash all the ingredients in a bowl.) Season with salt and pepper to taste. Serve with crackers, cucumbers or peppers, or keto focaccia. Store in an airtight container in the fridge for up to 4 days.

NUTRITION FACTS PER SERVING (¼ CUP/58 G/2 OZ):
Total carbs: 1.8 g / Fiber: 0.4 g / Net carbs: 1.4 g / Protein: 7.1 g / Fat: 12.3 g / Calories: 147 kcal
Macronutrient ratio: Calories from carbs (4%), protein (20%), fat (76%)

Multiseed Keto Crackers

MAKES: 24 crackers
HANDS-ON TIME: 10 minutes
OVERALL TIME: 1 hour

These crisp, dunkable crackers aren't just low in carbs: they're allergy-friendly, too. They contain no nuts, eggs, nightshades, or dairy. And that means everyone can enjoy them! Serve them with any of the high-fat dips in this chapter.

⅓ cup (56 g/2 oz) whole flaxseeds
¼ cup (38 g/1.3 oz) whole chia seeds
⅓ cup (43 g/1.5 oz) pumpkin seeds
⅓ cup (47 g/1.6 oz) sunflower seeds
⅓ cup (48 g/1.7 oz) sesame seeds
2 tablespoons (18 g/0.6 oz) poppy seeds
1 teaspoon sea salt
1 teaspoon coarse black pepper
1 cup (240 ml) water
Optional: 1 to 2 teaspoons onion powder, garlic powder, or Italian herbs

Preheat the oven to 360°F (180°C, or gas mark 4).

Place all the ingredients, except the water, in a bowl. Combine well. Place about ½ cup (120 g) of the mixture into a food processor and process until finely ground, scraping down the sides of the food processor as needed. Return the ground seed mixture to the bowl, mix again, and add the water. Mix with a spoon until well combined, then let the mixture sit for 5 to 10 minutes.

Place a silicone mat or a piece of heavy-duty parchment paper in a 10 x 14-inch (25 x 35-cm) baking sheet. Transfer the dough to the tray and spread with a rubber spatula, shaping it into the rectangular shape of the silicone mat, until it is about ⅛ inch (3 mm) thick. Use a pizza cutter to cut it into a total of 24 crackers (6 rows by 4 columns). Bake for 40 to 45 minutes, or until crispy and golden brown. When done, remove from the oven, and cut through the precut crackers. Let them cool down and crisp up on a cooling rack for 20 to 30 minutes before serving. Store for up to 2 weeks at room temperature in an airtight container.

NUTRITION FACTS PER CRACKER:
Total carbs: 2.6 g / Fiber: 1.8 g / Net carbs: 0.8 g / Protein: 2.2 g / Fat: 4.7 g / Calories: 57 kcal
Macronutrient ratio: Calories from carbs (6%), protein (16%), fat (78%)

Macadamia Cheese Dip

MAKES: 16 servings
HANDS-ON TIME: 10 minutes
OVERALL TIME: 5 hours

If you're vegan, or if you love cheese but can't tolerate dairy, try this rich, satisfying dip instead. It only takes a few minutes to whip up and it's very low in carbs. Plus, macadamias are very high in heart-healthy monounsaturated fats, so you can feel good about chowing down.

1½ cups (200 g/7.1 oz) macadamia nuts

3 tablespoons (45 ml) fresh lemon juice

1 tablespoon (12 g/0.4 oz) nutritional yeast, or more to taste

1 teaspoon onion powder

2 cloves garlic, crushed

½ cup (120 ml) filtered water

¼ cup (60 ml) extra-virgin olive oil

Sea salt and black pepper

Optional: freshly chopped herbs, such as chives, parsley, or basil

Crispy vegetables (ideal for induction), Multiseed Keto Crackers (page 84), or Garlic & Herb Focaccia (page 48) for serving

Soak the macadamia nuts in filtered water to cover for at least 4 hours, or overnight. Drain and discard the water. Place the nuts in the blender with the lemon juice, nutritional yeast, onion powder, garlic, water, and oil. Process until smooth and creamy. Season to taste with salt and pepper, and optionally add herbs of your choice. Serve with vegetables, crackers, or focaccia. Store in an airtight container for up to 5 days, or freeze for up to 6 months. To defrost, place in the fridge overnight and mix before serving.

NUTRITION FACTS PER SERVING (2 TABLESPOONS/28 G/1 OZ):
Total carbs: 2.5 g / Fiber: 1.3 g / Net carbs: 1.2 g / Protein: 1.4 g / Fat: 12.9 g / Calories: 125 kcal
Macronutrient ratio: Calories from carbs (4%), protein (5%), fat (91%)

Tyrokafteri (Spicy Greek Cheese & Pepper Dip)

MAKES: 12 servings
HANDS-ON TIME: 10 minutes
OVERALL TIME: 20 minutes

Made with feta cheese, peppers, and chile, this low-carb, Mediterranean-inspired dip is perfectly balanced between savory, sweet, and spicy. And because it's only got a handful of ingredients, it's easy to throw together in a hurry when last-minute guests drop in for drinks.

1 tablespoon (15 g/0.5 oz) ghee

1 small (85 g/3 oz) red pepper, chopped

1 (14 g/0.5 oz) mild green chile, such as jalapeño, chopped

2 cups (300 g/10.6 oz) crumbled feta cheese

½ cup plus 1 tablespoon (142 g/5 oz) 5% full-fat yogurt

3 tablespoons (45 ml) extra-virgin olive oil

2 pickles (90 g/3.2 oz), sliced

1 tablespoon (15 ml) fresh lemon juice

¼ teaspoon red pepper flakes, or more to taste

Crispy vegetables (ideal for induction), Multiseed Keto Crackers (page 84), or Garlic & Herb Focaccia (page 48) for serving

Heat a skillet greased with the ghee and add the red pepper and the chile. Cook for 8 to 10 minutes, or until tender and lightly browned. Place in a food processor and add all the remaining ingredients. (It's better to start with just ¼ teaspoon of red pepper flakes and add more to taste if you prefer more heat.) Process until smooth. Serve with vegetables, crackers, or focaccia. To store, refrigerate in an airtight container for up to 5 days.

NUTRITION FACTS PER SERVING (¼ CUP/57 G/2 OZ):
Total carbs: 2.3 g / Fiber: 0.3 g / Net carbs: 2 g / Protein: 4.8 g / Fat: 10.6 g / Calories: 122 kcal
Macronutrient ratio: Calories from carbs (7%), protein (16%), fat (77%)

Chapter 4

Nourishing Soups and Refreshing Salads

There's a chapter devoted to soups and salads in almost all of my books. That's partly because Czechs eat soup on just about every occasion and at any time of the day—as a starter or main dish, and even for breakfast. (Really!) But it's also because low-carb soups are so good for batch cooking. Make the Cream of Mushroom Soup on page 90, the Vietnamese-inspired Chicken Meatball Pho on page 98, or the Chilled Avocado-Coconut Soup on page 97 tonight, then store the leftovers in the fridge to tide you over for the rest of the week.

As for salads, I simply can't imagine my life without them. Don't get me wrong, I love bacon and eggs—and keto treats, too! But there's nothing like a big bowl of salad laced with a generous glug of extra-virgin olive oil, ideally served with fatty fish, to make my body feel great. Try it for yourself: start with the satisfying, stick-to-your-ribs Carne Asada Salad on page 100, The Easiest Cobb Salad on page 107, or the lemony, herb-strewn Zingy Fennel & Squid Salad on page 110.

Cream of Mushroom Soup

MAKES: 6 servings
HANDS-ON TIME: 15 minutes
OVERALL TIME: 45 minutes

Creamy, full of earthy flavor, and finished with a warming dash of freshly ground nutmeg, this dairy-free soup is just what you need on a chilly fall evening. Serve it with a handful of Multiseed Keto Crackers (page 84) or Garlic & Herb Focaccia (page 48).

1 cup (30 g/1.1 oz) dried porcini mushrooms

5 cups (1200 ml) chicken stock or vegetable stock, divided

2 tablespoons (30 g/1.1 oz) ghee or duck fat

1 medium (110 g/3.9 oz) yellow onion, chopped

2 cloves garlic, minced

½ medium (300 g/10.6 oz) cauliflower, cut into small florets

½ teaspoon freshly ground nutmeg

1 teaspoon dried thyme

1 cup (240 ml) coconut milk

¾ teaspoon sea salt, or to taste

¼ teaspoon black pepper, or to taste

Place the porcini mushrooms in a bowl, cover with 2 cups (480 ml) of the hot stock, and let them steep for about 30 minutes.

Grease a large saucepan with the ghee. Add the onion and cook over medium-high heat for 6 to 8 minutes, until lightly browned. Add the garlic and cook for 1 minute more. Add the cauliflower, nutmeg, thyme, and the remaining 3 cups (720 ml) stock. Pour in the mushrooms soaked in the stock and any remaining liquid. Bring to a boil, and cover with a lid. Cook for about 8 minutes, or until the cauliflower is tender.

Use an immersion blender to purée the mixture. For a smooth soup, purée until smooth. For a chunky texture, reserve some of the vegetable mixture, blend the remaining mixture, then add the reserved vegetables back to the saucepan. Add the coconut milk and remove from the heat. Stir and season with salt and pepper to taste. Serve immediately, or let the soup cool and refrigerate in an airtight container for up to 5 days.

NUTRITION FACTS PER SERVING (ABOUT 360 ML/1½ CUPS):
Total carbs: 9 g / Fiber: 1.9 g / Net carbs: 7.1 g / Protein: 6.3 g / Fat: 17.3 g / Calories: 207 kcal
Macronutrient ratio: Calories from carbs (14%), protein (12%), fat (74%)

Salmon Ramen

MAKES: 2 servings
HANDS-ON TIME: 15 minutes
OVERALL TIME: 20 minutes

This fragrant ramen soup is ideal for beating keto flu and boosting your electrolyte intake: salmon is high in potassium and omega-3s, and mushrooms are a good source of magnesium. Add a pinch of turmeric for a dose of anti-inflammatory curcumin—and extra flavor!

2 tablespoons (30 g/1.1 oz) ghee or coconut oil, divided

2 small (220 g/7.8 oz) salmon fillets

Sea salt and black pepper

2 medium (30 g/1.1 oz) spring onions, sliced, white and green parts separated

1 tablespoon (6 g/0.2 oz) grated ginger

1 small (14 g/0.5 oz) chile pepper, sliced, seeds removed

3 cups (720 ml) fish stock or chicken stock

1 tablespoon (15 ml) fish sauce

1 tablespoon (15 ml) coconut aminos

1 cup (70 g/2.5 oz) sliced shiitake or oyster mushrooms

Optional: 1 teaspoon grated turmeric root, or ½ teaspoon ground turmeric

4 ounces (113 g) Swiss chard or bok choy

8 ounces (225 g) kelp noodles, drained

2 large eggs

Optional: 1 teaspoon dried wakame seaweed flakes

2 teaspoons Sriracha sauce

1 tablespoon (15 ml) extra-virgin olive oil

1 teaspoon toasted sesame oil

2 teaspoons sesame seeds

Grease a pan with 1 tablespoon (15 g/0.5 oz) of the ghee and place over medium-high heat. Pat the salmon fillets dry with paper towels, and season with salt and pepper. Place the salmon, skin-side down, in the hot pan, and lower the heat to medium. Cook undisturbed for 3 to 4 minutes per side, until the fish is firm and cooked through. (Do not force the fish out of the pan: if the fish doesn't release when you try to flip it, cook it a bit longer until it releases easily.) Set the cooked fish aside and keep warm.

Place the white parts of the onions, plus the ginger and chile, in a medium saucepan greased with the remaining (15 g/0.5 oz) ghee. Cook over medium heat until fragrant. Add the stock, fish sauce, coconut aminos, and mushrooms. Add the turmeric, if using. Bring to a boil and add the Swiss chard. Cook for 1 to 2 minutes, then remove from the heat. Rinse the kelp noodles and add them to the pot.

Soft-boil the eggs by following the instructions on page 42. Season the stock with salt and pepper to taste, and add the wakame seaweed flakes, if using.

To assemble, ladle the soup into serving bowls. Add the salmon fillets (you can peel off the skin if you wish), the green parts of the onions, and the soft-boiled eggs cut in half. Drizzle the eggs and salmon with the Sriracha, olive oil, and sesame oil. Sprinkle with sesame seeds and serve immediately. Refrigerate the stock and noodles only, in an airtight container, for up to 5 days.

NUTRITION FACTS PER SERVING (2 CUPS/480 ML/16 FL OZ):
Total carbs: 13.1 g / Fiber: 5.6 g / Net carbs: 7.5 g / Protein: 38.1 g / Fat: 37.7 g / Calories: 543 kcal
Macronutrient ratio: Calories from carbs (6%), protein (29%), fat (65%)

Anti-Inflammatory Egg Drop Soup

MAKES: 6 servings
HANDS-ON TIME: 10 minutes
OVERALL TIME: 20 minutes

I've created a keto-friendly version of the Chinese take-out classic, and it's so much healthier than the original. Like the Salmon Ramen on page 93, it features turmeric, a powerful adaptogen that's immune-boosting, antioxidant, and anti-inflammatory.

2 quarts (2 L) chicken stock or vegetable stock

1 tablespoon grated turmeric root, or 1 teaspoon ground turmeric

1 tablespoon grated ginger, or 1 teaspoon ground ginger

2 cloves garlic, minced

1 small (14 g/0.5 oz) chile pepper, seeds removed and sliced

2 cups (144 g/5.1 oz) sliced brown mushrooms

4 cups (144 g/5.1 oz) chopped Swiss chard, collard greens, or spinach, stalks and leaves separated

2 tablespoons (30 ml) coconut aminos

4 large eggs, lightly beaten

2 medium (30 g/1.1 oz) spring onions, sliced

2 tablespoons (8 g/0.3 oz) chopped fresh cilantro or parsley

1 teaspoon sea salt, or to taste

Ground black pepper

6 tablespoons (90 ml) extra-virgin olive oil

Pour the chicken stock into a large pot and heat over medium heat until it starts to simmer. Add the turmeric, ginger, garlic, chile, mushrooms, chard stalks, and coconut aminos to the pot, and simmer for about 5 minutes.

Add the chard leaves and cook for 1 minute more. Slowly pour the beaten eggs into the simmering soup. Keep stirring until the egg is cooked, then remove the pot from the heat. Add the spring onions and cilantro. Season with salt and pepper to taste. Divide among serving bowls and drizzle with extra-virgin olive oil (1 tablespoon or 15 ml per serving). Eat immediately, or let the soup cool and refrigerate in an airtight container for up to 5 days.

NOTE: Need to up your protein intake? Just add 1 pound (450 g) cooked and shredded chicken to the soup at the end of the cooking process and warm through.

NUTRITION FACTS PER SERVING (2 CUPS/480 ML/16 FL OZ):
Total carbs: 3.7 g / Fiber: 0.8 g / Net carbs: 2.9 g / Protein: 10.8 g / Fat: 22.4 g / Calories: 255 kcal
Macronutrient ratio: Calories from carbs (5%), protein (17%), fat (79%)

Chilled Avocado—Coconut Soup

MAKES: 6 servings
HANDS-ON TIME: 10 minutes
OVERALL TIME: 10 minutes

Never had avocado in a soup before? It works beautifully, especially with equally creamy coconut milk. Spiked with chile and fresh lime juice, this smooth soup is perfect for summer days when it's way too hot to cook. Plus, it's allergy-free, and it's high in heart-healthy fats, fiber, and potassium.

2 large (400 g/14.1 oz) avocados,
  pitted and peeled
½ small (35 g/1.2 oz) yellow onion,
  roughly chopped
2 cloves garlic, crushed
1 medium (200 g/7.1 oz) cucumber,
  roughly chopped
¼ cup (60 ml) fresh lime juice
3 cups (720 ml) vegetable stock
1 cup (240 ml) coconut milk
Optional: 1 (14 g/0.5 oz) jalapeño
  pepper, seeds removed
1 medium (30 g/1.1 oz) spring onion,
  sliced
6 tablespoons (90 ml) extra-virgin
  olive oil
Optional: crumbled feta or cooked,
  crispy Spanish chorizo; Garlic &
  Herb Focaccia (page 48) for serving

Place all the ingredients except the spring onion and olive oil in a blender and process until smooth. Divide among serving bowls, sprinkle with spring onion, and drizzle with olive oil (1 tablespoon or 15 ml per serving). Serve on its own as a starter, or top with some feta or chorizo and eat with focaccia as a complete meal. Refrigerate (without toppings) in an airtight container for up to 5 days.

NUTRITION FACTS PER SERVING (1 CUP/240 ML/8 FL OZ):
Total carbs: 10.5 g / Fiber: 5.3 g / Net carbs: 5.2 g / Protein: 3.2 g / Fat: 36.8 g / Calories: 366 kcal
Macronutrient ratio: Calories from carbs (6%), protein (3%), fat (91%)

Chicken Meatball Pho

MAKES: 6 servings
HANDS-ON TIME: 20 minutes
OVERALL TIME: 50 minutes

If your energy levels are flagging, try this keto version of Vietnamese pho! It's the perfect cold-weather pick-me-up dish, and it's one of the best ways to fit extra electrolytes and nourishing collagen into your diet.

Broth:

1 medium (110 g/3.9 oz) yellow onion, quartered

2-inch (5-cm) piece fresh ginger, peeled and quartered

2 star anise

1 cinnamon stick

4 whole cloves

2 teaspoons coriander seeds

2 quarts (2 L) chicken stock or bone broth (page 42)

2 tablespoons (30 ml) fish sauce

1 tablespoon (15 ml) coconut aminos

2 cloves garlic, sliced

Sea salt and black pepper

2 packs (400 g/14.1 oz) shirataki noodles or kelp noodles

Meatballs:

1 tablespoon (15 g/0.5 oz) ghee or duck fat

1½ cups (180 g/6.3 oz) cauliflower rice (page 40)

1.1 pounds (500 g) ground chicken

1 large egg

2 tablespoons (16 g/0.6 oz) coconut flour

1 tablespoon (4 g/0.2 oz) chopped fresh cilantro

1 tablespoon (4 g/0.2 oz) chopped Thai basil

½ teaspoon sea salt

¼ teaspoon black pepper

Optional toppings: fresh herbs such as cilantro and Thai basil, sliced chile pepper, bean sprouts, sliced spring onion, lime wedges, and Sriracha sauce

TO MAKE THE BROTH: Either carefully char the onion and ginger over an open flame, or place them under a broiler preheated to its maximum for 5 to 7 minutes, until slightly blackened on the outside but partially raw inside. Set aside.

In a large pot, dry-roast the spices over medium heat until fragrant, stirring frequently. Pour in the stock, fish sauce, and coconut aminos, then add the charred onion, ginger, and garlic. Bring to a boil over high heat, then reduce the heat to medium-low. Cook, covered, for about 30 minutes. Then strain the soup through a sieve into another pot, return to the heat, and keep simmering. Season the stock with salt and pepper to taste.

Meanwhile, prepare the shirataki noodles (see page 41) and set aside. If you're using kelp noodles, simply rinse them and set aside.

TO MAKE THE MEATBALLS: Grease a pan with the ghee and cook the cauliflower rice for 5 to 7 minutes, stirring occasionally. When done, remove from the heat. Place the ground chicken and egg into a bowl. Add the coconut flour, cilantro, Thai basil, salt, and pepper, plus the cooked cauliflower rice. Mix until well combined. Shape into 18 medium meatballs. Add the meatballs to the pot with the strained stock and cook for 12 to 15 minutes.

To assemble, place about a sixth of the shirataki noodles into a bowl. Add about 1¼ cups (300 ml) of the stock and 3 meatballs, plus any of the suggested toppings, and serve hot. To store, let the soup cool and then refrigerate in an airtight container for up to 4 days. Reheat and add toppings just before serving.

NUTRITION FACTS PER SERVING (2 CUPS/480 ML/16 FL OZ):
Total carbs: 7.5 g / Fiber: 2.8 g / Net carbs: 4.7 g / Protein: 27.3 g / Fat: 13.1 g / Calories: 254 kcal
Macronutrient ratio: Calories from carbs (8%), protein (44%), fat (48%)

Carne Asada Salad

MAKES: 2 servings
HANDS-ON TIME: 10 minutes
OVERALL TIME: 15 minutes

High in electrolytes and low in carbs, this simple steak salad is ideal for keto adaptation. And thanks to its refreshing cilantro- and jalapeño-spiked dressing, it's so flavorful it practically jumps out of the bowl! To make it even more substantial, top it with sour cream and cheese.

Spicy Cilantro-Lime Vinaigrette:

- 1 small bunch (15 g/0.5 oz) fresh cilantro
- 1 (14 g/0.5 oz) jalapeño pepper
- 4 cloves garlic, chopped
- ½ teaspoon ground cumin
- ½ cup (120 ml) extra-virgin olive oil
- ¼ cup (60 ml) fresh lime juice
- Sea salt and black pepper

Salad:

- 1 large (300 g/10.6 oz) flank steak or skirt steak
- Sea salt and black pepper
- 1 tablespoon (15 g/0.5) ghee, lard, or coconut oil
- 1 head (200 g/7.1 oz) soft green lettuce, such as butterhead lettuce, or other leafy greens
- 1 medium (150 g/5.3 oz) avocado, pitted, peeled, and diced
- 1 medium (100 g/3.5 oz) tomato, diced
- Lime wedges and fresh cilantro for serving
- Optional toppings: shredded Cheddar cheese and sour cream

TO MAKE THE VINAIGRETTE: Place all the ingredients in a blender and process until smooth. Reserve ¼ cup (60 ml) for the salad. Store any leftover dressing in the fridge for up to a week.

TO MAKE THE SALAD: Pat dry the steak and season with salt and pepper. Set a large pan greased with the ghee over high heat. Once hot, cook the steak for 3 minutes on each side (flank steak), or 2 to 3 minutes on each side (skirt steak), depending on the thickness of the meat, until medium-rare. Do not overcook the steak. Remove from the pan and keep warm.

When ready to serve, slice the meat thinly against the grain. Place the lettuce leaves in a bowl, and top with the sliced steak, avocado, and tomato. Drizzle the vinaigrette (2 tablespoons/30 ml per serving) over the salad. Serve with lime wedges and cilantro, and, optionally, with cheese and sour cream. The cooked steak can be refrigerated for up to 3 days. The dressing can be refrigerated for up to 1 week in an airtight container. Always prepare the salad right before serving.

NUTRITION FACTS PER SERVING:
Total carbs: 14 g / Fiber: 7.3 g / Net carbs: 6.7 g / Protein: 35.5 g / Fat: 56.6 g / Calories: 694 kcal
Macronutrient ratio: Calories from carbs (4%), protein (21%), fat (75%)

Old Bay Salad

MAKES: 2 servings
HANDS-ON TIME: 10 minutes
OVERALL TIME: 10 minutes

With just one serving of this salad, you'll score 30 percent of your daily magnesium requirement, and 50 percent of your daily potassium. That means it's one of the best options if you just started following a ketogenic lifestyle, because both are essential for the induction phase. For extra points, sub some dark leafy greens for the iceberg lettuce!

5 ounces (142 g) cooked shrimp

5 ounces (142 g) cooked crabmeat (canned is fine)

⅓ cup (73 g/2.6 oz) mayonnaise (page 42)

1 tablespoon (15 ml) fresh lemon juice

1 tablespoon (15 ml) Sriracha

½ teaspoon Old Bay seasoning

1 medium (80 g/2.8 oz) celery stalk, sliced

Sea salt and black pepper

½ medium (200 g/7.1 oz) iceberg lettuce, or soft green lettuce such as butterhead

1 medium (150 g/5.3 oz) avocado, pitted, peeled, and sliced

2 medium (30 g/1.1 oz) spring onions, sliced

Place the shrimp, crabmeat, mayonnaise, lemon juice, Sriracha, Old Bay seasoning, and celery into a bowl and mix until well combined. Season with salt and pepper to taste. Tear the lettuce into bite-size pieces and divide between 2 bowls. Add half of the dressed shrimp-crab mixture to each and top with avocado and spring onions. Eat immediately or store the dressed shrimp-crab mixture in the fridge for up to 3 days. Assemble the salad just before serving.

NOTES:

• You can find my recipe for Sriracha plus more homemade ingredients such as Dijon mustard, ketchup, and BBQ sauce on my blog: www.ketodietapp.com/blog.

• Packing this salad for lunch? Place the dressed shrimp-crab mixture into a tall 1-quart (960-ml) jar. Add the celery, avocado, and spring onions, then top with salad greens. When ready to serve, tip the salad over into a serving bowl so that the dressing covers the greens. Or, simply shake the jar—keeping the lid closed—and then eat the salad right from the jar.

NUTRITION FACTS PER SERVING:
Total carbs: 14 g / Fiber: 7.5 g / Net carbs: 6.5 g / Protein: 31.3 g / Fat: 44.8 g / Calories: 570 kcal
Macronutrient ratio: Calories from carbs (5%), protein (23%), fat (72%)

Caesar Salad with Poached Egg

MAKES: 2 servings
HANDS-ON TIME: 30 minutes
OVERALL TIME: 30 minutes

Break your fast with this classic chicken Caesar salad. It's high in protein and healthy fats, and the low-carb croutons made from Garlic & Herb Focaccia (page 48) add plenty of texture and crunch. For a nigthshade-free dressing, use Mediterranean Vinaigrette (see Note, page 104) instead.

MCT Salad Dressing:

¼ cup (55 g / 1.9 oz) mayonnaise (page 42)
1 tablespoon (15 g / 0.5 oz) Dijon mustard
¼ cup (60 ml) extra-virgin olive oil
2 tablespoons (30 ml) MCT oil
2 tablespoons (30 ml) fresh lemon juice
2 cloves garlic, minced
2 tablespoons (8 g / 0.3 oz) chopped herbs of your choice
Sea salt and black pepper
Optional: 4 anchovies (16 g / 0.6 oz) and 1 tablespoon (5 g / 0.2 oz) grated Parmesan cheese

Salad:

2 large (200 g / 7.1 oz) chicken thighs, skin on, bone removed
Sea salt and black pepper
1 tablespoon (15 ml) duck fat or ghee
7.1 ounces (200 g) soft green lettuce, such as butterhead, or iceberg lettuce
2 large eggs, poached (see page 42)
2 slices (32 g / 1.1 oz) crispy bacon (see page 41)
2 ounces (57 g) shaved Parmesan cheese
Optional: croutons made from 1 slice of Garlic & Herb Focaccia (page 48), cubed and toasted in the oven

TO MAKE THE DRESSING: Process all the ingredients in a blender. Reserve ¼ cup (60 ml) for the salad. Any leftover salad dressing can be stored in the fridge for up to 5 days.

TO MAKE THE SALAD: Pat the chicken thighs dry with a paper towel, and season them with salt and pepper on both sides. Grease a skillet with the duck fat and heat over high heat. Place the chicken thighs, skin-side down, into the hot pan. Cook for about 2 minutes, then reduce the heat to medium and cook for another 3 minutes, or until the skin is golden brown. Flip the chicken thighs over and cook for about 5 minutes more. The thighs are done when a thermometer inserted into the thickest part of the thigh reads at least 165°F (74°C). When done, transfer to a plate. Set aside for 5 minutes, then slice into thin strips.

To assemble the salad, tear the lettuce into pieces and divide between 2 bowls. Add the sliced chicken, poached egg, bacon, Parmesan, and croutons, if using. Drizzle with the prepared dressing. Eat immediately. To store, keep the ingredients in separate containers in the fridge. Reheat and assemble before serving.

NUTRITION FACTS PER SERVING:
Total carbs: 5.1 g / Fiber: 1.5 g / Net carbs: 3.6 g / Protein: 37 g / Fat: 63.8 g / Calories: 742 kcal
Macronutrient ratio: Calories from carbs (2%), protein (20%), fat (78%)

Summer Asparagus & Halloumi Salad

MAKES: 4 servings
HANDS-ON TIME: 15 minutes
OVERALL TIME: 20 minutes

Rich in vitamins A, C, and K, watercress is a real nutritional powerhouse. And, of course, it's ultra-low in carbs. Serve it with a dressing made with healthy fats, and top with slices of warm, salty, grilled Halloumi—or, if you're dairy-free, poached eggs.

Pesto Dressing:

¼ cup (55 g/1.9 oz) mayonnaise (page 42)

2 tablespoons (30 g/1.1 oz) basil pesto (page 43)

1 tablespoon (15 ml) fresh lemon juice

Salad:

14.1 ounces (400 g) asparagus, woody ends removed

11.3 ounces (320 g) Halloumi cheese, or use 4 poached eggs (see page 42) for a dairy-free version

1 tablespoon (15 g/0.5 oz) ghee or duck fat

2 cups (70 g/2.5 oz) fresh watercress or arugula

1 pack (100 g/3.5 oz) fresh spinach

1 medium (200 g/7.1 oz) cucumber, spiralized or sliced

1 cup (150 g/5.3 oz) chopped tomatoes, or halved cherry tomatoes

1 medium (150 g/5.3 oz) avocado, pitted, peeled, and sliced

Sea salt and pepper

TO MAKE THE DRESSING: Combine all the ingredients in a small bowl. Set aside.

TO MAKE THE SALAD: Fill a saucepan with salted water and bring to a boil. Add the asparagus and cook for 3 to 5 minutes, until crisp-tender. Drain and set aside.

Slice the Halloumi into about ½-inch (1-cm) slices. Grease a regular or griddle skillet with ghee and heat over medium-high heat. Add the Halloumi and cook on both sides for 2 to 3 minutes. Do not flip the Halloumi too early: let it crisp up to prevent it from breaking. When done, set aside and keep warm.

To assemble the salad, place the watercress and spinach in a bowl. Add the cucumber, tomatoes, and avocado slices. Place the cooked asparagus in the middle and top with the grilled Halloumi. Add the prepared dressing, and season with salt and pepper if needed. Serve immediately.

NOTE: If you can't eat eggs, make a simple Mediterranean Vinaigrette instead of the pesto dressing. Place all of the following ingredients in a sealable jar: ½ cup (120 ml) extra-virgin olive oil, ¼ cup (60 ml) lemon juice, 1 clove minced garlic, 1 teaspoon dried Italian herbs, and salt and black pepper to taste. Shake until the vinaigrette is emulsified and use 2 tablespoons (30 ml) per serving. Store in the fridge for up to 5 days.

NUTRITION FACTS PER SERVING (SALAD + 2 TABLESPOONS/130 ML DRESSING):
Total carbs: 12.8 g / Fiber: 6.3 g / Net carbs: 6.5 g / Protein: 21 g / Fat: 47.7 g / Calories: 546 kcal
Macronutrient ratio: Calories from carbs (5%), protein (16%), fat (79%)

The Easiest Cobb Salad

MAKES: 4 servings
HANDS-ON TIME: 20 minutes
OVERALL TIME: 35 minutes

Based on the restaurant classic and topped with fun-to-eat bacon-wrapped asparagus parcels, this simple keto salad can serve as either an appetizer or a full meal. If you practice intermittent fasting (IF) and need a higher-protein, higher-calorie meal to keep you going, it's the obvious solution.

1 bunch (200 g/7.1 oz) asparagus

12 thin-cut slices (180 g/6.3 oz) bacon

2 large (400 g/14.1 oz) skinless, boneless chicken breasts

1 bay leaf

½ teaspoon whole black peppercorns

1 teaspoon sea salt

2 tablespoons (30 ml) fresh lemon juice or white wine vinegar

1 small head (200 g/7.1 oz) green lettuce, roughly chopped

2 cups (60 g/2.1 oz) baby spinach

2 large hard-boiled eggs (see page 42), sliced

¾ cup (100 g/3.5 oz) crumbled blue cheese

1 medium (150 g/5.3 oz) avocado, pitted, peeled, and diced

½ medium (100 g/3.5 oz) cucumber, peeled and sliced

1 cup (150 g/5.3 oz) cherry tomatoes, chopped

½ cup (50 g/1.8 oz) black or green olives, sliced

1 cup (232 g/8.2 oz) Ranch Dressing (page 81)

Prepare the bacon-wrapped asparagus. Preheat the oven to 400°F (200°C, or gas mark 6). Snip the woody ends from the asparagus spears. Wrap a thin slice (15 g/0.5 oz) of bacon around 2 or 3 asparagus spears at a time. Place the "parcels" on a baking sheet, and bake for about 20 minutes. Once the bacon is browned and the asparagus is cooked through, remove from the oven. Set aside.

Meanwhile, poach the chicken breasts. Place the chicken breasts, bay leaf, peppercorns, salt, and lemon juice in a saucepan and fill with water until the chicken is submerged. Bring to a boil over medium-high heat, then reduce to low, cover with a lid, and cook for 10 to 12 minutes. The chicken is ready when an instant-read thermometer inserted into the thickest part of the chicken reads 165°F (74°C). Remove the chicken breasts from the poaching liquid and place on a cutting board. Dice the chicken breasts once they have cooled slightly.

To assemble the salad, place the lettuce and spinach in a bowl. Arrange the chicken, eggs, blue cheese, avocado, cucumber, tomatoes, and olives side by side in rows. Serve with the Ranch Dressing and the bacon-wrapped asparagus spears.

NUTRITION FACTS PER SERVING:
Total carbs: 12.1 g / Fiber: 5.9 g / Net Carbs: 6.2 g / Protein: 41.5 g / Fat: 48.5 g / Calories: 646 kcal
Macronutrient ratio: Calories from carbs (4%), protein (26%), fat (70%)

Nordic Salad

MAKES: 4 servings
HANDS-ON TIME: 15 minutes
OVERALL TIME: 15 minutes

This Scandinavian-style sweet-and-sour salad is a family favorite. Different variations turn up in almost every Czech deli, but the traditional version uses carb-heavy potatoes and mayonnaise made with inferior oils. Swap the potatoes for rutabaga, make your own mayo, and you've got a healthy, keto- and paleo-friendly version that's full of omega-3s!

1 medium (350 g/12.3 oz) rutabaga, peeled and diced into ½-to 1-inch (1 to 2.5-cm) pieces

3 whole allspice berries

1 teaspoon whole black peppercorns

2 bay leaves

2 tablespoons (30 ml) apple cider vinegar

1 teaspoon sea salt

14.1 ounces (400 g) cooked canned or smoked fatty fish, such as herring, salmon, sardine, or mackerel, broken up with a fork or cut into pieces

½ cup (110 g/3.9 oz) mayonnaise (page 42)

1 medium (60 g/2.1 oz) celery stalk, chopped

1 small (60 g/2.1 oz) red onion, sliced

1 tablespoon (15 ml) fresh lemon juice

1 teaspoon fresh lemon zest

2 tablespoons (8 g/0.3 oz) chopped fresh parsley

1 tablespoon (4 g/0.2 oz) chopped fresh dill

Optional: 2 teaspoons (10 g/0.4 oz) powdered erythritol or Swerve, or 3 to 5 drops stevia

Sea salt and black pepper

1 head (400 g/14.1 oz) iceberg lettuce

Place the rutabaga in a pot filled with enough water to cover it. Add the allspice, peppercorns, bay leaves, vinegar, and salt. Bring to a boil over high heat, and then reduce the heat to medium. Cook for about 15 minutes, or until the rutabaga is tender. Remove from the heat and strain through a colander. Discard the spices. Set the rutabaga aside to cool down.

Place the cooked rutabaga in a mixing bowl with the fish, mayonnaise, celery, onion, lemon juice, lemon zest, parsley, and dill (reserve some herbs for garnish). Mix until well combined. Add the sweetener, if using, and season with salt and pepper to taste.

To assemble the salad, break the lettuce into leaves and fill each with the fish mixture. Garnish with the remaining herbs and serve. Store the fish-rutabaga mixture in the fridge in an airtight container for up to 3 days.

NOTE: This salad is great with pickled herring in place of the cooked or smoked fish. If you use pickled fish, make sure you avoid products with added sugar: some versions of pickled herring are very sweet. Always be sure to read the label!

NUTRITION FACTS PER SERVING:
Total carbs: 13 g / Fiber: 3.9 g / Net carbs: 9.1 g / Protein: 25.6 g / Fat: 34.8 g / Calories: 464 kcal
Macronutrient ratio: Calories from carbs (8%), protein (23%), fat (69%)

Wedge Salad with Blue Cheese Dressing

MAKES: 4 servings
HANDS-ON TIME: 10 minutes
OVERALL TIME: 10 minutes

Cool, crisp iceberg lettuce is the best vehicle for creamy blue cheese dressing, isn't it? This refreshing—but highly addictive—salad gets extra flavor from onion, crumbled bacon, and walnuts. It makes an excellent light summer meal, or it can do double duty as a side dish for Induction Burger Stacks (page 169).

Blue Cheese Dressing:

- ½ cup (67 g/2.4 oz) crumbled blue cheese
- ¼ cup (58 g/2 oz) sour cream
- ¼ cup (55 g/1.9 oz) mayonnaise (page 42)
- 1 clove garlic, minced
- 1 tablespoon (15 ml) fresh lemon juice
- 2 tablespoons (30 ml) heavy whipping cream
- Sea salt and black pepper

Salad:

- 1 head (400 g/14.1 oz) iceberg lettuce
- 1 small (60 g/2.1 oz) red onion, sliced
- 1 cup (150 g/5.3 oz) chopped tomatoes
- ½ cup (68 g/2.4 oz) crumbled blue cheese
- 4 slices (64 g/2.3 oz) crispy bacon (see page 41), crumbled
- ½ cup (59/2 oz) chopped walnuts, ideally activated (see page 42)

TO MAKE THE DRESSING: Combine all the ingredients in a small bowl. Add a splash of water if it's too thick.

TO MAKE THE SALAD: Cut the lettuce into quarters and remove the hard core. Top with the onion, tomatoes, blue cheese, bacon, and walnuts. Drizzle with ⅔ cup (180 ml) of the dressing and serve. Store the remaining dressing in the fridge for up to 5 days.

NUTRITION FACTS PER SERVING (¼ SALAD PLUS 3 TABLESPOONS/45 ML DRESSING):
Total carbs: 9.3 g / Fiber: 3.1 g / Net carbs: 6.2 g / Protein: 15.5 g / Fat: 33.9 g / Calories: 392 kcal
Macronutrient ratio: Calories from carbs (6%), protein (16%), fat (78%)

Zingy Fennel & Squid Salad

MAKES: 4 servings
HANDS-ON TIME: 10 minutes
OVERALL TIME: 25 minutes

Craving something light, summery, and refreshing? This cool, lightly spiced salad is the solution. Seafood, which is a great source of B vitamins, phosphorus, potassium, and selenium, is a natural match for sweet, crunchy fennel, and they share the spotlight effortlessly in this quick-prep salad.

Juice (about ¼ cup/60 ml) and zest
   of 1 lemon
2 cloves garlic, crushed
¼ cup plus 2 tablespoons (90 ml)
   extra-virgin olive oil
2 medium (400 g/14.1 oz) fennel bulbs
4 ounces (113 g) soft greens, such as
   chard or spinach, chopped
½ small (30 g/1.1 oz) red onion, sliced
1 small (14 g/0.5 oz) mild chile pepper,
   finely chopped
2 tablespoons (8 g/0.3 oz) chopped
   fresh dill or reserved fennel fronds
2 tablespoons (8 g/0.3 oz) chopped
   fresh parsley
½ teaspoon sea salt
¼ teaspoon black pepper
7.1 ounces (200 g) cooked shrimp
7.1 ounces (200 g) cooked baby squid
   tentacles and bodies sliced into
   rings

Combine the lemon juice, lemon zest, garlic, and olive oil in a small bowl and set aside. Trim off the hard tops and bottoms of the fennel (reserve the fennel fronds for garnish). Halve the fennel and slice as thinly as you can (or use a mandoline or a food processor). Place the fennel in a bowl and add the chard, onion, chile, dill (or reserved fennel fronds), parsley, and the prepared dressing. Season with salt and pepper, and mix well. Set aside for 15 minutes to let the flavors combine. Add the shrimp and squid pieces, and mix until well combined. Season with salt and pepper to taste. Serve immediately, or refrigerate for up to 1 day.

NUTRITION FACTS PER SERVING:
Total carbs: 12.7 g / Fiber: 4 g / Net carbs: 8.7 g / Protein: 17.2 g / Fat: 21.7 g / Calories: 305 kcal
Macronutrient ratio: Calories from carbs (12%), protein (23%), fat (65%)

Chapter 5

Quick and Easy Lunchbox Dishes

Following a new diet can be challenging, even if you have plenty of time to cook nutritious meals at home. And if, like so many of us, you're busy all day—working, going to school, or taking care of the kids—eating well becomes even trickier. So, what do you do if you're new to keto eating and have a busy lifestyle, but still want lunchbox options that never get boring?

Check out this chapter for the answers! It's full of make-ahead, portable, quick-prep lunch options that have the right amounts of protein, fat, and micronutrients. They will help you feel satisfied and control cravings. Try the Unwiches on page 114: they're bread-free sandwiches with all of the fillings and none of the carbs. Or grab a grain-free Three-Cheese Crustless Mini Quiche (page 19): they're so sating, and they make a great quick snack as well as a light meal. If you're dying for a "traditional" sandwich, use a fresh batch of keto focaccia to make a Focaccia Sandwich Four Ways (page 118), featuring both meat and veggie options. Whether you're eating at home or on the run, you'll be able to enjoy keto-friendly lunch options that'll keep you going all afternoon.

Induction Unwich Two Ways

MAKES: 1 unwich
HANDS-ON TIME: 5 minutes
OVERALL TIME: 5 minutes

"Unwiches" are essentially sandwiches in which bread is replaced by lettuce. They are becoming increasingly popular: Even fast-food chains offer them. Make yours at home, and skip the hidden carbs and unhealthy vegetable oils!

8 large (100 g/3.5 oz) leaves soft green lettuce, such as butterhead

Salmon & Cream Cheese Unwich:

4.2 ounces (120 g) smoked salmon

1 teaspoon fresh lemon juice

2 tablespoons (30 g/1.1 oz) cream cheese

Chopped fresh dill and black pepper to taste

1 medium (150 g/5.3 oz) avocado, pitted, peeled, and sliced

Club Unwich:

2 slices (57 g/2 oz) quality ham

2 slices (43 g/1.5 oz) Monterey Jack or Swiss cheese (or 2 more slices of ham for dairy-free)

1 large egg, hard-boiled (see page 42), sliced

1 small (85 g/3 oz) tomato, sliced and seeds removed

2 tablespoons (16 g/0.6 oz) crumbled crispy bacon (see page 41)

1 tablespoon (15 g/1.1 oz) mayonnaise (page 42)

1 teaspoon Dijon mustard

Black pepper

Place a piece of parchment down on your work surface. Place the lettuce on top in a single layer slightly overlapping.

TO MAKE THE SALMON & CREAM CHEESE UNWICH: Top the lettuce with the smoked salmon and drizzle with lemon juice. Spread the cream cheese on top, and add the dill and black pepper. Top with the sliced avocado.

TO MAKE THE CLUB UNWICH: Place the ham and cheese slices on top of the lettuce. Add the egg and tomato slices (remove the seeds first, or the unwich will get soggy). Top with the bacon, mayonnaise, and mustard. Season with black pepper.

Roll the wrap like you would a sushi roll, pulling the parchment up and out as you fold it over so you're not tucking the paper into the wrap. Roll tightly, tucking in the edges as you go. Once wrapped, cut in half with a sharp knife. To eat, simply pull the parchment away like you would when eating a burrito.

NUTRITION FACTS PER SERVING (SALMON & CREAM CHEESE/CLUB):
Total carbs: 17.2/7.6 g / Fiber: 11.5/2.5 g / Net carbs: 5.7/5.1 g / Protein: 28.5/33.4 g / Fat: 35.8/34.7 g / Calories: 472/475 kcal / Macronutrient ratio: Calories from carbs (5/4%), protein (25/29%), fat (70/67%)

Quick Tuna Melt Pockets

MAKES: 2 servings
HANDS-ON TIME: 10 minutes
OVERALL TIME: 30 minutes

Inspired by the popular "Fat Head" dough, which uses almond flour, cheese, and other low-carb ingredients to make "dough" for pizzas and other traditionally high-carb dishes, these speedy tuna melt pockets taste like the real deal. Eat half of a pocket as a regular meal; if you're breaking your fast, eat the whole thing.

4 ounces (113 g) drained canned tuna

1 tablespoon (15 g/0.5 oz) mayonnaise (page 42)

1 teaspoon fresh lemon juice

1 medium (15 g/0.5 oz) spring onion, sliced

Sea salt and black pepper

¾ cup (85 g/3 oz) shredded mozzarella

2 tablespoons (28 g/1 oz) cream cheese

3 tablespoons (24 g/0.8 oz) coconut flour

3 ounces (85 g) provolone or Cheddar cheese slices

2 teaspoons (10 g/0.4 oz) melted ghee or duck fat

Place the tuna in a bowl. Add the mayonnaise, lemon juice, and spring onion. Combine well. Season with salt and pepper, and set aside.

Prepare the dough. Melt the mozzarella and cream cheese in the microwave for 1 minute. Alternatively, you can melt this in the oven at 300°F (150°C, or gas mark 2) for 8 to 10 minutes. Mix and add the coconut flour. Stir until the dough is well combined.

Preheat the oven to 360°F (180°C, or gas mark 4). Roll out the dough thinly between 2 sheets of parchment paper or use a nonstick mat and nonstick rolling pin. (When rolled out, the dough should be about 8 x 11 inches [20 x 30 cm].) Add the tuna filling to the center of the dough and top with provolone cheese, then fold over like an envelope and seal the dough with your fingers. Do not press too hard or the filling will spill out. Using a sharp knife, poke some holes into the dough to release the steam while baking, then brush with the ghee. Bake for 18 to 20 minutes, or until golden brown and firm to the touch. When done, remove from the oven and let cool for a few minutes. Cut in half and enjoy while still hot, or let the tuna melt cool, place it an airtight container, and refrigerate for up to 5 days.

NOTE: Instead of coconut flour, you can use ¼ cup (28 g/1 oz) flax meal. Alternatively, use ⅓ cup (33 g/1.2 oz) almond flour and skip the cream cheese. (This version has been adapted from the recipe for Hot Morning Pockets by Vicky and Rami, fellow bloggers at Tasteaholics.com.)

NUTRITION FACTS PER SERVING (½ POCKET):
Total carbs: 7.2 g / Fiber: 2.4 g / Net carbs: 4.8 g / Protein: 36.2 g / Fat: 37.4 g / Calories: 509 kcal
Macronutrient ratio: Calories from carbs (4%), protein (29%), fat (67%)

Mexican Pockets

MAKES: 2 servings
HANDS-ON TIME: 10 minutes
OVERALL TIME: 40 minutes

The dough for the "pocket" in this recipe is a simplified version of my keto tortilla dough, so it's especially easy to make. That's why these Mexican Pockets are ideal as a quick-prep dinner, or for tossing into your lunchbox. If you need to up your electrolytes, serve them with sliced avocado. Eat half of a pocket as a regular meal; if you're breaking your fast, eat the whole thing.

⅓ cup (50 g/1.8 oz) flax meal

1 tablespoon (4 g/0.1 oz) whole psyllium husks

3 tablespoons (24 g/0.8 oz) coconut flour

¼ teaspoon sea salt

½ cup (120 ml) lukewarm water

5.3 ounces (150 g) Mexican chorizo

1 small (90 g/3.2 oz) green pepper, diced

1 tablespoon (15 g/0.5 oz) unsweetened tomato paste

2 teaspoons (10 g/0.4 oz) duck fat

Optional: 1 medium (150 g/5.3 oz) avocado, sliced

Combine all the dry ingredients in a bowl. Add the lukewarm water and mix well. Let the dough sit for 15 minutes.

Meanwhile, place a skillet over high heat. Add the chorizo and dry-fry for 1 to 2 minutes, or until it begins to release its juices. Add the pepper and tomato paste. Cook for about 5 minutes, or until the chorizo is cooked through and the pepper is tender.

Preheat the oven to 400°F (200°C, or gas mark 6). Roll out the dough thinly between 2 sheets of parchment paper or use a nonstick mat and nonstick rolling pin. (When rolled out, the dough should be about 8 x 11 inches [20 x 30 cm].) Add the chorizo-pepper filling to the center of the dough, then fold over like an envelope and seal the dough with your fingers. Do not press too hard or the filling will spill out. Using a sharp knife, poke some holes into the dough for releasing the steam while baking, then brush with the ghee. Bake for 20 to 25 minutes, or until golden brown and firm to the touch. When done, remove from the oven and let cool for a few minutes. Cut in half and enjoy while still hot, or let it cool and refrigerate for up to 3 days. Serve with avocado, if desired.

NOTE: Make sure you weigh the dry ingredients for this recipe, as volume amounts may vary. Also, whole psyllium husks work better than powder here, but if you must substitute, use 2 teaspoons (5 g/0.2 oz) of psyllium powder instead.

NUTRITION FACTS PER SERVING (½ POCKET):
Total carbs: 17.3 g / Fiber: 12.2 g / Net carbs: 5.1 g / Protein: 19.2 g / Fat: 27.2 g / Calories: 382 kcal
Macronutrient ratio: Calories from carbs (6%), protein (22%), fat (72%)

Focaccia Sandwich Four Ways

MAKES: 1 sandwich
HANDS-ON TIME: 5 minutes
OVERALL TIME: 5 minutes

If you've got some leftover Garlic & Herb Focaccia (page 48) lurking in the fridge, you're a single step away from making a quick, versatile low-carb lunch. Enjoy one or two as a regular meal, or double it if you're doing intermittent fasting (IF).

1 slice Garlic & Herb Focaccia (page 48) for each sandwich, cut widthwise

Egg-Avocado Salad Sandwich:

1 hard-boiled egg (see page 42)
1 tablespoon (15 g/0.5 oz) mayonnaise (page 42)
½ teaspoon Dijon mustard
1 tablespoon (4g/0.2 oz) chopped chives or spring onion
Sea salt and black pepper
½ small (50 g/1.8 oz) avocado, pitted, peeled, and sliced

Ham & Cheese Sandwich:

2 teaspoons (10 g/0.4 oz) butter
1 slice (2 oz/57 g) quality ham
2 slices (2 oz/57 g) Cheddar or provolone cheese
Optional: handful of fresh spinach or arugula

Caprese Sandwich:

2 tablespoons (20 g/0.7 oz) marinara sauce (page 43) or basil pesto (page 43)
2 ounces (57 g) fresh mozzarella, sliced
2 to 3 slices (50 g/1.8 oz) tomato, seeds removed
2 to 4 fresh basil leaves

BLT Sandwich:

1 tablespoon (15 g/0.5 oz) mayonnaise (page 42)
2 (1 oz/28 g) soft green lettuce leaves
2 to 3 slices (50 g/1.8 oz) tomato, seeds removed
4 thin-cut slices (32 g/1.2 oz) cooked bacon (page 41)

TO MAKE THE EGG-AVOCADO SANDWICH: Place the egg in a bowl. Using a fork, mash it with the mayo, mustard, and chives. Season with salt and pepper. Spread the mixture on the inside of the focaccia, and top with avocado and the other half of focaccia.

TO MAKE THE THE HAM & CHEESE SANDWICH: Spread a teaspoon of butter inside each of the focaccia halves. Add the sliced ham, cheese, and spinach (if using). Top with the other half of the focaccia.

TO MAKE THE CAPRESE SANDWICH: Spread ½ tablespoon (10 g) of marinara sauce inside each of the focaccia halves. Add the mozzarella, tomato slices (with seeds removed: otherwise the sandwich would be soggy), and basil leaves. Top with the other half of the focaccia.

TO MAKE THE BLT SANDWICH: Spread ½ tablespoon (about 8 g) of mayo inside each of the focaccia halves. Place some lettuce on top of each half, and fill with the tomato slices and crisp bacon. Refrigerate prepared sandwiches for up to 1 day.

NUTRITION FACTS PER SERVING (1 EGG-AVOCADO/HAM & CHEESE/CAPRESE/BLT SANDWICH):
Total carbs: 12.2/8/11.7/9.8 g / Fiber: 9.4/5.8 /6.7/6.8 g / Net carbs: 2.8/2.2/5/3.1 g / Protein: 11.3/27.1/18/ 14.1 g / Fat: 34.6/38.4/22.2/25.6 g / Calories: 381/471/301/305 kcal / Macronutrient ratio: Calories from carbs (3/2/7/4%), protein (12/23/25/19%), fat (85/75/68/77%)

Three-Cheese Crustless Mini Quiches

MAKES: 12 mini quiches
HANDS-ON TIME: 20 minutes
OVERALL TIME: 45 minutes

These low-carb vegetarian quiches are surprisingly filling, and they're super-portable, too: pop a couple into your lunchbox, or grab one as a snack as you're running out the door. If you have time, though, they're best served drizzled with homemade pesto and paired with a simple side salad.

1 tablespoon (15 g/0.5 oz) ghee or duck fat

1 large (150 g/5.3 oz) yellow onion, chopped

2 cloves garlic, minced

8.5 ounces (240 g) fresh spinach or chopped Swiss chard

1.1 pounds (500 g) ricotta cheese

1 cup (90 g/3.2 oz) finely grated Parmesan cheese

1 large egg

4 egg yolks

8.5 ounces (240 g) blue cheese, feta, or goat cheese, crumbled

Optional: 1 teaspoon (5 g/0.2 oz) basil pesto (page 43) per quiche

Preheat the oven to 375°F (190°C, or gas mark 5). Grease a large saucepan (big enough to fit all the spinach) with the ghee. Heat over medium-high heat, add the onion, and cook for 6 to 8 minutes, or until lightly browned. Add the garlic and cook for 1 minute more. Add the spinach and cook for 1 to 2 minutes, stirring frequently, until wilted. Remove from the heat and set aside.

In a bowl, combine the ricotta, Parmesan, egg, and egg yolks. Spoon about 1 ounce (28 g) of the ricotta cheese mixture into each cup of a silicone muffin pan (or a regular muffin pan greased with ghee). Top each with a dollop of the spinach-onion mixture and about 1 tablespoon (15 g) of blue cheese. Finally, top each with the remaining ricotta cheese mixture and bake for 20 to 25 minutes, or until the quiches are set and the tops are lightly browned. Let the quiches cool for a few minutes before serving. Optionally, top each with homemade pesto. Store in the fridge to up to 5 days, or freeze for up to 6 months.

NUTRITION FACTS PER SERVING (1 MINI QUICHE):
Total carbs: 3.6 g / Fiber: 0.6 g / Net carbs: 3 g / Protein: 1.1 g / Fat: 17.7 g / Calories: 233 kcal
Macronutrient ratio: Calories from carbs (5%), protein (26%), fat (69%)

Avocado-Stuffed Power Balls

MAKES: 4 servings
HANDS-ON TIME: 20 minutes
OVERALL TIME: 30 minutes

These spicy, allergy-friendly chorizo-beef meatballs hide chunks of electrolyte-rich avocado. They're best served over a bed of cauliflower rice and kale, and doused in a homemade chimichurri sauce that takes just seconds to make.

Chimichurri:

1 large bunch (60 g/2.1 oz) fresh parsley

¼ cup (15 g/0.5 oz) fresh oregano

4 cloves garlic, chopped

1 small (5 g/0.2 oz) red chile pepper, seeds removed

2 tablespoons (30 ml) apple cider vinegar or fresh lime juice

½ cup (120 ml) extra-virgin olive oil

½ teaspoon salt

¼ teaspoon black pepper

Meatballs:

12.3 ounces (350 g) ground beef

5.3 ounces (150 g) Mexican chorizo or ground 20% fat pork

2 tablespoons (8 g/0.3 oz) chopped fresh parsley

½ teaspoon sea salt

½ medium (75 g/2.7 oz) avocado, chopped into 16 pieces

1 tablespoon (15 g/0.5 oz) ghee or duck fat

Cauliflower-Chard Rice:

½ recipe chimichurri sauce (above)

3 cups (360 g/12.7 oz) cauliflower rice (page 40)

7.1 ounces (200 g) chopped Swiss chard or dark-leaf kale, stems removed

Sea salt and black pepper

TO MAKE THE CHIMICHURRI: Place all the ingredients in a blender and process until smooth.

TO MAKE THE MEATBALLS: In a bowl, combine the beef, chorizo, parsley, and salt. Mix until well combined. Using your hands, create 16 patties (about 32 g/1.1 oz each). Place a piece of avocado in the middle of each patty and wrap the meat around it until you create a meatball. Grease a large skillet with the ghee. Once hot, add the meatballs in a single layer. Cook for 2 minutes per side, turning with a fork until browned on all sides and cooked through. Remove from the heat.

TO MAKE THE CAULIFLOWER-CHARD RICE: Pour half of the chimichurri sauce into a large saucepan and heat over medium heat. Add the cauliflower rice and kale. Cook for 5 to 7 minutes, or until the kale is tender. Season with salt and pepper.

To assemble, place a quarter of the cauli-chard rice into a bowl, top with 4 meatballs, and serve with the remaining chimichurri sauce (about 3 tablespoons/45 ml per serving). Refrigerate the meatballs and cauliflower rice in an airtight container for up to 4 days, and refrigerate the chimichurri in an airtight container for up to 1 week.

NUTRITION FACTS PER SERVING (4 MEATBALLS + CAULI-KALE RICE + CHIMICHURRI):
Total carbs: 13.9 g / Fiber: 6.2 g / Net carbs: 7.6 g / Protein: 24.7 g / Fat: 59.6 g / Calories: 683 kcal
Macronutrient ratio: Calories from carbs (5%), protein (15%), fat (80%)

Greek Keftedes Bowls

MAKES: 4 servings
HANDS-ON TIME: 30 minutes
OVERALL TIME: 30 minutes

This well-balanced Mediterranean meal is perfect for breaking your fast. It's really nutritious and will keep you fuller for longer. Absolutely starving? Serve it with a slice of Garlic & Herb Focaccia (page 48)!

Tzatziki:

½ medium (100 g/3.5 oz) cucumber
1 cup (250 g/8.8 oz) 5% full-fat yogurt
1 clove garlic, crushed
1 tablespoon (15 ml) fresh lemon juice
½ teaspoon fresh lemon zest
2 tablespoons (30 ml) extra-virgin olive oil
1 tablespoon (4 g/0.2 oz) chopped fresh dill
Sea salt and black pepper

Greek Salad:

1 small (150 g/5.3 oz) cucumber, grated
1⅓ cups (200 g/7.1 oz) halved cherry tomatoes
1 small (75 g/2.6 oz) green pepper, sliced
½ small (30 g/1.1 oz) red onion, sliced
½ cup (75 g/2.6 oz) crumbled feta cheese
12 (36 g/1.3 oz) pitted black or green olives
1 teaspoon dried oregano
2 tablespoons (30 ml) extra-virgin olive oil

Meatballs:

1.1 pounds (500 g) ground lamb
½ teaspoon sea salt
¼ teaspoon black pepper
½ small (35 g/1.2 oz) yellow onion, finely chopped
2 cloves garlic, crushed
2 tablespoons (8 g/0.3 oz) chopped fresh parsley, or 2 teaspoons dried parsley
1 tablespoon (4 g/0.2 oz) chopped fresh oregano, or 1 teaspoon dried oregano
1 tablespoon (4 g/0.2 oz) chopped fresh mint, or 1 teaspoon dried mint
1 large egg
½ cup (50 g/1.8 oz) almond flour, or 2½ tablespoons (20 g/0.7 oz) coconut flour

1 tablespoon (15 g/0.5 oz) ghee or duck fat

TO MAKE THE TZATZIK: Grate the cucumber into a bowl and drain any excess liquid. Add the yogurt, garlic, lemon juice, lemon zest, olive oil, and dill. Add salt and pepper to taste. Mix until combined. Cover and store in an airtight container in the fridge for up to 3 days.

TO MAKE THE SALAD: Place all the vegetables in a bowl. Add the feta, olives, and oregano. Drizzle with the olive oil.

TO MAKE THE MEATBALLS: In a bowl, combine all the ingredients for the meatballs. Using your hands, form the mixture into 20 meatballs (about 33 g/1.2 oz each). Grease a large skillet with ghee. Once hot, add the meatballs in a single layer. Cook for 2 minutes per side, turning with a fork until browned on all sides and cooked through. Remove from the heat.

To assemble, place a quarter of the Greek salad in a bowl, add 5 meatballs, and serve with tzatziki (about ⅓ cup/80 ml per serving). Refrigerate the meatballs and tzatziki in separate airtight containers for up to 4 days.

NUTRITION FACTS PER SERVING (5 MEATBALLS + ⅓ CUP/80 ML TZATZIKI + ¼ GREEK SALAD):
Total carbs: 13.6 g / Fiber: 3.9 g / Net carbs: 9.7 g / Protein: 35.6 g / Fat: 60.7 g / Calories: 732 kcal
Macronutrient ratio: Calories from carbs (5%), protein (20%), fat (75%)

Bacon-Wrapped Beef Patties with "Chimiole"

MAKES: 4 servings
HANDS-ON TIME: 20 minutes
OVERALL TIME: 40 minutes

"Chimiole" isn't as weird as it sounds: it's a combination of chimichurri and guacamole. I created it when I had some leftover chimichurri sauce from a barbecue, plus loads of avocados. And guess what? The combination works so well that it's been a favorite in my house ever since! And it's the perfect side for these oven-baked, bacon-wrapped beef burgers.

Patties:

- 1 pound (450 g) ground beef
- ¼ teaspoon black pepper
- ½ small (35 g/1.2 oz) yellow onion, finely chopped
- 1 clove garlic, crushed
- 16 slices (240 g/8.5 oz) thin-cut bacon (about 15 g/0.5 oz per slice)

"Chimiole":

- 2 large (400 g/14.1) avocados, pitted and peeled
- 1 small (70 g/2.5 oz) yellow onion, finely chopped
- 1⅓ cups (200 g/7.1 oz) chopped regular or cherry tomatoes
- ½ cup (120 ml) Chimichurri (page 120)
- Sea salt and black pepper
- Optional: lettuce and freshly chopped vegetables such as tomatoes, bell peppers, or cucumber for serving

TO MAKE THE PATTIES: Preheat the oven to 400°F (200°C, or gas mark 6). Combine the beef, pepper, onion, and garlic in a bowl. Using your hands, form the mixture into 8 medium patties (about 60 g/2.1 oz each). Wrap each of the patties with 2 slices of bacon. Place on a baking tray lined with parchment paper. Bake for 25 to 30 minutes, or until the patties are golden brown.

TO MAKE THE "CHIMIOLE": Place 1 avocado into a bowl and mash well with a fork. Add the onion, tomatoes, and chimichurri. Stir to combine. Dice the second avocado and mix it into the "chimiole," but do not mash it. Season with salt and black pepper to taste.

Serve 2 patties with about 1 cup/240 g of the "chimiole." Optionally, serve with lettuce and vegetables. To store, place the patties and "chimiole" in separate airtight containers, and store in the fridge for up to 3 days.

NUTRITION FACTS PER SERVING (2 PATTIES + 1 CUP/240 G "CHIMIOLE"):
Total carbs: 14.9 g / Fiber: 8.8 g / Net carbs: 6.1 g / Protein: 30.5 g / Fat: 66.3 g / Calories: 768 kcal
Macronutrient ratio: Calories from carbs (3%), protein (16%), fat (81%)

Turkey Nuggets with Kale Slaw and Italian Dressing

MAKES: 4 servings
HANDS-ON TIME: 10 minutes
OVERALL TIME: 20 minutes

Ever wondered what to do with all those leftover broccoli stalks? Don't throw them out: uUse them to make this tasty superfood slaw. Then serve it with crispy turkey nuggets and a creamy Italian dressing for a potassium-rich, induction-friendly meal.

Italian Dressing:

- ½ cup (110 g/3.9 oz) mayonnaise (page 42)
- ¼ cup (58 g/2 oz) sour cream
- 1 tablespoon (15 g/0.5 oz) tomato paste
- 4 pieces (12 g/0.4 oz) sun-dried tomatoes, chopped
- 2 tablespoons (8 g/0.3 oz) chopped fresh herbs such as parsley, basil, or thyme
- Sea salt and black pepper

Superfood Kale Slaw:

- 7.1 ounces (200 g) green cabbage
- 3.5 ounces (100 g) dark-leaf kale or baby kale
- 3 to 4 (100 g/3.5 oz) broccoli stalks, peeled or kohlrabi
- 1 small (70 g/2.5 oz) red onion, sliced
- 2 tablespoons (30 ml) fresh lemon juice
- ½ teaspoon celery seeds
- 2 tablespoons (8 g/0.3 oz) chopped herbs such as parsley, basil, or thyme
- Sea salt and black pepper

Turkey Nuggets:

- 1.3 pounds (600 g) turkey leg (dark) meat
- 1 large egg, beaten
- Pinch of sea salt and black pepper
- 1½ cups (135 g/4.8 oz) finely grated Parmesan cheese
- 2 tablespoons (30 g/1.1 oz) ghee or duck fat

TO MAKE THE DRESSING: Combine all the ingredients in a small bowl. Set aside.

TO MAKE THE SLAW: Using your food processor's slicing blade, thinly slice the cabbage, kale, and broccoli stalks (or kohlrabi), then place in a large mixing bowl. Add the red onion, lemon juice, celery seeds, and herbs. Add half of the prepared dressing and combine well. Season with salt and pepper to taste, and mix well again.

TO MAKE THE TURKEY NUGGETS: Slice the turkey into pieces about ½ inch (1 cm) thick. In a bowl, beat the egg with a pinch of salt and pepper. Place the Parmesan in a separate bowl. Dip each of the turkey pieces in the egg, then dip into the bowl with the Parmesan and roll to coat well. Heat a pan greased with the ghee over medium-high heat. Once hot, add the turkey nuggets, and fry until golden brown on both sides. Work in batches: do not overfill the pan. Use a rubber spatula to flip the turkey halfway through cooking, keeping as much of the Parmesan crust as possible on the nuggets. Serve the turkey nuggets with the slaw and the remaining dressing on the side.

NUTRITION FACTS PER SERVING (6 OZ/180 G NUGGETS + ¾ CUP/150 G SLAW + ¼ CUP/60 ML DRESSING):
Total carbs: 10.4 g / Fiber: 3.6 g / Net carbs: 6.8 g / Protein: 45.9 g / Fat: 54.2 g / Calories: 709 kcal
Macronutrient ratio: Calories from carbs (4%), protein (26%), fat (70%)

Mexican Chicken Bowls

MAKES: 4 servings
HANDS-ON TIME: 20 minutes
OVERALL TIME: 1 hour 30 minutes

Banish cravings and keto flu by making these potassium-rich, Mexican-inflected lunch bowls. Prepare them in advance for a quick-prep lunchbox solution that'll keep you going all the way to dinnertime.

Marinated Chicken:

- 1.3 pounds (600 g) chicken breasts, cut into 1½-inch (4-cm) pieces
- 2 tablespoons (30 ml) extra-virgin olive oil
- 1 tablespoon (15 ml) fresh lemon juice
- 1 tablespoon (15 ml) white wine vinegar
- 1 tablespoon (5 g/0.2 oz) dried oregano
- ½ teaspoon chipotle powder
- ½ teaspoon sea salt
- ¼ teaspoon black pepper

Avocado-Feta Salsa:

- 3 tablespoons (45 ml) extra-virgin olive oil
- 2 tablespoons (30 ml) fresh lime juice
- 1 clove garlic, crushed
- 1 large (200 g/7.1 oz) avocado, diced
- 2 cups (300 g/10.6 oz) halved cherry or chopped regular tomatoes
- 1 small (60/2.1 oz) red onion, sliced
- 2 teaspoons dried oregano
- 2 tablespoons (8 g/0.3 oz) chopped cilantro or parsley
- ¾ cup (113 g/4 oz) crumbled feta cheese or queso fresco
- Sea salt and black pepper
- 1 tablespoon (15 g/0.5 oz) ghee or duck fat
- 1 head (200 g/7.1 oz) romaine, or any green lettuce

Optional: salsa verde for serving

TO MAKE THE CHICKEN: Place the chicken pieces in a bowl. Add the olive oil, lemon juice, vinegar, oregano, chipotle powder, salt, and pepper. Mix until well coated, cover, and let the chicken marinate in the fridge for at least 1 hour, or overnight.

TO MAKE THE AVOCADO-FETA SALSA: In a bowl, combine the olive oil, lime juice, and garlic. Place the avocado, tomatoes, onion, herbs, and cheese in a bowl, and pour over the prepared oil mixture. Season with salt and pepper to taste. Place in the fridge while you cook the chicken, or store covered for up to 2 days (but best served fresh).

Heat a large skillet greased with the ghee over medium-high heat. Add the marinated chicken pieces and cook until they are browned on all sides and cooked through, about 10 minutes. To serve, fill 2 to 3 lettuce leaves with some avocado-feta salsa and serve with the chicken and, optionally, salsa verde. Leftover chicken and salsa verde can be stored in an airtight container in the fridge for up to 4 days.

NUTRITION FACTS PER SERVING (CHICKEN + AVOCADO-FETA SALSA):
Total carbs: 13.5 g / Fiber: 6.8 g / Net carbs: 6.7 g / Protein: 38 g / Fat: 48.3 g / Calories: 635 kcal
Macronutrient ratio: Calories from carbs (4%), protein (25%), fat (71%)

Mackerel Fat Stacks

MAKES: 2 servings
HANDS-ON TIME: 10 minutes
OVERALL TIME: 15 minutes

These fish stacks are rich in omega-3 fatty acids, magnesium, and potassium, so they're great for keto induction. Plus, even though they're filling enough to act as a full meal, they're a snap to make: you'll be able to whip them up in less than fifteen minutes.

2 large (180 g/6.3 oz) portobello mushrooms

Sea salt and black pepper

1 tablespoon (15 g/0.5 oz) ghee or duck fat

2 medium (220 g/7.8 oz) smoked mackerel fillets, skin removed

1 small (50 g/1.8 oz) red onion, finely chopped

¼ cup (60 g/2.1 oz) crème fraîche or sour cream

2 tablespoons (30 g/1.1 oz) mayonnaise (page 42)

1 tablespoon (15 ml) fresh lemon juice

1 small head (100 g/3.5 oz) green lettuce, such as butterhead

2 cups (60 g/2.1 oz) fresh spinach, arugula, or watercress

½ medium (100 g/3.5 oz) cucumber, peeled and sliced

½ medium (75 g/2.7 oz) avocado, pitted, peeled, and sliced

Clean the mushrooms with a damp paper towel. Remove the stems and reserve for another recipe (for instance, add them to an omelet or egg muffins, page 57). Season the mushrooms with salt and pepper. Place, bottom-side up, in a hot ovenproof pan greased with ghee. Cook for 1 to 2 minutes, then flip over. Cover with a lid and cook for 5 to 7 minutes more, or until tender. Turn the mushrooms bottom-side up and remove from the heat. Set aside.

Break the mackerel into small pieces. In a bowl, combine the mackerel, onion, crème fraîche, mayonnaise, and lemon juice. Season with salt and pepper to taste.

To assemble the stacks, divide the lettuce, spinach, and cucumber between 2 bowls. Top each with a portobello mushroom and add the mackerel mixture. Top with avocado and serve. The mackerel mixture can be stored in the fridge for up to 4 days. It's best to assemble the salad just before serving, or the night before (drizzle the avocado with some lemon or lime juice to prevent browning).

NUTRITION FACTS PER SERVING (1 STACK):
Total carbs: 13.9 g / Fiber: 5.8 g / Net carbs: 8.1 g / Protein: 26.4 g / Fat: 51.3 g / Calories: 611 kcal
Macronutrient ratio: Calories from carbs (5%), protein (18%), fat (77%)

California Sushi Wraps

MAKES: 4 wraps
HANDS-ON TIME: 10 minutes
OVERALL TIME: 10 minutes

Every ingredient in these ten-minute rice-free sushi wraps is packed with goodness! Eggs are a fantastic source of quality protein and choline; seaweed is a great source of iodine; fatty salmon is high in omega-3s; and avocado provides heart-healthy monounsaturated fats.

2 large eggs

Salt and pepper

2 teaspoons (10 g/0.4 oz) ghee or duck fat, divided

2 nori sheets

4.2 ounces (120 g) smoked salmon

1 small (110 g/3.9 oz) avocado, pitted, peeled, and sliced

2 teaspoons (10 ml) fresh lemon juice

3 ounces (85 g) peeled cucumber, cut into matchsticks

2 tablespoons (30 g/1.1 oz) mayonnaise (page 42)

2 teaspoons (6 g/0.2 oz) sesame seeds

Crack one egg into a bowl. Season with salt. Whisk and then pour into a hot pan greased with 1 teaspoon (5 g/0.2 oz) of the ghee. Cook over medium-high heat for about a minute, or until the top is firm and opaque. Transfer to a plate (don't worry too much if the shape of the omelet isn't perfectly round). Repeat for the second egg, greasing the pan with the remaining 1 teaspoon (5 g/0.2 oz) ghee before cooking the second egg. When done, cut each omelet in half. Cut the nori sheets in half. To assemble, top each of the nori halves with half an omelet and a quarter each of the smoked salmon, avocado slices, lemon juice, cucumber, mayonnaise, and sesame seeds. Using your hands, tightly roll each wrap into a cone shape, starting from the bottom left corner. Wet the edges of the seaweed to seal. Repeat with the remaining nori wraps. Eat immediately or store in the fridge for up to a day. The nori sheets get soft quickly, so if you prefer the wraps crispy, assemble them just before serving.

NUTRITION FACTS PER SERVING (2 WRAPS):
Total carbs: 7.9 g / Fiber: 5.2 g / Net carbs: 2.8 g / Protein: 20.2 g / Fat: 34.5 g / Calories: 413 kcal
Macronutrient ratio: Calories from carbs (3%), protein (20%), fat (77%)

Keto Power Bars

MAKES: 12 bars
HANDS-ON TIME: 20 minutes
OVERALL TIME: 1 hour 20 minutes

Sometimes—and especially if you're on the go all day—you just want to grab a quick bar for lunch. It's best to make your own, because most store-bought options either contain too much protein and too little fat, or are high-fat options that melt at room temperature. None of that is an issue with these nutty, chocolaty beauties, though!

1¼ cups (124 g/4.4 oz) pecan halves

½ cup (60 g/2.1 oz) coconut flour

¼ cup (38 g/1.3 oz) whole chia seeds

½ cup (80 g/2.8 oz) powdered erythritol or Swerve

1 cup (100 g/3.5 oz) collagen powder (see page 31 for alternatives)

1 teaspoon vanilla powder, or
1 tablespoon sugar-free vanilla extract

1 teaspoon ground cinnamon

3 ounces (85 g) unsweetened chocolate

3 ounces (85 g) cacao butter

½ cup (120 g/4.2 oz) almond butter or sunflower seed butter

1 teaspoon sugar-free maple extract

Chop most of the pecan halves, reserving a few for topping. Combine the chopped pecans, coconut flour, chia seeds, erythritol, collagen powder, vanilla, and cinnamon in a bowl. Melt the unsweetened chocolate and cacao butter in a double boiler, or in a heatproof bowl placed over a small saucepan filled with 1 cup (235 ml) of water, placed over medium heat. Once melted, carefully remove the bowl from the saucepan. Mix in the almond butter, maple extract, and the dry ingredients. Combine well with a spatula until you have created a cookie dough–like mixture. Transfer the dough to an 8 x 8-inch (20 x 20-cm) parchment-lined pan or silicone pan. Top with the reserved pecan halves. Refrigerate for about 1 hour, or until set and ready to slice. Create bars by cutting the mixture into 6 rows by 2 columns. Store in an airtight container at room temperature for up to 2 weeks.

WHAT IS UNSWEETENED CHOCOLATE?

Unsweetened chocolate—also known as cacao liquor or cacao paste—is pure cocoa mass and becomes liquid when heated. It contains both cacao solids and cacao butter. Unsweetened chocolate can be substituted with dark chocolate (at least 85% cocoa, or ideally more). All are low in carbs and will not significantly affect nutrition facts.

NUTRITION FACTS PER SERVING (1 BAR):
Total carbs: 8.9 g / Fiber: 5.7 g / Net carbs: 3.2 g / Protein: 10.3 g / Fat: 27.3 g / Calories: 326 kcal
Macronutrient ratio: Calories from carbs (4%), protein (14%), fat (82%)

Vegetable Rose Pie

MAKES: 12 servings
HANDS-ON TIME: 30 minutes
OVERALL TIME: 1 hour 30 minutes

This beautifully keto pie is made with low-carb vegetable ribbons in place of high-carb potato and carrot. And a little goes a long way: mascarpone and pesto are high in fat, so you won't need a large slice to feel full.

Crust:

1½ cups (150 g/5.3 oz) almond flour

1 cup (90 g/3.2 oz) grated Parmesan cheese

1 large egg

2 tablespoons (30 g/1.1 oz) butter

Filling:

3 medium (600 g/1.3 oz) zucchini (use green and yellow for a "rainbow" effect)

1 large (400 g/14.1 oz) eggplant

1 tablespoon (15 ml) fresh lemon juice

1 tablespoon (15 ml) melted ghee

Sea salt and black pepper

1 cup (240 g/8.5 oz) mascarpone cheese

½ cup (125 g/4.4 oz) basil pesto (page 43)

1 cup (120 g/4.2 oz) grated Swiss cheese

⅓ cup (30 g/1.1 oz) grated Parmesan cheese

2 large eggs

1 tablespoon (15 ml) extra-virgin olive oil

Fresh basil or thyme for garnish

TO MAKE THE CRUST: Preheat the oven to 350°F (175°C, or gas mark 4). Place all the ingredients for the crust in a bowl, and mix until well combined. Press into a pie pan toward the edges to create a bowl shape so that the pie can hold the filling. The edges should be at least 1¼ inches (3 cm) tall. Bake for 10 to 12 minutes, or until golden brown. Watch it carefully, because almonds can burn easily.

TO MAKE THE FILLING: Slice the zucchini into long, thin ribbons. Do the same for the eggplant, then halve the ribbons lengthwise to create thinner ribbons. Lay the zucchini and eggplant ribbons on baking trays lined with parchment paper. Drizzle with the lemon juice and brush with the melted ghee. Season with salt and pepper. When the crust is ready, remove from the oven and cool on a rack. Increase the temperature to 400°F (200°C, or gas mark 6), and bake the ribbons for 15 to 18 minutes, until soft. Remove from the oven and let them cool down for a few minutes.

Place the mascarpone, pesto, Swiss cheese, Parmesan, eggs, and salt and pepper to taste into a bowl, and mix until well combined. Spoon the filling into the prepared crust.

Reduce the temperature to 300°F (150°C). Stack 2 slices of zucchini and eggplant on top of each other. Starting from one end, roll the stack into a spiral and press it into the filling so that it stands up in the center of the pie. Create a layer from another three vegetable slices and wrap these stacks around the spiral in the center. Repeat until the pie is complete: you will have created a rose effect and very little of the filling will be visible. Bake for 35 to 40 minutes, until the filling has set. Remove from the oven and let it cool down for 15 minutes. Drizzle with the olive oil and garnish with fresh herbs. Serve warm or cold. Store refrigerated for up to 5 days.

NUTRITION FACTS PER SERVING (1 SLICE):
Total carbs: 7.4 g / Fiber: 3 g / Net carbs: 4.4 g / Protein: 13.3 g / Fat: 32 g / Calories: 361 kcal
Macronutrient ratio: Calories from carbs (5%), protein (15%), fat (80%)

Chapter 6

Energy-Boosting, Fat-Fueled Dinners

What's on the dinner menu when you're eating keto? Just about everything! The recipes in this chapter are proof that you'll never feel bored or deprived on a ketogenic lifestyle. I love variety, which is why I've come up with low-carb versions of lots of your favorite meals. In this chapter, you'll find everything from American classics to Indian-style curries and Mediterranean one-pot wonders— and I've made sure to keep them simple, so lots of them call for just a few basic ingredients.

And, of course, these recipes have been designed specially to help you meet your macros and stay nourished, particularly during the induction phase of the keto diet. Lots of them are high in electrolytes, which are great for keeping cravings at bay. And, if you practice intermittent fasting (IF), they are substantial enough for when you're breaking your fast and need an extra-satisfying meal. If you miss pasta, try the Superfood Pesto Zoodles & Eggs on page 135: it's just as comforting, but with way fewer carbs. The Bacon-Wrapped Monkfish with Creamed Spinach on page 144 is elegant enough to serve to guests, and the vegetarian Masala Cauli-Rice with Grilled Halloumi on page 136 is just the thing when you're craving Indian food. These healthy, low-stress dinners are sure to keep the whole family happy—all week long.

Mushroom Stroganoff

MAKES: 4 servings
HANDS-ON TIME: 20 minutes
OVERALL TIME: 30 minutes

Hearty keto dishes don't have to include meat. Here's proof: this low-carb vegetarian version of the Russian classic is just as rich and creamy as the original, but it gets its bulk from mushrooms and spinach. It's also a great way to use those leftover egg yolks from your keto focaccia (page 48)!

2 packs (400 g/14.1 oz) shirataki
  noodles
4 egg yolks
1¼ cups (300 ml) heavy whipping
  cream or coconut milk
2 tablespoons (30 g/1.1 oz) ghee or
  coconut oil
½ small (35 g/1.2 oz) yellow onion,
  chopped
2 cloves garlic, minced
1.1 pounds (500 g) white mushrooms,
  sliced
1 tablespoon (15 g/0.5 oz) Dijon
  mustard
Sea salt and black pepper
4 cups (120 g/4.2 oz) fresh spinach
2 tablespoons (8 g/0.3 oz) chopped
  fresh parsley

Prepare the shirataki noodles according to the instructions on page 41.

In a bowl, mix the egg yolks with the cream and set aside. Grease a saucepan with the ghee. Once hot, add the onion and cook over medium-high heat for about 5 minutes, until lightly browned. Then add the garlic and cook for 1 minute more. Add the mushrooms and cook for about 5 minutes. Reduce the heat to medium and pour in the cream–egg yolk mixture while stirring. Cook for about 5 minutes, stirring constantly, until it thickens. Add the mustard, and season with salt and pepper to taste. Add the spinach and cook for 1 minute, until wilted. Add the prepared shirataki noodles and cook for a minute to heat through. Finally, top with the fresh parsley and serve, or let it cool and refrigerate in an airtight container for up to 5 days.

NUTRITION FACTS PER SERVING:
Total carbs: 12.2 g / Fiber: 3.7 g / Net carbs: 8.5 g / Protein: 9.2 g / Fat: 41.4 g / Calories: 444 kcal
Macronutrient ratio: Calories from carbs (8%), protein (8%), fat (84%)

Superfood Pesto Zoodles & Eggs

MAKES: 4 servings
HANDS-ON TIME: 15 minutes
OVERALL TIME: 20 minutes

I can't remember the last time I bought pesto. Once you make your own, you'll never go back to the store-bought stuff. Homemade pesto is the key ingredient in this comforting vegetarian meal, which is packed with micronutrients and heart-healthy monounsaturated fatty acids.

Avocado-Pesto Sauce:

1 medium (150 g/5.3 oz) avocado, pitted and peeled
2 cups (60 g/2.1 oz) fresh spinach, watercress, or arugula
2 cloves garlic, minced
2 tablespoons (30 ml) fresh lemon or lime juice
¼ cup (60 ml) extra-virgin olive oil
¼ cup (34 g/1.2 oz) pine nuts or sunflower seeds
1 cup (15 g/0.5 oz) basil leaves
Sea salt and black pepper

Zoodles & Eggs:

4 medium (800 g/1.76 lb) zucchini
Salt
1 tablespoon (15 g/0.5 oz) ghee or duck fat
4 large eggs, fried or poached (see page 42)
Optional: chopped cherry tomatoes and more eggs

TO MAKE THE AVOCADO-PESTO SAUCE: Place the avocado, spinach, garlic, lemon juice, olive oil, and pine nuts in a food processor, and process until smooth. Add the basil and pulse a few more times. Season with salt and pepper, then spoon into a small bowl and set aside.

TO MAKE THE ZOODLES AND EGGS: Use a julienne peeler or a spiralizer to turn the zucchini into thin "noodles." Sprinkle the noodles with salt and let them sit for 10 minutes. Use a paper towel to pat them dry. Set aside.

Grease a pan with the ghee and cook the zoodles for 2 to 5 minutes. Add half of the prepared avocado-pesto sauce and cook for just a minute, or until heated through. Top with fried or poached eggs, and tomatoes and more eggs, if desired, and serve with the remaining avocado-pesto sauce. Store in the fridge for 2 to 3 days.

NOTE: Bulk up the recipe by adding cooked shirataki noodles (see page 41), or substitute them for part of the zucchini noodles. Or try it with cooked salmon instead of eggs for an extra dose of omega-3s.

NUTRITION FACTS PER SERVING:
Total carbs: 12.4 g / Fiber: 5.2 g / Net carbs: 7.2 g / Protein: 11.2 g / Fat: 34 g / Calories: 384 kcal
Macronutrient ratio: Calories from carbs (8%), protein (12%), fat (80%)

Masala Cauli-Rice with Grilled Halloumi

MAKES: 4 servings
HANDS-ON TIME: 20 minutes
OVERALL TIME: 20 minutes

Craving Indian food, minus the unhealthy carbs? You've got to try this vegetarian keto masala. It's made with cauli-rice, and it gets a hit of protein and good fats from a topping of crispy, salty Halloumi cheese. To keep the Halloumi juicy and tender inside, always remember to serve it warm.

⅓ cup (73 g/2.6 oz) ghee or virgin coconut oil, divided

1 small (70 g/2.5 oz) yellow onion, chopped

1 clove garlic, minced

1 small (5 g/0.2 oz) red or green chile pepper, chopped, seeds removed

½ teaspoon garam masala

½ teaspoon ground turmeric

½ teaspoon ground cumin

½ teaspoon ground coriander

⅛ to ¼ teaspoon chili powder

6 cups (720 g/1.6 lb) cauliflower rice (see page 40)

1 medium (120 g/4.2 oz) tomato, chopped

Sea salt and black pepper

11.3 ounces (320 g) Halloumi cheese, about 80 g/2.8 oz per serving

Grease a large skillet with the ghee (reserve about a tablespoon [15 g] for cooking the Halloumi). Cook the onion over medium-high heat for 5 to 7 minutes, until lightly browned and fragrant. Then add the garlic and chile. Add all the spices, cook for a minute, and then add the cauli-rice. Cook for 5 minutes, stirring frequently. Then add the tomato and cook for another 2 to 3 minutes, or until the cauli-rice is tender. Season with salt and pepper to taste. Set aside and keep warm.

Grease a skillet (regular or griddle) with the remaining ghee. Slice the Halloumi into about ½-inch (1-cm) slices. Add the Halloumi to the skillet, and cook over medium-high heat on both sides for 2 to 3 minutes. Do not flip too early: let the cheese become crisp and brown to prevent it from breaking. When done, serve immediately with the prepared masala cauli-rice. To store, let it cool and refrigerate in an airtight container for up to 5 days. Reheat before serving.

NUTRITION FACTS PER SERVING:
Total carbs: 14.1 g / Fiber: 4.6 g / Net carbs: 9.5 g / Protein: 20.1 g / Fat: 40.7 g / Calories: 491 kcal
Macronutrient ratio: Calories from carbs (8%), protein (17%), fat (75%)

Bibimbap Veggie Bowl

MAKES: 2 servings
HANDS-ON TIME: 10 minutes
OVERALL TIME: 20 minutes

Never had bibimbap? You've got to try this Korean dish of rice mixed with vegetables, eggs, and meat. This keto vegetarian version is served with cauli-rice and good-for-your-gut kimchi!

Marinated Halloumi:

4 ounces (113 g) Halloumi, cut into
  1-inch (2-cm) cubes
2 tablespoons (30 ml) coconut aminos
1 tablespoon (15 ml) coconut vinegar
  or fresh lime juice
1 clove garlic, minced
1 tablespoon (10 g/0.4 oz) powdered
  erythritol or Swerve
1 teaspoon grated fresh ginger
1 teaspoon toasted sesame oil

Bibimbap Bowl:

¼ cup (60 ml) virgin coconut oil or
  ghee, divided
1 teaspoon grated fresh ginger
1 clove garlic, crushed
1 medium (15 g/0.5 oz) spring onion,
  sliced
2 cups (240 g/8.5 oz) cauliflower rice
  (see page 40)
Sea salt and Korean red pepper or
  black pepper
3 cups (90 g/3.2 oz) chopped chard
  or spinach, stalks and leaves
  separated
2 large eggs
¼ cup (29 g/1 oz) sliced radishes
¼ cup (35 g/1.2 oz) kimchi (without
  fish sauce for vegetarians)
1 teaspoon toasted sesame oil
2 teaspoons (6 g/0.2 oz) sesame seeds

TO MAKE THE MARINATED HALLOUMI: Place the Halloumi cubes in a bowl. In a separate bowl, combine the coconut aminos, vinegar, garlic, erythritol, ginger, and sesame oil. Add the marinade to the bowl with the Halloumi and mix until well coated. Marinate for at least 30 minutes, or overnight.

TO MAKE THE BIBIMBAP BOWL: Grease a skillet with 1 tablespoon (15 ml) of the coconut oil. Fry the ginger, garlic, and spring onion over medium heat for 1 to 2 minutes. Add the cauliflower rice and cook for 5 to 7 minutes, stirring frequently. Season with salt and pepper. When done, divide the cauliflower rice between 2 bowls.

Grease the skillet with another tablespoon (15 ml) of the coconut oil. Add the chard stalks and cook for 1 to 2 minutes. Then add the chopped leaves and cook for 1 minute more. Season with salt and pepper. Divide between the 2 bowls.

Grease the skillet with another tablespoon (15 ml) of the coconut oil. Add the marinated cheese (reserve the marinade for topping) and cook over high heat, turning the cubes as they crisp up, for 4 to 5 minutes. Divide between the 2 bowls.

Finally, grease the skillet with the remaining 1 tablespoon (15 ml) coconut oil and fry the eggs until the whites are opaque and the yolks still runny. Top each bowl with one fried egg. Add the radishes and kimchi. Drizzle with the sesame oil and the remaining marinade, and sprinkle with the sesame seeds. Serve immediately.

NOTE: For extra protein, serve bibimbap with leftover steak (page 170), or Bacon-Wrapped Beef Patties (page 124).

NUTRITION FACTS PER SERVING:
Total carbs: 14.1 g / Fiber: 4.6 g / Net carbs: 9.5 g / Protein: 22.5 g / Fat: 53.8 g / Calories: 612 kcal
Macronutrient ratio: Calories from carbs (6%), protein (15%), fat (79%)

Taverna-Style Greek Butterflied Sea Bass

MAKES: 2 servings
HANDS-ON TIME: 15 minutes
OVERALL TIME: 25 minutes

The traditional Greek diet is so healthy: it's chockfull of fish, seafood, fresh vegetables, and extra-virgin olive oil every day. This is one of the most common ways to serve freshly caught fish in Greece—cooked simply and served with lemon juice, loads of olive oil, and *chorta*, or wild greens. Butterflying the sea bass results in tender, juicy fish with plenty of flavor.

1 (500 g/1.1 lb) sea bass or sea bream, cleaned and butterflied

Sea salt and black pepper

6 tablespoons (90 ml) extra-virgin olive oil, divided

1 clove garlic, sliced

10.6 ounces (300 g) Swiss chard, collard greens, or kale, roughly chopped, stalks and leaves separated

2 tablespoons (8 g/0.3 oz) chopped fresh parsley, divided

1 tablespoon (4 g/0.2 oz) chopped fresh oregano, divided

Juice from 1 lemon (about 60 ml/ ¼ cup)

Preheat the oven to 400°F (200°C, or gas mark 6). Butterfly the sea bass (or ask your fishmonger to do it for you): Remove the insides, the scales, and the fins. Leave the tail and the head on. Cut it along the backbone and all the way through the head. Do not cut it all the way through the belly; this is where it should remain connected, at least partially. Butterflying the sea bass will help it cook faster and will crisp up the meat inside.

Season the fish with salt and pepper on the inside and outside. Open the fish and place it in a baking dish. Drizzle with 1 tablespoon (15 ml) of the olive oil. Place in the oven and bake for about 20 minutes or until the fish is opaque and flakes easily.

Meanwhile, cook the Swiss chard. Heat a large skillet greased with 2 tablespoons (30 ml) of the olive oil over medium heat. Once hot, add the garlic, and cook for a minute. Then add the chard stalks and cook for 2 to 3 minutes. Finally, add the chard leaves and half of the herbs. Cook for a minute or until wilted. Season with salt and pepper to taste.

In a bowl, mix the remaining 3 tablespoons (45 ml) olive oil with the lemon juice, then pour the mixture over the cooked sea bass. Garnish with the reserved herbs, and serve with the cooked chard.

NUTRITION FACTS PER SERVING:
Total carbs: 9.2 g / Fiber: 3.2 g / Net carbs: 6 g / Protein: 39.3 g / Fat: 48 g / Calories: 620 kcal
Macronutrient ratio: Calories from carbs (4%), protein (26%), fat (70%)

Buttered Mahimahi with Green Beans

MAKES: 2 servings
HANDS-ON TIME: 10 minutes
OVERALL TIME: 10 minutes

Homemade Flavored Butter (page 44) is a great way to add fats—and flavor—to meals that feature white fish and lean meat, which you'll need to do when you follow a ketogenic diet. So be sure to keep a couple of your favorites on hand in the fridge. Then you'll be ready to make this simple five-ingredient dish, which takes just ten minutes to conjure up.

10.6 ounces (300 g/10.6 oz) green beans

2 fillets (250 g/8.5 oz) mahimahi (or use any white fish)

Pinch of sea salt and black pepper

1 tablespoon (15 g/0.5 oz) ghee or duck fat

½ recipe Jalapeño & Lime Flavored Butter (page 44), or any savory flavored butter

Bring a saucepan filled with salted water to a boil. Add the green beans, and cook for 2 to 4 minutes, until crisp-tender. Drain and keep warm.

Pat dry the fish fillets with a paper towel, and lightly season with salt and pepper. Heat a skillet greased with the ghee over medium-high heat. Once hot, add the fish, skin-side down, and cook for about 4 minutes, or until the fillets can be easily released with a spatula. Flip over and cook for another 3 minutes. Divide the green beans between 2 plates. Top with the cooked fish, and top the fish with slices of flavored butter while still hot. Serve immediately.

NUTRITION FACTS PER SERVING:
Total carbs: 11.1 g / Fiber: 4.3 g / Net carbs: 6.9 g / Protein: 30.9 g / Fat: 31.9 g / Calories: 439 kcal
Macronutrient ratio: Calories from carbs (6%), protein (28%), fat (66%)

Scandinavian Fish Tray Bake

MAKES: 4 servings
HANDS-ON TIME: 10 minutes
OVERALL TIME: 30 minutes

Baking fish and vegetables in the same tray is a major time-saver: I make keto tray bakes just about every week! This is my go-to meal when I don't have time to cook but want to keep my diet clean. After all, you can never go wrong with meat, fish, and low-carb vegetables flavored with simple herbs, lemon juice, and olive oil—or in this case, a simple horseradish-flavored dressing.

Fish & Veg Bake:

1 small (60 g/2.1 oz) red onion, sliced

2 medium (400 g/14.1 oz) zucchini, sliced

7.1 ounces (200 g) broccoli florets or broccolini

1½ cups (200 g/7.1 oz) radishes, quartered

Few sprigs of fresh dill

¼ cup (60 ml) extra-virgin olive oil, divided

½ teaspoon sea salt

¼ teaspoon black pepper

4 small (500 g/1.1 oz) salmon fillets

1 tablespoon (15 ml) fresh lemon juice

Horseradish Dressing:

⅓ cup (73 g/2.6 oz) mayonnaise (page 42)

1 tablespoon (15 ml) fresh lemon juice

1 teaspoon (5 g/0.2 oz) grated horseradish

TO MAKE THE TRAY BAKE: Preheat the oven to 400°F (200°C, or gas mark 6). Place the onion, zucchini, broccoli, radishes, and dill (reserve some for later) in a baking dish. Drizzle with 3 tablespoons (45 ml) of the olive oil, and season with salt and pepper. Place in the oven, and bake for about 10 minutes. Then add the salmon, drizzle with the remaining 1 tablespoon (15 ml) olive oil and the lemon juice, and transfer back into the oven. Bake for 12 to 15 minutes or until the fish is opaque and flakes easily.

TO MAKE THE DRESSING: Simply combine the mayonnaise, lemon juice, and horseradish in a small bowl. Serve with the baked salmon and vegetables. To store, let the salmon and vegetables cool, then refrigerate for up to 3 days.

NUTRITION FACTS PER SERVING:
Total carbs: 10.2 g / Fiber: 3.5 g / Net carbs: 6.7 g / Protein: 30.5 g / Fat: 36.8 g / Calories: 488 kcal
Macronutrient ratio: Calories from carbs (6%), protein (25%), fat (69%)

Bacon-Wrapped Monkfish with Creamed Spinach

MAKES: 3 servings
HANDS-ON TIME: 15 minutes
OVERALL TIME: 20 minutes

Another way to turn lean fish and meat into a healthy keto meal is to wrap it in bacon and serve it with a side of creamed spinach. It's a handy way to work extra greens into your diet: just one serving covers most of your daily potassium needs, and provides half of your magnesium, too!

Fish:

3 fillets (375 g/8.5 oz) monkfish or
    other white fish
Few sprigs of fresh thyme
6 thin-cut slices (90 g/3.2 oz) bacon
1 tablespoon (15 ml) melted ghee or
    duck fat

Creamed Spinach:

1.2 pounds (600 g) fresh spinach
2 tablespoons (28 g/1 oz) butter
⅓ cup (80 g/2.8 oz) mascarpone
    cheese
¼ teaspoon ground nutmeg
Sea salt and black pepper
⅓ cup (30 g/1.1 oz) grated Parmesan
    cheese

TO MAKE THE FISH: Preheat the oven to 400°F (200°C, or gas mark 6). Pat dry the fish fillets and top with the sprigs of fresh thyme. Wrap 2 slices of bacon around each fillet. Place in a baking dish, drizzle with melted ghee, and transfer to the oven. Bake for about 12 minutes, and then crisp up for 5 minutes under the broiler.

TO MAKE THE CREAMED SPINACH: Bring a large pot of water to a boil. Blanch the spinach for 30 to 60 seconds. Immediately plunge the spinach into a bowl filled with ice water. Drain well, pat dry, and set aside.

Place the butter and mascarpone in a saucepan, and add the blanched spinach, nutmeg, and salt and pepper to taste. Gently heat until it begins to simmer. Then mix in the Parmesan. (Alternatively, divide the spinach between 3 single-serving baking dishes and top each with a third of the Parmesan.) Place under the broiler for 2 to 3 minutes, until crisp and lightly golden. When done, serve alongside the fish. The fish is best served immediately, but it can be refrigerated with the spinach for up to 3 days.

NUTRITION FACTS PER SERVING:
Total carbs: 8.3 g / Fiber: 4.5 g / Net carbs: 3.8 g / Protein: 33.2 g / Fat: 35 g / Calories: 474 kcal
Macronutrient ratio: Calories from carbs (3%), protein (29%), fat (68%)

Pan-Fried Salmon with Superfood Mash

MAKES: 4 servings
HANDS-ON TIME: 15 minutes
OVERALL TIME: 20 minutes

If you're short on time but need a good-for-you keto meal that's also impressive enough to serve to guests, you can't do better than these juicy salmon fillets served with a buttery herbed spinach-and-cauliflower mash. It's the perfect balance of healthy fats and nutrient-dense vegetables.

Cauliflower Mash:

1 tablespoon (15 g/0.5 oz) ghee
　or duck fat
1 small (70 g/2.5 oz) yellow onion,
　chopped
1 clove garlic, minced
1 medium (600 g/1.3 lb) cauliflower,
　cut into medium-size florets
7.1 ounces (200 g) fresh spinach,
　or a combination of spinach and
　watercress
¼ cup (55 g/1.9 oz) butter, ghee, or
　extra-virgin olive oil
2 tablespoons (8 g/0.3 oz) chopped
　fresh herbs, such as basil, parsley,
　thyme, or dill
Sea salt and black pepper

Salmon:

1 tablespoon (15 g/0.5 oz) ghee
　or duck fat
4 fillets (500 g/1.1 lb) salmon
Sea salt and black pepper
1 tablespoon (15 ml) fresh lemon juice
2 tablespoons (30 ml) extra-virgin
　olive oil

TO MAKE THE CAULIFLOWER MASH: In a pan greased with the ghee, cook the onion over medium-high heat until lightly browned, 5 to 7 minutes. Add the garlic, and cook for 1 minute more. Take off the heat and set aside. Place the cauliflower florets in a steamer, and cook for about 10 minutes. Remove from the heat and place in a blender with the spinach, cooked onion and garlic, butter, and fresh herbs, plus salt and pepper to taste. Process until smooth and set aside. To store, let it cool, cover, and refrigerate for up to 5 days.

TO MAKE THE SALMON: Grease a pan with the ghee and place over medium-high heat. Pat the salmon fillets dry with paper towels, and season with salt and pepper. Place the salmon, skin-side down, in the hot pan, and reduce the heat to medium. Cook for 3 to 4 minutes per side, until the fish is firm and cooked through. (Do not force the fish out of the pan: if you try to flip the fillet and it doesn't release, wait a few more seconds until it becomes crisp, then try again.) When done, drizzle with the lemon juice and olive oil and serve with the mash.

NUTRITION FACTS PER SERVING (SALMON FILLET + 1 CUP/220 G MASH):
Total carbs: 11.3 g / Fiber: 4.5 g / Net carbs: 6.8 g / Protein: 31.8 g / Fat: 33.8 g / Calories: 470 kcal
Macronutrient ratio: Calories from carbs (6%), protein (28%), fat (66%)

Butter-Stuffed Spatchcock Chicken

MAKES: 4 servings
HANDS-ON TIME: 10 minutes
OVERALL TIME: 1 hour

Spatchcocking is the absolute tastiest (and fastest) way to make roast chicken: by removing the backbone and flattening the chicken, its skin gets really crispy and it cooks more quickly. And pressing flavored butter under the skin ensures extra-crispy skin and moist and tender meat.

1 whole chicken (about 1.4 kg/3 lb, bones included)

1 tablespoon (15 ml) fresh lemon juice

½ teaspoon sea salt

¼ teaspoon black pepper

1 recipe flavored butter of your choice (page 44) or dairy-free alternative

1 tablespoon (15 ml) melted ghee or duck fat

1 medium (600 g/1.3 lb) cauliflower, cut into florets

Preheat the oven to 400°F (200°C, or gas mark 6). Remove the giblets and string from the chicken. Splay open the chicken, breast-side down, with the drumsticks facing toward you. Run your finger down the spine of the chicken to identify the soft outside of the rib cage. Cut up one side of the spine using strong kitchen scissors. Repeat on the other side of the spine and remove the backbone (reserve for making bone broth, page 42 or chicken stock).

Rub the lemon juice inside the chicken, and season with salt and pepper all over (beware of the salt already included in the butter: don't overseason). Flip the chicken over, splay open the legs, and, using the palm of your hand, press down firmly to flatten the chicken. Pull up the skin and rub the butter (reserve some butter for serving into the flesh.) Brush the skin with melted ghee: this will help the skin become crispy.

Push the tips of the wings behind the breastbone where the neck is. Place the chicken, cut-side down, on a rimmed baking sheet and add ¼ cup (60 ml) water. Bake for about 50 minutes, basting the juices over the chicken once or twice during cooking. Add the cauliflower during the last 10 to 15 minutes, and baste the juices over it. The chicken is done when a meat thermometer inserted into the breast meat reaches 150°F (65°C) and the thighs reach 170°F (77°C). Top with the remaining flavored butter, letting it melt over the chicken. Serve immediately.

NUTRITION FACTS PER SERVING (¼ CHICKEN + SIDE):
Total carbs: 8.9 g / Fiber: 3.3 g / Net carbs: 5.6 g / Protein: 31.3 g / Fat: 50.5 g / Calories: 603 kcal
Macronutrient ratio: Calories from carbs (4%), protein (21%), fat (75%)

NOTE: For even crispier chicken, line a rimmed baking sheet with parchment paper or aluminum foil. Place a roasting rack on the tray, place the chicken on the rack, and bake. The rack allows air to circulate under the chicken as it cooks, ensuring that the skin becomes as crispy as possible.

Butter Chicken

MAKES: 6 servings
HANDS-ON TIME: 30 minutes
OVERALL TIME: 3 hours

If you're a fan of mildly spicy Indian cuisine, you'll love this keto-friendly take on butter chicken. Chunks of chicken breast are marinated in yogurt, lemon juice, and fragrant spices, then cooked with fresh ginger and other aromatics, tomato paste, and cream. It's rich, creamy, and utterly delicious!

Marinated Chicken:

2 pounds (900 g) chicken breasts
¾ cup (188 g/6.6 oz) 5% full-fat yogurt
2 tablespoons (30 ml) fresh lemon juice
1 tablespoon (7 g/0.2 oz) ground turmeric
1 tablespoon (6 g/0.2 oz) garam masala
1 tablespoon (5 g/0.2 oz) ground cumin
1 teaspoon ground cinnamon

Stew:

¼ cup (55 g/1.9 oz) ghee or duck fat
1 small (70 g/2.5 oz) yellow onion, finely chopped
2 cloves garlic, minced
2 tablespoons (12 g/0.4 oz) grated fresh ginger
1 to 2 (14 g/0.5 oz) red or green chiles, seeds removed, chopped
3 tablespoons (45 g/1.6 oz) tomato paste
1 cup (240 ml) chicken stock or water
¼ cup (57 g/2 oz) butter
1 teaspoon sea salt
½ teaspoon black pepper
1¼ cups (300 ml) heavy whipping cream

Fresh cilantro for garnish
Serving suggestions: cauliflower rice (see page 40) or shirataki rice (see page 41)

TO MAKE THE CHICKEN: Cut the chicken into 1½-inch (4-cm) pieces. In a bowl, combine all the ingredients for the marinade. Add the chicken, cover with plastic wrap, and refrigerate for 2 hours or up to 24 hours.

TO MAKE THE STEW: Heat a large pot greased with the ghee over medium-high heat. Add the onion and cook for about 7 minutes, until fragrant and lightly browned. Add the garlic, ginger, and chiles. Cook for another 2 to 3 minutes. Add the marinated chicken, and cook for about 10 minutes, stirring frequently. Then add the tomato paste, chicken stock, butter, salt, and black pepper. Bring to a boil, then reduce the heat to medium. Cook, uncovered, for 15 minutes. Pour in the cream, and cook for another 5 to 10 minutes. Remove from the heat and let sit for 5 minutes. Serve with cilantro and cauliflower rice or shirataki rice.

NUTRITION FACTS PER SERVING (DOES NOT INCLUDE SIDE):
Total carbs: 7.3 g / Fiber: 1.2 g / Net carbs: 6.1 g / Protein: 37.2 g / Fat: 42.5 g / Calories: 569 kcal
Macronutrient ratio: Calories from carbs (4%), protein (27%), fat (69%)

Harissa Skillet Chicken

MAKES: 4 servings
HANDS-ON TIME: 10 minutes
OVERALL TIME: 35 minutes

All you need to pull this no-fuss Moroccan-style meal together is a skillet, a baking dish, a batch of Spicy Harissa Flavored Butter (page 44), and a few common ingredients. In barely half an hour, you'll be digging into crispy chicken thighs on a bed of low-carb veggies. (Minimal cleanup required!)

1 medium (450 g/1lb) cauliflower, cut into small florets

1 medium (300 g/10.6 oz) eggplant, cut into ½-inch (2-cm) pieces

8 (2 lb/900 g) chicken thighs, skin on and bone in

Sea salt and black pepper

1 tablespoon (15 g/0.5 oz) ghee or duck fat

¼ cup (60 ml) water

1 recipe (160 g/5.6 oz) Spicy Harissa Flavored Butter (page 44), sliced

Preheat the oven to 400°F (200°C, or gas mark 6). Place the cauliflower florets and eggplant in a baking dish.

Pat the chicken thighs dry with a paper towel. Season with salt and pepper. Heat a large skillet greased with the ghee. Once hot, add the chicken thighs, skin-side down, and cook in batches for about 5 minutes, or until the skin is golden and crisp. Then flip over and cook for just 1 minute more. Place the chicken on top of the vegetables in the baking dish, skin-side up. Deglaze the skillet by pouring the water into it, then pour over the vegetables on the tray. Top the vegetables and chicken with slices of the flavored butter. Bake for 20 to 25 minutes, tossing halfway through. The chicken is done when an instant-read thermometer inserted into the thickest part of the thigh reads 165°F (75°C). Crispy chicken thighs are best served immediately. To store, let the chicken and vegetables cool, then store in the fridge for up to 4 days.

NUTRITION FACTS PER SERVING (2 THIGHS + VEGETABLES):
Total carbs: 12.3 g / Fiber: 5.4 g / Net carbs: 6.9 g / Protein: 32.5g / Fat: 34.9 g / Calories: 485 kcal
Macronutrient ratio: Calories from carbs (6%), protein (28%), fat (66%)

Turkey Meatballs with Sautéed Kale & Gremolata Dressing

MAKES: 4 servings
HANDS-ON TIME: 20 minutes
OVERALL TIME: 25 minutes

Meatballs are the last word in convenience. They can be made ahead, frozen, and then used weeks or even months later to whip up quick, nutritious one-pot meals. Take this Italian-style dish, for instance: it's very low in carbs, but high in heart-healthy fats and electrolytes.

Gremolata Dressing:

1 tablespoon (6 g/0.2 oz) finely grated lemon zest
⅓ cup (20 g/0.7 oz) chopped parsley
⅓ cup (80 ml) extra-virgin olive oil
2 cloves garlic, crushed

Meatballs:

1.1 pounds (500 g) ground turkey
1 large egg
3 tablespoons (24 g/0.8 oz) coconut flour, or ½ cup (50 g/1.8 oz) almond flour
½ medium (55 g/1.9 oz) yellow onion, finely chopped
1 clove garlic, minced
½ teaspoon sea salt
¼ teaspoon black pepper
1 tablespoon (15 ml) duck fat or ghee

Sautéed Kale:

1 tablespoon (15 ml) duck fat or ghee
1 clove garlic, sliced
14.1 ounces (400 g) dark-leaf kale, chopped, stems removed
¼ teaspoon chili red pepper flakes
1 tablespoon (15 ml) fresh lemon juice
⅓ cup (80 ml) chicken stock
Sea salt and black pepper

TO MAKE THE GREMOLATA: Simply place all the ingredients in a bowl and mix well. Set aside.

TO MAKE THE MEATBALLS: Place the ground turkey, egg, coconut flour, onion, garlic, and salt and pepper in a mixing bowl. Mix until well combined. Using your hands, create 20 meatballs (about 1.1 oz/31 g each) from the mixture. Grease a large pan with the duck fat, and place it over medium heat. When hot, add the meatballs in a single layer. Cook for 2 minutes on each side, turning with a fork until browned on all sides and cooked through. Transfer the meatballs to a plate and keep warm.

TO MAKE THE SAUTÉED KALE: Grease the pan with the duck fat. Add the garlic and cook for a minute, then add the kale, red pepper flakes, and lemon juice. Cook for 1 to 2 minutes, tossing well. Then add the chicken stock, cover with a lid, and cook until tender, about 5 minutes. Season with salt and pepper. Return the meatballs to the pan, on top of the kale. Spoon the gremolata dressing over the meatballs and kale, or serve it on the side. To store, let the meatballs and kale cool, then refrigerate for up to 4 days.

NUTRITION FACTS PER SERVING (5 MEATBALLS + KALE + GREMOLATA):
Total carbs: 9.5 g / Fiber: 5 g / Net carbs: 4.5 g / Protein: 28.1 g / Fat: 45.4 g / Calories: 545 kcal
Macronutrient ratio: Calories from carbs (3%), protein (21%), fat (76%)

Mediterranean Chicken Tray Bake

MAKES: 4 servings
HANDS-ON TIME: 10 minutes
OVERALL TIME: 35 minutes

Homemade Lemon & Herb Flavored Butter (page 44) graces this easy, colorful, Italian-style chicken dish, in which panfried chicken tops low-carb veggies like fennel, zucchini, and broccoli. Twenty minutes and a dash of lemon later, and dinner is on the table!

1 small (70 g/2.5 oz) onion, sliced

1 medium (200 g/7.1 oz) fennel bulb, sliced

1 medium (120 g/4.2 oz) red pepper, sliced

1 medium (200 g/7.1 oz) green or yellow zucchini, sliced

1 bunch (7.1 oz/200 g) broccolini, or broccoli cut into florets

8 (900 g/2 lb) chicken thighs, skin on and bone in

Sea salt and black pepper

1 tablespoon (15 g/0.5 oz) ghee or duck fat

¼ cup (60 ml) water

2 tablespoons (30 ml) fresh lemon juice

1 recipe (150 g/5.3 oz) Lemon & Herb Flavored Butter (page 44), sliced

2 tablespoons (8 g/0.3 oz) chopped fresh herbs, such as parsley, basil, and fennel fronds

Preheat the oven to 400°F (200°C, or gas mark 6). Place the onion, fennel, pepper, zucchini, and broccoli in a baking dish.

Pat the chicken thighs dry with a paper towel, and season with salt and pepper. Heat a large skillet greased with the ghee. Once hot, add the chicken thighs, skin-side down, and cook in batches for about 5 minutes, or until the skin is golden and crispy. Turn on the other side and cook for just 1 minute. Place the chicken on top of the vegetables in the baking dish, skin-side up. Deglaze the skillet by pouring the water into it, then pour over the vegetables in the tray. Drizzle with the lemon juice and top the vegetables and chicken with slices of the flavored butter. Bake for 20 to 25 minutes, tossing halfway through. The chicken is done when an instant-read thermometer inserted into the thickest part of the thigh reads 165°F (75°C). Top with the herbs and serve. Crispy chicken thighs are best served immediately. To store, let the chicken and vegetables cool, then store in the fridge for up to 4 days.

NUTRITION FACTS PER SERVING (2 THIGHS + VEGETABLES):
Total carbs: 13.3 g / Fiber: 4.6 g / Net carbs: 8.7 g / Protein: 32.5 g / Fat: 33.5 g / Calories: 479 kcal
Macronutrient ratio: Calories from carbs (7%), protein (28%), fat (65%)

Crispy Five-Spice Duck Breasts

MAKES: 2 servings
HANDS-ON TIME: 15 minutes
OVERALL TIME: 30 minutes

Duck breasts always feel like a luxury, but they're so easy to make and so delicious. Here, they're coated in garlic and Asian spices on one side, while the fatty skin on the other side gets wonderfully crispy—one of the perks of eating keto!

½ teaspoon Chinese five-spice mix

¼ teaspoon ground ginger

½ teaspoon sea salt, plus more as needed

⅛ teaspoon black pepper, plus more as needed

1 clove garlic, crushed

2 (300 g/10.6 oz) duck breasts

10.6 ounces (300 g) asparagus, woody stems removed

1 tablespoon (15 ml) balsamic vinegar

2 tablespoons (30 ml) extra-virgin olive oil

Combine the spices, salt, and pepper on a small plate. Rub the crushed garlic into the skinless part of the duck breasts, and then dredge in the spices (keeping the skin clean). Cover with aluminum foil and refrigerate for at least an hour, or overnight.

When ready to cook, preheat the oven to 430°F (220°C, or gas mark 7). Remove the duck breasts from the fridge. Score the skin, and season with salt and pepper. Heat a medium ovenproof skillet over medium-high heat. Place the duck breasts skin-side down in the hot dry pan (no oil needed), and reduce the heat. As the duck fat is released, use a spoon to baste the breasts with it regularly, and cook for 6 to 8 minutes, or until lightly golden. Flip over and cook for about 30 seconds, just to "seal" them on the other side.

Place the skillet into the preheated oven. Cook for 10 minutes (rare), 15 minutes (medium), or 18 minutes (well done). Add the asparagus for the last 7 to 8 minutes of the cooking process, coating it in the rendered fat and seasoning it with a pinch of salt. Let the duck breasts rest on a cooling rack for 10 minutes before serving. Drizzle the asparagus with the balsamic vinegar and olive oil. Duck breasts are best served while still warm but can be refrigerated in an airtight container for up to 4 days.

NUTRITION FACTS PER SERVING:
Total carbs: 8.3 g / Fiber: 3.5 g / Net carbs: 4.8 g / Protein: 29.6 g / Fat: 36.5 g / Calories: 478 kcal
Macronutrient ratio: Calories from carbs (4%), protein (25%), fat (71%)

Chicken Parmesan Casserole

MAKES: 4 servings
HANDS-ON TIME: 15 minutes
OVERALL TIME: 1 hour

After a long day at work, you need a warming, comforting dinner to help you relax. Don't be tempted to grab carb- and additive-laden take-out. Make this no-stress chicken Parm instead. Topped with three kinds of cheese and then baked until golden and bubbling, it's the perfect family meal.

¾ cup (180 ml) marinara sauce
   (page 43)

⅓ cup (80 ml) extra-virgin olive oil

¼ teaspoon red pepper flakes

4 medium (500 g/1.1 lb) boneless,
   skinless chicken breasts

½ teaspoon sea salt

¼ teaspoon black pepper

1.1 pounds (500 g) green beans,
   trimmed

½ cup (57 g/2 oz) shredded
   mozzarella cheese

½ cup (57 g/2 oz) shredded fontina,
   Gouda, or provolone cheese

½ cup (45 g/1.6 oz) grated Parmesan
   cheese

Fresh herbs, such as basil, oregano,
   and thyme, for garnish

Combine the marinara, olive oil, and red pepper flakes in a medium bowl. Place half the mixture into a second bowl, and set aside.

Using a sharp knife, make 3 or 4 shallow, diagonal slits in the chicken breasts (do not cut all the way through). Place the chicken breasts into the first bowl with half of the marinara marinade and the salt and pepper. Coat on all sides, making sure the sauce also gets into the slits. Cover and refrigerate for an hour, or overnight.

Preheat the oven to 400°F (200°C, or gas mark 6). Bring a saucepan filled with salted water to a boil. Add the green beans. Cook for 2 to 4 minutes, until crisp-tender, then plunge them into a bowl of ice water. Drain well and place them in a large ovenproof casserole dish. Add the reserved marinara sauce and combine well until coated. Layer the marinated chicken with the marinade on top of the green beans. Cover with a piece of parchment paper and transfer to the oven. Bake for about 30 minutes.

After 30 minutes, remove the parchment paper, and top the chicken with the mozzarella, fontina, and Parmesan. Return to the oven and cook for another 15 to 20 minutes, until the cheese is golden and bubbly and the chicken is cooked through. To serve, garnish with fresh herbs. Eat warm, or let it cool down and refrigerate for up to 4 days.

NUTRITION FACTS PER SERVING:
Total carbs: 12.6 g / Fiber: 4.1 g / Net carbs: 8.5 g / Protein: 39.4 g / Fat: 38.1 g / Calories: 545 kcal
Macronutrient ratio: Calories from carbs (6%), protein (29%), fat (65%)

Chicken Piccata

MAKES: 4 servings
HANDS-ON TIME: 15 minutes
OVERALL TIME: 30 minutes

There's nothing as nourishing and comforting as crisp skillet chicken dressed in a tangy lemon and caper sauce over a tangle of electrolyte-rich baby spinach. It's guaranteed to brighten up even the coldest winter evening!

2 large (500 g/1.1 lb) boneless chicken breasts, skin on

3 tablespoons (45 ml) melted ghee, divided

1 small (70 g/2.5 oz) yellow onion, chopped

2 cloves garlic, minced

1 tablespoon (15 ml) white wine vinegar or apple cider vinegar

¼ cup (60 ml) fresh lemon juice

3 tablespoons (43 g/1.5 oz) butter

¼ cup (34 g/1.2 oz) capers, drained

2 tablespoons (8 g/0.3 oz) chopped fresh parsley (plus more for optional garnish)

1 pound (450 g) fresh spinach

Sea salt and black pepper

¼ cup (60 ml) extra-virgin olive oil

Lemon slices, for garnish

To butterfly the chicken breasts, place them on a chopping board. Placing your hand flat on top of one chicken breast, use a sharp knife to slice into one side, starting at the thicker end and ending at the thinner point. Be careful not to cut all the way through to the other side. Open the breast so that it resembles a butterfly, about ½ inch (1 cm) thick.

Heat a large skillet greased with 1 tablespoon (15 ml) of the ghee over medium-high heat. Once hot, add the butterflied chicken, skin-side down. Cook undisturbed for 5 to 7 minutes. Rotate the pan halfway through to ensure even cooking. Then flip the chicken over and cook for another 2 to 3 minutes. When done, transfer to a plate, skin-side up.

Grease the pan with the remaining 2 tablespoons (30 ml) ghee, and add the onion. Cook for 5 to 7 minutes, or until golden brown. Add the garlic and cook for 1 minute more. To deglaze the pan, add the vinegar, lemon juice, and butter, scraping the browned bits from the bottom of the skillet. Add the capers and parsley. Return the cooked chicken to the pan and heat for 1 to 2 minutes. Remove from the heat and set aside.

To blanch the spinach, bring a large saucepan filled with salted water to a boil. Add the spinach and cook for 30 to 60 seconds, until wilted. Use a slotted spoon to transfer the spinach to a large bowl of ice water, then drain and squeeze out any excess water. Season with salt and pepper and drizzle with the olive oil. Serve with the crispy chicken and sauce. Garnish with lemon slices and more fresh parsley if desired. Crispy chicken is best served immediately, but can be refrigerated in an airtight container for up to 4 days.

NUTRITION FACTS PER SERVING:
Total carbs: 7.6 g / Fiber: 3.2 g / Net carbs: 4.4 g / Protein: 29.9 g / Fat: 45.5 g / Calories: 554 kcal
Macronutrient ratio: Calories from carbs (3%), protein (22%), fat (75%)

Sautéed Chicken Livers with Creamy Mash

MAKES: 4 servings
HANDS-ON TIME: 20 minutes
OVERALL TIME: 35 minutes + soaking

My mom used to make this quick stew all the time: as a kid, I refused to eat liver any other way! It gets lots of flavor from onion and garlic—which turn up in most Czech gravies—plus crispy bacon and a final flourish of fresh thyme.

2 cups (480 ml) water

1 tablespoon (15 ml) fresh lemon juice or apple cider vinegar

1 pound (450 g) chicken livers, sliced

1 medium (1.3 lb/600 g) cauliflower, cut into florets

¼ cup (57 g/2 oz) butter, ghee, or duck fat

Sea salt and black pepper

2 tablespoons (30 g/1.1 oz) ghee or duck fat, divided

4 slices (120 g/4.2 oz) bacon, chopped

1 medium (110 g/3.5 oz) yellow onion, sliced

1 clove garlic, minced

1 cup (240 ml) chicken stock or bone broth (page 42), divided

2 tablespoons (30 g/1.1 oz) tomato paste

3 egg yolks

Few sprigs fresh thyme

Combine the water and lemon juice in a bowl. Add the livers and refrigerate overnight. This helps remove any gamey, metallic taste.

Prepare the cauliflower mash. Place the cauliflower florets in a steamer and cook for about 10 minutes. Remove from the heat. Place in a blender with the butter, plus salt and pepper to taste. Process until smooth and set aside.

While the cauliflower is cooking, heat a skillet greased with 1 tablespoon (15 g/0.5 oz) of the ghee over medium-high heat. Add the chicken livers and cook for 1 to 2 minutes, stirring frequently, until browned on all sides. Transfer to a plate with a slotted spoon.

Grease the skillet with the remaining 1 tablespoon (15 g/0.5 oz) ghee, and add the bacon and onion. Cook for 8 to 10 minutes, or until the onion is lightly browned and the bacon is crisp. Then add the garlic and cook for 1 minute more. Add ¾ cup (180 ml) of the stock and the tomato paste, and bring to a boil. Add the chicken livers back to the skillet and cook for 2 to 3 minutes. Mix the egg yolks with the remaining ¼ cup (60 ml) stock. Slowly drizzle into the skillet with the liver while stirring, and cook until it thickens slightly. Season with salt and pepper to taste. Garnish with the fresh thyme, and serve with the prepared cauli-mash. To store, let the livers and mash cool, then refrigerate for up to 4 days.

NUTRITION FACTS PER SERVING (LIVERS + GRAVY + ⅔ CUP MASH):
Total carbs: 12.1 g / Fiber: 3.8 g / Net carbs: 8.3 g / Protein: 29.8 g / Fat: 37 g / Calories: 497 kcal
Macronutrient ratio: Calories from carbs (7%), protein (25%), fat (68%)

Keto Pad Thai

MAKES: 4 servings
HANDS-ON TIME: 20 minutes
OVERALL TIME: 30 minutes

Thanks to low-carb shirataki noodles, it's totally possible to enjoy take-out-style Pad Thai on a keto diet! This healthier version takes less than half an hour to make. If you can't eat nuts, just replace the almond butter with coconut butter.

Sauce:

¼ cup (60 ml) fish sauce

1 tablespoon (15 ml) coconut aminos

1 tablespoon (15 g/0.5 oz) Sriracha

2 cloves garlic, crushed

¼ cup (64 g/2.3 oz) almond butter or coconut butter

Optional: 1 to 2 tablespoons (10 to 20 g/0.3 to 0.6 oz) erythritol, or 5 to 7 drops stevia extract

Stir-Fry:

2 packs (400 g/14.1 oz) shirataki noodles

5 tablespoons (70 g/2.5 oz) ghee, divided

4 large eggs

1.1 pounds (500 g) boneless, skinless chicken thighs

2 medium (30 g/1.1 oz) spring onions, sliced

2 cups (100 g/3.5 oz) bean sprouts

Sea salt and black pepper

¼ cup (15 g/0.5 oz) flaked almonds or coconut

2 cups (140 g/4.9 oz) shredded red cabbage

2 tablespoons (30 ml) fresh lime juice

Small bunch cilantro, chopped

TO MAKE THE SAUCE: Combine all the ingredients for the sauce in a bowl, including the erythritol, if using. Set aside.

TO MAKE THE STIR-FRY: Prepare the shirataki noodles by following the steps on page 41.

Prepare the omelets. Heat a pan greased with ½ tablespoon of the ghee. Beat 2 eggs, pour into the hot pan, and swirl to coat the surface in order to make a very thin omelet. Cook over medium-high heat for a couple of minutes or until firm on top. Flip over with a spatula and cook for 30 seconds more. When done, transfer to a plate. Grease the pan ½ tablespoon more ghee and repeat with the remaining 2 eggs. Set aside to cool down, then roll up the omelets and cut into thin strips.

Cut the chicken thighs into 1-inch (2.5-cm) pieces. Heat a large pan greased with the remaining ¼ cup (55 g/1.9 oz) ghee and cook over medium-high heat until pale and cooked through, about 5 to 7 minutes, stirring occasionally. Add the spring onions. Cook over medium-high heat for 1 to 2 minutes. Then add the omelet strips and bean sprouts and cook for 1 minute more while stirring. Add the prepared sauce and shirataki noodles, cook briefly until heated through, and remove from the heat. Season with salt and pepper to taste.

To toast the almond flakes, place them in a dry hot pan and cook over medium-high heat until fragrant, 1 to 2 minutes. Keep stirring to prevent burning. Serve the pad thai with the cabbage, lime juice, cilantro, and toasted almonds.

NUTRITION FACTS PER SERVING:
Total carbs: 14.1 g / Fiber: 5.4 g / Net carbs: 8.7g / Protein: 36.6 g / Fat: 37.8 g / Calories: 547 kcal
Macronutrient ratio: Calories from carbs (7%), protein (28%), fat (65%)

Chicken Satay with Superfood Tabbouleh

MAKES: 4 servings
HANDS-ON TIME: 20 minutes
OVERALL TIME: 35 minutes + marinating

Herbs are fantastic sources of micronutrients like vitamin A, calcium, iron, and potassium. Why not use them to make a big bowl of lemony, low-carb tabbouleh? Serve it alongside tender baked chicken drenched in an almond satay sauce.

Satay Dip:

¼ cup (64 g/2.2 oz) almond butter

2 tablespoons (32 g/1.1 oz) tahini

1 tablespoon (6 g/0.2 oz) grated fresh ginger

1 clove garlic, minced

1 tablespoon (15 ml) lime juice

1 tablespoon (15 ml) coconut aminos

1 tablespoon (15 ml) fish sauce

2 tablespoons (30 ml) coconut milk

1 teaspoon chopped red chile

Sea salt and black pepper

Optional: 1 tablespoon (10 g/0.3 oz) erythritol, or 2 to 3 drops stevia

Chicken:

4 medium (500 g/1.1 lb) skinless, boneless chicken breasts

Sea salt and black pepper

TO MAKE THE SATAY DIP: Combine all the ingredients in a medium bowl. Set aside.

TO MAKE THE CHICKEN: Using a sharp knife, make 3 to 4 shallow, diagonal slits in the chicken breasts (do not cut all the way through). Season the chicken with salt and pepper. Place the chicken breasts into a bowl with half of the satay sauce, reserving the rest for serving. Coat on all sides, making sure the sauce also gets into the slits. Cover and refrigerate for an hour, or overnight.

When ready to cook, preheat the oven to 360°F (180°C, or gas mark 4). Place the chicken, slits-side up, into a baking dish, and top with any remaining sauce. Bake for 25 to 30 minutes. The chicken is done when an instant-read thermometer inserted into the thickest part reads 165°F (74°C).

TO MAKE THE TABBOULEH: Heat a large pan greased with the ghee over medium-high heat. Add the cauliflower rice and cook for about 5 minutes. Remove from the heat and set aside. To the bowl with the cooked cauliflower rice, add the greens, tomatoes, cucumber, parsley, mint, spring onions, lemon juice, olive oil, and red pepper flakes. Mix, and season with salt and pepper to taste. Serve immediately with the baked chicken breasts and reserved satay dip. To store, let the chicken and tabbouleh cool, and store in separate airtight containers in the fridge for up to 4 days.

NUTRITION FACTS PER SERVING:
Total carbs: 15.2 g / Fiber: 6.3 g / Net carbs: 8.9 g / Protein: 34.4 g / Fat: 35.1 g / Calories: 517 kcal
Macronutrient ratio: Calories from carbs (7%), protein (28%), fat (65%)

Tabbouleh:

1 tablespoon (15 g/0.5 oz) ghee or
   coconut oil

2½ cups (300 g/10.6 oz) cauliflower
   rice (see page 40)

4.2 ounces (120 g) soft dark greens,
   such as baby kale or spinach,
   chopped

1 cup (150 g/5.3 oz) chopped cherry or
   regular tomatoes

½ medium (100 g/3.5 oz) cucumber,
   peeled and finely diced

½ cup (30 g/1.1 oz) chopped parsley,
   or to taste

¼ cup (15 g/0.5 oz) chopped mint, or
   to taste

2 medium (30 g/1.1 oz) spring onions,
   sliced

¼ cup (60 ml) fresh lemon juice

¼ cup (60 ml) extra-virgin olive oil

¼ teaspoon red pepper flakes

Sea salt and black pepper

Salisbury Steak with Quick Mash

MAKES: 4 servings
HANDS-ON TIME: 30 minutes
OVERALL TIME: 30 minutes

Salisbury steak may not be "real" steak—it bears a closer resemblance to hamburgers—but who cares. It's so easy to make and so delicious. Served with cauliflower mash and onion gravy, this is cold-weather keto comfort food at its best!

Cauliflower Mash:

1 medium (600 g/1.3 lb) cauliflower
2 tablespoons (30 ml) extra-virgin olive oil
Sea salt and black pepper

Salisbury Steak:

1.1 pounds (500 g) ground beef
2 teaspoons onion powder
1 egg yolk
2 tablespoons (16 g/0.6 oz) coconut flour
½ teaspoon sea salt
¼ teaspoon black pepper
1 tablespoon (15 g/0.5 oz) ghee or duck fat

Onion Gravy:

3 tablespoons (45 g/1.6 oz) ghee or duck fat
1 large (150 g/5.3 oz) yellow onion, sliced
1 tablespoon (15 g/0.5 oz) tomato paste
1 tablespoon (15 g/0.5 oz) Dijon mustard
1 tablespoon (15 ml) coconut aminos
1 cup (240 ml) bone broth (page 42) or chicken stock

TO MAKE THE CAULIFLOWER MASH: Cut the cauliflower into medium-size florets and place in a steamer. Cook for about 10 minutes. Remove from the heat, and place in a blender with the olive oil and season with salt and pepper to taste. Process until smooth, set aside, and keep warm.

TO MAKE THE SALISBURY STEAK: In a bowl, combine the beef, onion powder, egg yolk, coconut flour, salt, and pepper. Using your hands, create 4 patties (about 135 g/4.8 oz each) from the mixture. Grease a large skillet with the ghee. Once hot, add the burgers. Reduce the heat to medium and cook for about 3 minutes on each side. Do not flip the burgers too soon or they will stick to the pan. When done, set aside and keep warm.

TO MAKE THE GRAVY: Grease the pan in which you cooked the patties with the ghee. Add the onion and cook over medium-high heat for about 7 minutes, or until lightly browned and fragrant. Add the tomato paste, mustard, and coconut aminos, and cook for 1 minute. Pour in the bone broth, bring to a boil, then remove from the heat. Let the gravy cool down for a few minutes, then pour into a blender and process until smooth.

Serve the cauliflower mash (about ¾ cup/160 g per serving) with the patties and pour over the gravy (about ¼ cup/60 ml per serving). Eat immediately, or store the patties and cauliflower mash in separate containers in the fridge for up to 4 days.

NUTRITION FACTS PER SERVING (1 STEAK + ¼ CUP/60 ML GRAVY + ¾ MASH):
Total carbs: 14.1 g / Fiber: 4.9 g / Net carbs: 9.2 g / Protein: 27.4 g / Fat: 49.7 g / Calories: 613 kcal
Macronutrient ratio: Calories from carbs (6%), protein (18%), fat (76%)

Induction Burger Stacks

MAKES: 4 servings
HANDS-ON TIME: 15 minutes
OVERALL TIME: 20 minutes

An amazing burger restaurant in my neighborhood offers "skinny" burgers, in which the buns are replaced by a vegetable salad. It's always packed, and for a very good reason: they use top-quality ingredients. These meaty, induction-friendly burger stacks are inspired by one of my favorite picks: a smoky burger topped with jalapeños and chipotle mayo.

Vegetable Salad:

3 tablespoons (45 ml) extra-virgin olive oil

1 tablespoon (15 ml) fresh lemon or lime juice

1 large (400 g/14.1 oz) head lettuce

2 cups (60 g/2.1 oz) fresh spinach

1 small (60 g/2.1 oz) red onion, sliced

1 cup (150 g/5.3 oz) halved cherry tomatoes

1 medium (120 g/4.2 oz) green pepper, sliced

Chipotle Mayo:

¼ cup (55/1.9 oz) mayonnaise (page 42)

1 tablespoon (15 g/0.5 oz) tomato paste or sugar-free ketchup

1 teaspoon fresh lime or lemon juice

¼ teaspoon garlic powder

¼ teaspoon chipotle powder

Sea salt and black pepper

Burgers:

1.1 pounds (500 g) ground beef

Sea salt and black pepper

1 tablespoon (15 g/0.5 oz) ghee or lard

Optional: 4 slices (80 g/2.8 oz) smoked Cheddar or provolone cheese

Optional extras: preserved jalapeño pepper slices, sliced cucumber, pickled cucumbers, or Pickled Red Onion (page 181)

TO MAKE THE SALAD: Combine the olive oil and lemon juice in a small bowl. Roughly chop the lettuce (reserve 4 to 8 whole lettuce leaves for the burgers). Add the vegetables to a bowl, pour over the dressing, mix well, and set aside.

TO MAKE THE CHIPOTLE MAYO: Combine all the ingredients in a small bowl. Set aside.

TO MAKE THE BURGERS: Gently divide the ground meat into 4 equal parts. Use your hands to shape each piece into a loose burger, about 4 inches (10 cm) in diameter. (Do not squeeze or pack the meat too tightly, or the burgers will lose their juiciness as they are cooked.) Season with salt and pepper on each side.

Grease a large pan with the ghee and heat over high heat. Use a spatula to transfer the burgers to the hot pan. Cook for 3 minutes, then flip over with the spatula, and cook for an additional 2 to 3 minutes. If using cheese, place it on top of the burgers for the last minute of the cooking process. Set aside.

To assemble, simply place 1 to 2 lettuce leaves on a plate and top with a burger. Serve with the chipotle mayo and vegetable salad. Optionally, top with jalapeños, cucumber, or pickles.

NUTRITION FACTS PER SERVING (BURGER + VEGETABLE SALAD):
Total carbs: 8.4 g / Fiber: 3.1 g / Net carbs: 5.3 g / Protein: 29.2 g / Fat: 55.5 g / Calories: 647 kcal
Macronutrient ratio: Calories from carbs (3%), protein (18%), fat (79%)

The Perfect Skirt Steak

MAKES: 4 servings
HANDS-ON TIME: 15 minutes
OVERALL TIME: 30 minutes

Five ingredients are all you need to make this nutritious keto version of steak frites! Here, skirt steak is panfried on a layer of coarse salt, which seals the juices in the meat, keeping it moist inside. (Don't worry: the steak won't end up too salty.) Then it's topped with flavored butter and served with oven-baked zucchini "fries." There's no better way to break your fast!

2 large (600 g/1.3 lb) skirt steaks

4 medium to large (900 g/2 lb) zucchini

1 tablespoon (15 ml) melted ghee or duck fat

1 tablespoon (17 g/0.6 oz) coarse sea salt, plus a pinch of fine salt

1 recipe Salty Anchovy Flavored Butter, or other flavored butter of your choice (page 44)

Preheat the oven to 450°F (230°C, or gas mark 8). Pat the steaks dry. To tenderize them, place them on a cutting board, cover with plastic wrap, and pound with a tenderizer until about ½ inch (1 cm) thick. Let sit at room temperature for about 20 minutes.

Wash the zucchini, then cut them into thick sticks resembling French fries. Drizzle with the melted ghee, and season with a pinch of fine salt. Place them on a parchment-lined baking sheet. Bake for 10 to 15 minutes, until golden brown and tender.

Meanwhile, cook the steaks. Spread the coarse salt evenly over the surface of a large cast-iron skillet. Heat over medium-high heat. When the skillet is hot, add one steak at a time and cook on top of the coarse salt for 2 to 3 minutes per side. (The salt will char or burn, but don't be alarmed: you will scrape it off the steaks after cooking.) When done, transfer to a chopping board, scraping off any salt crystals that have not melted. Add more salt to the pan if needed, and repeat with the other steak. Let them rest for 5 minutes before slicing thinly against the grain. Serve with the prepared flavored butter and zucchini "fries."

NOTE: In addition to other flavored butters (page 44), you can serve skirt steak with Chimichurri (page 120), Blue Cheese Dressing (page 109), or Spicy Cilantro-Lime Vinaigrette (page 100).

NUTRITION FACTS PER SERVING:
Total carbs: 7.6 g / Fiber: 2.3 g / Net carbs: 5.3 g / Protein: 36 g / Fat: 45.9 g / Calories: 576 kcal
Macronutrient ratio: Calories from carbs (4%), protein (25%), fat (71%)

Steak Fajitas with Avocado Salsa Verde

MAKES: 4 servings
HANDS-ON TIME: 25 minutes
OVERALL TIME: 25 minutes + marinating

Looking for a quick dinner solution? These grain-free "fajitas" take less than half an hour to make. Steak and crunchy vegetables get marinated in lime juice and cumin before being fried quickly in a hot pan. Then, they're served on top of crisp lettuce with homemade avocado salsa verde.

Marinade:

2 cloves garlic, minced
½ cup (120 ml) extra-virgin olive oil
¼ cup (60 ml) fresh lime juice
1 teaspoon ground cumin
1 teaspoon chili powder
½ teaspoon red pepper flakes
1 teaspoon sea salt
¼ teaspoon black pepper

Fajitas:

1 medium (110 g/3.9 oz) yellow onion,
  sliced
1 medium (120 g/4.2 oz) red bell
  pepper, sliced
1 medium (120 g/4.2 oz) yellow bell
  pepper, sliced
1 medium (120 g/4.2 oz) green bell
  pepper, sliced
1. 3 pounds (600 g) flank or skirt steak
2 tablespoons (30 g/1.1 oz) ghee or
  lard, divided
8 leaves (143 g/5 oz) lettuce
2 tablespoons (30 ml) extra-virgin
  olive oil

Avocado Salsa Verde:

½ cup (120 ml) (sugar-free) salsa
2 small (200 g/7.1 oz) avocados, pitted,
  peeled, and sliced

TO MAKE THE MARINADE: Combine all the ingredients for the marinade in a bowl and set aside.

TO MAKE THE FAJITAS: Place the onion and peppers in one bowl, and the flank steak in another. Divide the marinade between the 2 bowls. Combine until the meat and vegetables are thoroughly coated. Refrigerate for at least 1 hour or up to 24 hours.

When ready to cook, remove the steak from the marinade and pat dry. Place a large pan greased with 1 tablespoon (15 g) of the ghee over high heat. Once hot, cook the steak for 2 to 3 minutes on each side, depending on its thickness, until medium-rare. Do not overcook the steak. Remove from the pan and keep warm.

Grease the same pan with the remaining ghee and place over high heat. Use a slotted spoon to add the vegetables to the pan. Cook for 3 to 5 minutes, stirring occasionally. (The leftover marinade can be used for making another batch of vegetables.)

TO MAKE THE SALSA: Combine teh salsa and avocado in a bowl and stir to mix. When ready to serve, slice the meat thinly against the grain. (If you use sirloin or rib eye, you won't need to cut the meat as thinly as you would with flank or skirt steak.) Serve on top of lettuce leaves (2 per serving) and drizzle with ½ tablespoon (7 ml) of olive oil, plus a quarter of the pepper mixture and the avocado salsa verde. Refrigerate the steak and peppers for up to 4 days (reheat gently to avoid overcooking), and refrigerate the avocado salsa in an airtight container for up to 3 days.

NUTRITION FACTS PER SERVING:
Total carbs: 16.1 g / Fiber: 7.2 g / Net carbs: 8.9 g / Protein: 35.1 g / Fat: 40 g / Calories: 560 kcal
Macronutrient ratio: Calories from carbs (7%), protein (26%), fat (67%)

Induction Carbonara

MAKES: 4 servings
HANDS-ON TIME: 20 minutes
OVERALL TIME: 30 minutes

Induction is the initial phase of the ketogenic diet, and if you're in the midst of it, you might be struggling with cravings. If you're jonesing for pasta, here's the solution: this just-as-hearty low-carb version of spaghetti carbonara has almost no carbs, but it's got plenty of flavor!

2 packs (400 g/14.1 oz) shirataki
   noodles
2 small (200 g/7.1 oz) zucchini,
   spiralized
4 egg yolks
1 cup (240 ml) heavy whipping cream
8 large slices (240 g/8.5 oz) bacon,
   chopped
½ cup (45 g/1.6 oz) grated Parmesan
   cheese
½ cup (8 g/0.3 oz) basil leaves
Sea salt and black pepper

Prepare the shirataki noodles following the instructions on page 41. Spiralize the zucchini according to the instructions on page 40 and set aside. In a small bowl, combine the egg yolks with the cream and set aside.

Place the bacon pieces in a large heatproof casserole dish. Add ½ cup (120 ml) water. Cook over medium-high heat until the water starts to boil. Reduce the heat to medium, and cook until the water evaporates and the bacon fat is rendered. Reduce the heat to low and cook until the bacon is lightly browned and crispy.

Add the prepared shirataki noodles, and toss through with the bacon. Slowly start pouring the cream–egg yolk mixture, stirring constantly, until it thickens. Add the spiralized zucchini and cook for 2 to 3 minutes. Finally, add the Parmesan, basil (chopped or whole), and season with salt and pepper, if needed. Eat immediately, or let it cool and refrigerate for up to 2 days.

NUTRITION FACTS PER SERVING:
Total carbs: 7.9 g / Fiber: 2.2 g / Net carbs: 5.7 g / Protein: 17.1 g / Fat: 45.7 g / Calories: 505 kcal
Macronutrient ratio: Calories from carbs (5%), protein (14%), fat (81%)

Thai Shredded Beef Bowls

MAKES: 4 servings
HANDS-ON TIME: 30 minutes
OVERALL TIME: 4 hours 30 minutes

Dust off your slow cooker and make a batch of this Thai shredded beef in advance, and you'll be able to pull these low-carb, beef-and-noodle bowls together in less than fifteen minutes!

Thai Beef:

2.65 pounds (1.2 kg) boneless beef chuck roast

Sea salt and black pepper

2 tablespoons (30 g/1.1 oz) virgin coconut oil or duck fat, divided

1 small (70 g/2.5 oz) yellow onion, chopped

2 cloves garlic, minced

4 lemongrass stalks, tough outer stalks removed and finely chopped

2-inch (5-cm) piece (18 g/0.7 oz) ginger or galangal, grated

1 (14 g/0.5 oz) Thai chile, chopped

2 star anise

1 cinnamon stick

½ cup (120 ml) bone broth (page 42) or water

¼ cup (60 ml) coconut aminos

2 tablespoons (30 ml) fish sauce

Bowls:

4 medium (60 g/2.1 oz) spring onions

2 tablespoons (30 ml) virgin coconut oil or duck fat

1 clove garlic, minced

1 medium (120 g/4.2 oz) red bell pepper, sliced

1 small (300 g/10.6 oz) broccoli or broccolini, chopped

3.5 ounces (100 g) drained kelp noodles or prepared shirataki noodles (see page 41)

½ recipe of Thai Shredded Beef (see above)

Fresh herbs such as Thai basil, parsley, or cilantro

Lime wedges and few slices of fresh chiles

TO MAKE THE THAI BEEF: Preheat the slow cooker. Cut the roast in half (large roasts cook better this way), and season with salt and pepper. Grease a large heavy saucepan or Dutch oven with 1 tablespoon (15 g) of the coconut oil. Cook the beef until browned on all sides, then transfer to the slow cooker.

Grease the saucepan with the remaining 1 tablespoon (15 g) coconut oil. Add the onion and cook over medium-high heat for 5 to 8 minutes, until lightly browned. Add the garlic, lemongrass, ginger, and chile, and cook for 1 to 2 minutes. Add the star anise and cinnamon, and pour in the bone broth, coconut aminos, and fish sauce to deglaze the saucepan, scraping the browned bits off the bottom. Pour into the slow cooker over the beef. Cover and cook on high for 4 hours, or on low for 8 hours. (You'll end up with 8 servings of beef and will only use half of it for this recipe: the other half can be stored in the fridge for up to 4 days or freezer for up to 3 months.)

TO ASSEMBLE THE 4 BOWLS: Slice the spring onions and separate the white parts from the green parts. Heat another large saucepan greased with the coconut oil. Add the white parts of the spring onion, and cook over medium-high heat for a minute. Then add the garlic, pepper, and broccoli, and cook until crisp-tender, about 5 minutes. Rinse the kelp noodles, add them to the saucepan, and heat through. Add the prepared beef—remember to add only 4 servings—and remove from the heat. Serve with herbs, lime wedges, and chiles.

NUTRITION FACTS PER SERVING (1 BOWL):
Total carbs: 12.2 g / Fiber: 4.2 g / Net carbs: 8 g / Protein: 32 g / Fat: 32.9 g / Calories: 465 kcal
Macronutrient ratio: Calories from carbs (7%), protein (28%), fat (65%)

Pork Medallions with Asparagus and Hollandaise

MAKES: 4 servings
HANDS-ON TIME: 20 minutes
OVERALL TIME: 35 minutes

Think of hollandaise sauce as your most powerful secret weapon. It's so versatile and so delicious, and it's packed to the gills with heart-healthy fats, thanks to the extra-virgin olive oil. Plus, it really adds elegance to this simple keto meal of pork paired with blanched asparagus.

Pork Medallions:

1 pound (450 g) pork tenderloin

Sea salt and black pepper

1 tablespoon (15 g/0.5 oz) ghee or duck fat

1.3 pounds (600 g) asparagus, woody ends removed

Hollandaise Sauce:

4 egg yolks

¼ cup (60 ml) fresh lime or lemon juice

1 teaspoon Dijon mustard

2 to 4 tablespoons (30 to 60 ml) water

½ cup (120 ml) extra-virgin olive oil, melted butter, or ghee

4 slices (64 g/2.2 oz) crispy bacon, crumbled

TO MAKE THE PORK: Preheat the oven to 375°F (190°C, or gas mark 5). Pat the tenderloin dry with a paper towel, and season with salt and pepper. Heat a large ovenproof skillet greased with the ghee over high heat. Add the tenderloin and cook until browned on all sides, about 3 to 4 minutes. Transfer to the oven, and bake for 20 to 25 minutes (estimate 5 minutes per every 100 grams). When done, remove from the oven, cover with aluminum foil, and place on a cooling rack.

Bring a saucepan filled with salted water to a boil. Add the asparagus and cook for about 2 minutes, until crisp-tender. Drain and keep warm.

TO MAKE THE HOLLANDAISE SAUCE: Fill a medium saucepan with 1 cup of water (240 ml) and bring to a boil. Mix the egg yolks with the lime juice, mustard, and water. (Use the leftover egg whites to make Garlic & Herb Focaccia on page 48.) Place the bowl over the saucepan filled with water. The water should not touch the bottom of the bowl. Keep mixing until the sauce starts to thicken. Slowly pour the olive oil into the mixture, stirring constantly until it becomes thick and creamy. If the sauce is too thick, add a splash of water.

To serve, slice the tenderloin and place on top of the asparagus. Pour over the hollandaise, sprinkle with the bacon, and serve immediately. The tenderloin can be stored in the fridge for up to 4 days.

NOTE: Hollandaise should be served within 1 hour of preparation. Do not reheat the sauce or it will separate. If you're only making it for yourself, halve this recipe, or prepare it one serving at a time.

NUTRITION FACTS PER SERVING (PORK + ASPARAGUS + ¼ CUP/60 ML HOLLANDAISE):
Total carbs: 7.8 g / Fiber: 3.3 g / Net carbs: 4.5 g / Protein: 34.5 g / Fat: 39.5 g / Calories: 518 kcal
Macronutrient ratio: Calories from carbs (4%), protein (27%), fat (69%)

Pork Chops with Mushroom & Mustard Sauce

MAKES: 4 servings
HANDS-ON TIME: 25 minutes
OVERALL TIME: 45 minutes

When it comes to dinner in my house, quick-prep meat-and-veg trays always save the day. They're healthy and hearty, but so simple. You just toss a few basic ingredients into a baking dish, then sit back and wait. Panfrying the pork chops here adds extra flavor, but you can always skip it if you're short on time.

½ cup (120 ml) warm bone broth (page 42) or water

⅓ cup (10 g/0.4 oz) dried porcini mushrooms

1 medium (350 g/12.3 oz) broccoli, cut into florets

7.1 ounces (200 g) chopped dark-leaf kale, stems removed

¼ cup (60 ml) melted ghee or lard, divided

Sea salt and black pepper

4 pieces (500 g/1.1 lb) thick-cut boneless pork chops (about 1-inch/2-cm thick)

1 medium (85 g/3 oz) yellow onion, chopped

1 teaspoon (5 g/0.2 oz) grated horseradish

1 tablespoon (15 g/0.5 oz) Dijon mustard

1 tablespoon (15 ml) fresh lemon juice

¼ cup (60 ml) heavy whipping cream or coconut milk

Pour the warm broth over the porcini mushrooms in a bowl. Let them soak for 20 to 30 minutes.

Preheat the oven to 450°F (230°C, or gas mark 8). Place the broccoli florets in a deep-dish baking tray. Add the kale, and mix to combine. Drizzle with 2 tablespoons (30 ml) of the ghee, and season with salt and pepper.

Pat the pork chops dry with a paper towel, and season with salt and pepper. Heat a skillet greased with 1 tablespoon (15 ml) of the ghee over high heat. Brown the pork chops quickly on each side for 1 minute, then place them into the tray on top of the broccoli and kale. Bake for 12 to 15 minutes.

Meanwhile, prepare the mustard-horseradish sauce. Grease the skillet in which you cooked the pork chops with the remaining 1 tablespoon (15 ml) ghee. Add the onion and cook over medium heat for 8 to 10 minutes, until golden brown. Add the horseradish, mustard, lemon juice, cream, and the soaked mushrooms (including the stock). Bring to a boil. Cook for 3 to 5 minutes, or until the mushrooms are tender. Remove from the heat, and set aside for 5 minutes. Use a blender to process the sauce until smooth. Add a dash of water if the sauce is too thick.

Serve the sauce with the baked pork chops and vegetables. Store the meat and vegetables and the sauce in separate airtight containers in the refrigerator for up to 4 days.

NUTRITION FACTS PER SERVING:
Total carbs: 12.8 g / Fiber: 4.7 g / Net carbs: 8.1 g / Protein: 31.2 g / Fat: 33.9 g / Calories: 476 kcal
Macronutrient ratio: Calories from carbs (7%), protein (27%), fat (66%)

Irish Pork Pie

MAKES: 6 servings
HANDS-ON TIME: 20 minutes
OVERALL TIME: 3 hours 30 minutes + marinating

Once I wanted to make a keto shepherd's pie, but all I had on hand was pork belly, pork loin, and leftover shredded cabbage. So, I ended up making tender, slow-cooked pork belly topped with a creamy, low-carb, Irish-style colcannon instead, and it's become one of our favorite dishes!

Pork Layer:

- 14.1 ounces (400 g) pork belly, cut into 1½-inch (4-cm) pieces
- 14.1 ounces (400 g) boneless pork loin, cut into 1½-inch (4-cm) pieces
- 3 cloves garlic, minced
- 2 bay leaves, crumbled
- 1 tablespoon (7 g/0.2 oz) paprika
- ¼ teaspoon allspice
- ¾ teaspoon sea salt
- ½ teaspoon black pepper
- 1 small (70 g/2.5 oz) yellow onion, sliced
- 1 tablespoon (15 ml) extra-virgin olive oil
- ¼ cup (60 ml) bone broth (page 42) or water

Topping:

- 1 medium (600 g/1.3 oz) cauliflower, cut into florets
- ½ cup (120 ml) heavy whipping cream or coconut milk
- ½ head (300 g/10.6 oz) green cabbage, tough stems removed, shredded
- 2 medium (30 g/1.1 oz) spring onions, sliced
- Sea salt and black pepper

TO MAKE THE PORK: Place the pork belly and pork loin into a bowl. Add the garlic, bay leaves, paprika, allspice, salt, pepper, onion, and olive oil. Mix until well coated, then place in the fridge for at least 2 hours, or up to 24 hours.

Preheat the oven to 300°F (150°C, or gas mark 2). Remove the marinated pork from the fridge, and place it in a baking dish deep enough to fit the topping. Add the broth, cover with aluminum foil or a lid, and bake for 3 hours. After 2½ hours, remove from the oven, and place on a cooling rack. Use a spoon to collect most of the juices (there will be plenty of grease from the pork belly). Use half of the juices to grease a large saucepan. Then cover and return to the oven.

TO MAKE THE TOPPING: Place the cauliflower florets on a steaming rack inside a pot filled with 1 to 2 cups of water. Bring to a boil and cook for 8 to 10 minutes. When the cauliflower is tender, remove from the heat, uncover, and let cool for 5 minutes. Transfer the cauliflower to a blender, add the cream and the reserved juices, and process until smooth.

Place the cabbage into the greased saucepan, stir to combine, and cover. Cook over medium-low heat for about 5 minutes, or until tender. Add the spring onions and cook for 1 minute more. When done, remove from the heat and add to the puréed cauliflower. Combine, and season with salt and pepper if needed.

Finally, spread the cauliflower-cabbage topping on top of the pork and return to the oven. Bake for another 20 minutes. When done, place on a cooling rack for 10 minutes. Serve hot, or let it cool and refrigerate for up to 4 days.

NUTRITION FACTS PER SERVING:
Total carbs: 11 g / Fiber: 4.1 g / Net carbs: 6.9 g / Protein: 23.3 g / Fat: 51.8 g / Calories: 599 kcal
Macronutrient ratio: Calories from carbs (5%), protein (16%), fat (79%)

Lamb Steaks with Mint Pesto and Pickled Onion

MAKES: 4 servings
HANDS-ON TIME: 20 minutes
OVERALL TIME: 20 minutes

A refreshing cucumber salad and homemade mint-walnut pesto add contrast to these easy low-carb lamb steaks. Add some pickled onions to the salad for extra zing!

Pickled Red Onion:

1¼ cups (300 ml) apple cider vinegar

¼ cup (60 ml) water

2 tablespoons (20 g/0.7 oz) erythritol or Swerve

1 teaspoon salt

10 black peppercorns

4 whole allspice berries

2 medium (220 g/7.7 oz) red onions, sliced

2 cloves garlic, sliced

Few sprigs of fresh thyme (optional)

Cucumber Salad:

2 large (500 g/1.1 lb) cucumbers, peeled and sliced into half-moons

1 medium (100 g/3.5 oz) red onion, or an equivalent amount of Pickled Red Onion (see above)

⅔ cup (100 g/3.5 oz) crumbled feta cheese

1 tablespoon (15 ml) extra-virgin olive oil

1 recipe mint-walnut pesto (page 43), divided

1 tablespoon (4 g/0.2 oz) chopped fresh mint

Lamb Cutlets:

4 large (600 g/1.2 lb) boneless lamb steaks (150 g/5.3 oz each)

½ teaspoon sea salt

¼ teaspoon black pepper

1 tablespoon (15 g/0.5 oz) ghee or duck fat

TO MAKE THE PICKLED ONION: Fill a small saucepan with the vinegar, water, erythritol, salt, peppercorns, and allspice. Cover and bring to a boil. Place the onions and garlic into a glass jar. Once the vinegar is boiling, pour it over the onions and garlic. Press the onions down until completely submerged. Optionally, add a few sprigs of thyme. Let the mixture cool to room temperature. The onions are ready to serve once cool, but taste better after a few hours in the fridge. Cover and store refrigerated for up to 3 weeks. This method results in crunchy onions. If you prefer the onions soft, add them to the pot with the vinegar mixture and boil for 1 to 2 minutes.

TO MAKE THE CUCUMBER SALAD: Place the cucumbers in a bowl and add the onion. Top with the feta cheese, olive oil, and half of the prepared mint pesto. Garnish with mint, and set aside.

TO MAKE THE LAMB CUTLETS: Season the lamb with salt and pepper. Grease a skillet with the ghee and cook the steaks on both sides for 3 to 4 minutes, or until browned and cooked through. Serve with the remaining mint pesto and cucumber salad. The pesto can be stored in the fridge for up to 2 weeks (to keep it fresh, pour a thin layer of olive oil on top after each use).

NOTE: Don't skip the pickled onions! They're the perfect accompaniment to keto burgers (page 169), sandwiches (page 114), and steaks (page 170). Plus, they're easy to make and keep in the fridge for weeks.

NUTRITION FACTS PER SERVING (1 CUTLET + SALAD + MINT PESTO):
Total carbs: 8.6 g / Fiber: 2.4 g / Net carbs: 6.2 g / Protein: 33 g / Fat: 57.9 g / Calories: 686 kcal
Macronutrient ratio: Calories from carbs (4%), protein (19%), fat (77%)

Cheese-Stuffed Greek Bifteki

MAKES: 8 servings
HANDS-ON TIME: 35 minutes
OVERALL TIME: 55 minutes

On a trip to Athens, my partner and I found an amazing street food stall with meat skewers and fresh salads. We all ordered cheese-stuffed "bifteki," oval-shaped meat patties flavored with fresh herbs, and we liked them so much that I recreated the recipe as soon as we got home!

Bifteki:

2 pounds (900 g) ground lamb or beef
1 small (60 g/2.1 oz) red onion, minced
2 cloves garlic, crushed
1 large egg, white only, yolk reserved
1 large egg
2 tablespoons (8 g/0.3 oz) chopped fresh parsley
1 teaspoon dried oregano
2 tablespoons (30 ml) white wine vinegar
¾ teaspoon sea salt
½ teaspoon black pepper
⅓ cup (40 g/1.4 oz) coconut flour
1 tablespoon (15 ml) melted ghee or duck fat

Bifteki Filling:

1 cup (240 g/8.5 oz) cream cheese
1 egg yolk (reserved from the bifteki)
2 tablespoons (8 g/0.3 oz) chopped fresh parsley
1 teaspoon dried oregano
½ cup (75 g/2.6 oz) feta

Greek-Style Salad:

½ cup (120 ml) extra-virgin olive oil
2 tablespoons (30 ml) fresh lemon juice
1 clove garlic, crushed
1.3 pounds (600 g) green beans, trimmed
2 cups (300 g/10.6 oz) halved cherry tomatoes
1 small (60 g/2.1 oz) red onion, sliced
1 cup (150 g/5.3 oz) feta
1 teaspoon each dried oregano and mint
¼ cup (34 g/1.2 oz) capers or olives, drained

TO MAKE THE BIFTEKI: Preheat the oven to 400°F (200°C, or gas mark 6). Place all the ingredients for the bifteki, except the ghee, in a bowl. Mix until well combined, then use your hands to form the mixture into 8 oval-shaped patties (about 150 g/5.3 oz each).

TO MAKE THE FILLING: Combine the cream cheese, egg yolk, parsley, oregano, and crumbled feta in a bowl. Spoon about 2 tablespoons (42 g/1.5 oz) of the cheese filling along the middle of the long side of each bifteki. Using your hands, fold each bifteki over gently without squeezing the cheese out. Place on a baking tray and brush each with the melted ghee. Transfer to the oven and bake for 30 to 35 minutes, until lightly browned on top and cooked through.

TO MAKE THE SALAD: Combine the olive oil, lemon juice, and crushed garlic in a small bowl and set aside. Bring a large pot filled with salted water to a boil. Add the green beans and cook for 3 to 4 minutes until crisp-tender. Drain the beans, then immediately plunge them into ice water for 30 seconds. Drain and place into a bowl. Add the tomatoes, onion, crumbled feta, herbs, and capers. Drizzle with the dressing. Serve immediately alongside the bifteki. Refrigerate the cooked bifteki in an airtight container for up to 4 days, or freeze for up to 3 months. Refrigerate the salad in an airtight container for up to 2 days.

NUTRITION FACTS PER SERVING (1 BIFTEKI + SALAD):
Total carbs: 13.1 g / Fiber: 4.3 g / Net carbs: 8.8 g / Protein: 29.9 g / Fat: 55.4 g / Calories: 652 kcal
Macronutrient ratio: Calories from carbs (5%), protein (18%), fat (77%)

cut 1 more line

Lamb, Coconut, and Okra Curry

MAKES: 8 servings
HANDS-ON TIME: 15 minutes
OVERALL TIME: 2 hours 30 minutes

When the weather gets colder, nothing beats a bowl of creamy curry made with tender meat and warming spices. This version calls for okra: it's rich in vitamin C, vitamin K, and magnesium, and thanks to its silky texture, it acts as a natural grain-free thickener.

¼ cup (60 g/2.1 oz) ghee or duck fat, divided

2.6 pounds (1.2 kg) lamb, cut into 1½-inch (4-cm) chunks

1 small (70 g/2.5 oz) yellow onion, diced

4 cloves garlic, minced

1 tablespoon (6 g/0.2 oz) grated ginger

1 small (14 g/0.5 oz) red or green chile pepper, chopped

1 tablespoon (6 g/0.2 oz) garam masala

2 teaspoons ground cumin

1½ teaspoons ground turmeric

½ teaspoon fennel seeds

1 teaspoon sea salt

½ teaspoon black pepper

1 tablespoon (15 g/0.5 oz) tomato paste

¼ cup (60 ml) fresh lime juice

4 cups (960 ml) water

1 can (400 ml/13.5 oz) coconut milk

1 pound (450 g) okra, trimmed and halved

Small bunch fresh cilantro

Suggested side: 1 cup (120 g/4.2 oz) cauliflower rice (see page 40), or 1 serving (100 g/3.5 oz) shirataki rice (see page 41)

Heat a large, heavy-bottomed pot with 2 tablespoons (30 g/1.1 oz) of the ghee and add the lamb. Cook over medium-high heat for 3 to 5 minutes, until browned on all sides. Transfer to a plate. Grease the same pot with the remaining 2 tablespoons (30 g/1.1 oz) ghee and add the onion. Cook for about 7 minutes, until lightly browned, then add the garlic, ginger, chile, garam masala, cumin, turmeric, fennel seeds, salt, and pepper. Cook for 1 to 2 minutes, until fragrant.

Return the browned lamb to the pan and mix to coat well. Add the tomato paste, lime juice, and water, and bring to a boil. Once simmering, reduce the heat to low and cover. Cook for 1 hour and 45 minutes. Add the coconut milk and okra, and return to a boil. Once simmering, cover again and cook for 15 to 20 minutes, or until the okra is tender. Garnish with the cilantro, and serve warm with cauliflower rice or shirataki rice. To store, let the curry cool, then refrigerate for up to 4 days, or freeze for up to 3 months.

NOTE: If you've got a slow cooker, this dish is even easier to make! Simply place the browned lamb in a preheated slow cooker. Brown the onion, garlic, ginger, chile, and spices in a pot as directed above, then pour in the lime juice and 1 cup (240 ml) water. Then pour the mixture over the browned lamb in the slow cooker. Cook on high for 3 to 4 hours (or on low for 6 to 8 hours). Add the coconut milk and okra in the last 60 minutes of the cooking process. If the sauce is too thick, add ½ to 1 cup (120 to 240 ml) more water. Serve immediately.

NUTRITION FACTS PER SERVING (CURRY WITHOUT CAULIFLOWER RICE):
Total carbs: 8.8 g / Fiber: 2.5 g / Net carbs: 6.3 g / Protein: 29.3 g / Fat: 43.5 g / Calories: 539 kcal
Macronutrient ratio: Calories from carbs (5%), protein (22%), fat (73%)

Chapter 7

Drinks and Desserts

We all need a little something sweet from time to time, and the good news is you don't have to give up treats just because you're following a ketogenic lifestyle. That's why this chapter features low-carb goodies and drinks that are great for any occasion. Make the Mexican Chocolate Fudgesicles on page 202 if it's too hot to cook, but you're still craving chocolate. Or if you're in the mood for a good old-fashioned pound cake, you can't do better than my Czech Butter Cake on page 195. And if you need something exceptional for a special event such as a birthday or a family party, check out the stunning (and delicious!) Tiramisu Crepe Cake on page 196.

Still, remember that treats are treats, and they can cause cravings even though they're sugar-free. Before you try the recipes in this chapter, ask yourself: Do I often eat more than one serving? Do sweet foods make me crave more sweets? Has my weight been stalling for over two weeks? If you answered "yes" to any of these questions, avoid most of these recipes, at least during the induction phase (apart from a few exceptions that are marked as "induction-friendly"), or when you reach a weight-loss plateau.

Electrolyte Agua Fresca

MAKES: 6 cups (1.4 L)
HANDS-ON TIME: 5 minutes
OVERALL TIME: 30 minutes

Mexican *agua fresca* is usually made from botanicals like fruits or flowers combined with sugar and water, but this version is much healthier and even more refreshing. Inspired by one of the most popular recipes on my blog, it's packed with electrolytes, which means it's a naturally effective keto flu remedy—and it's great for rehydrating during exercise, too.

5 cups (1.2 L) still or sparkling water, or herbal tea of your choice

½ cup (120 ml) fresh lime or lemon juice

2 tablespoons (12 g/0.4 oz) Natural Calm magnesium (see Note)

½ teaspoon food-grade potassium chloride (see Note)

¼ teaspoon pink Himalayan salt

¼ cup (40 g/1.4 oz) powdered erythritol or Swerve, or stevia to taste

1 small (100 g/3.5 oz) cucumber, sliced

Bunch of fresh mint

Optional: ice cubes

Combine the water, lime juice, Natural Calm magnesium, potassium chloride, salt, and erythritol in a jug. Stir until no crystals are visible. Add the cucumber slices and mint, then refrigerate for at least 30 minutes before serving to allow the water to infuse with the cucumber and mint. Serve over ice, if you like. Store in the fridge for 3 to 4 days.

NOTE: For best results and to avoid stomach distress, always drink Electrolyte Agua Fresca with meals, and do not consume more than 2 cups (480 ml) per day; ideally, start with 1 cup (240 ml) per day. Sweeteners can be omitted; use them to taste. If you can't find potassium chloride, you can use ¾ teaspoon of Morton Lite Salt and skip the sea salt. For information about magnesium and potassium supplements, read more on page 27.

NUTRITION FACTS PER SERVING (1 CUP/240 ML):
Total carbs: 2 g / Fiber: 0.1 g / Net carbs: 1.9 g / Protein: 0.1 g / Fat: 0 g / Calories: 6 kcal
Macronutrient ratio: Calories from carbs (94%), protein (4%), fat (2%)

Superfood Smoothies Two Ways

MAKES: 1 serving
HANDS-ON TIME: 5 minutes
OVERALL TIME: 5 minutes

You might have had avocados in a green smoothie before—but what about zucchini? It's not as weird as it sounds: low-carb zucchini can add a silky, extra-creamy texture to just about any kind of smoothie. Try it for yourself in these nutritious keto smoothies, which act as quick meals when you're too busy to cook. (Use sweeteners to taste or skip them altogether, especially during the induction phase.)

Golden Milk Smoothie:

½ cup (120 ml) coconut milk
½ to ¾ cup (120 to 180 ml) water
¼ medium (75 g/2.6 oz) peeled and grated zucchini
2 tablespoons (14 g/0.5 oz) collagen powder (see page 31 for alternatives)
1 tablespoon (10 g/0.4 oz) erythritol or Swerve, or 3 to 5 drops liquid stevia
1 tablespoon (15 ml) MCT oil or MUFA-based mild-tasting oil (see page 18)
¾ teaspoon ground turmeric
½ teaspoon ground ginger
¼ teaspoon ground cinnamon
¼ teaspoon vanilla bean powder
Pinch of black pepper
Optional: few ice cubes

Green Smoothie:

½ cup (120 ml) coconut milk
½ to ¾ cup (120 to 180 ml) water
½ medium (75 g/2.6 oz) avocado
½ cup (15 g/0.5 oz) fresh spinach
1 tablespoon (15 ml) MCT oil or MUFA-based mild-tasting oil (see page 18)
2 tablespoons (14 g/0.5 oz) collagen powder (see page 31 for alternatives)
2 tablespoons (20 g/0.7 oz) erythritol or Swerve, or 5 to 8 drops liquid stevia

½ teaspoon vanilla powder or 1 teaspoon sugar-free vanilla extract
Optional: ½ to 1 teaspoon matcha green tea powder, a few ice cubes, or 1 tablespoon (5 g/0.2 oz) cacao powder

Place all the ingredients to make the Golden Milk Smoothie or Green Smoothie in a blender. Process until smooth. Serve immediately.

NOTE: Whenever you use turmeric, always remember to add a pinch of black pepper. Black pepper helps your body absorb turmeric, and it also increases its anti-inflammatory, antioxidant, and immune-boosting properties!

NUTRITION FACTS PER SERVING (GOLDEN/GREEN SMOOTHIE):
Total carbs: 8.4/11.4 g / Fiber: 1.6/5.4 g / Net carbs: 6.8/6 g / Protein: 15.4/16.2 g / Fat: 38.2/48.2 g / Calories: 415/515 kcal / Macronutrient ratio: Calories from carbs (6/5%), protein (14/12%), fat (80/83%)

Strawberry Cream Soda

MAKES: 1 serving
HANDS-ON TIME: 10 minutes
OVERALL TIME: 20 minutes + chilling

Making Strawberry Cream Soda from scratch is easier than you think. And you won't find any sugar or artificial sweeteners here: just real-food, low-carb ingredients. Feel free to get creative with this recipe: use raspberries, blackberries, or blueberries instead of strawberries, and add fruit-friendly spices such as vanilla or cinnamon.

Strawberry Simple Syrup (makes about 300 ml/ 1¼ cups):

½ cup (120 ml) water

½ cup (100 g/3.5 oz) erythritol or Swerve

2 cups (300 g/10.6 oz) chopped strawberries, fresh or frozen

Strawberry Cream Soda:

Ice

½ cup (120 ml) club soda or sparkling water

2 tablespoons (30 ml) Strawberry Simple Syrup (recipe above)

2 tablespoons (30 ml) heavy whipping cream or coconut milk

Optional: whipped cream or coconut cream (see page 73), for topping

TO MAKE THE STRAWBERRY SIMPLE SYRUP: Combine the water, erythritol, and strawberries in a small saucepan. Bring to a simmer over a medium heat. Once simmering, reduce the heat to low. Mash the strawberries with a fork as they soften and cook for 15 to 20 minutes. Remove from the heat, and pour the mixture through a sieve placed over a bowl. Discard the strawberries, or reserve them and use them like berry jam: as a yogurt topping or in smoothies. Transfer the syrup to a glass jar, and let it cool. Refrigerate before using and use within 2 weeks.

TO MAKE THE SODA: Fill a glass with ice. Pour in the club soda, and add 2 tablespoons (30 ml) of the strawberry syrup and 2 tablespoons (30 ml) of heavy whipping cream. Top with whipped cream or coconut cream, if you like. Serve immediately.

NOTE: If you prefer a sweeter soda, add a few drops of stevia, or an additional tablespoon (15 ml) of strawberry syrup.

NUTRITION FACTS PER SERVING:
Total carbs: 3.6 g / Fiber: 0.6 g / Net carbs: 3 g / Protein: 0.8 g / Fat: 11.5 g / Calories: 121 kcal
Macronutrient ratio: Calories from carbs (10%), protein (3%), fat (87%)

Keto Lemon Curd

MAKES: about 1¾ cups (420 ml)
HANDS-ON TIME: 20 minutes
OVERALL TIME: 30 minutes

Got some leftover egg yolks from that batch of Garlic & Herb Focaccia (page 48) you just made? You can use them to make healthy homemade mayonnaise (page 42) or Hollandaise Sauce (page 176), but if you're after something sweeter, you can convert them into this sweet-and-tangy, high-fat lemon curd! Try it in the Pavlova Lemon Curd Sandwiches on page 190.

6 large egg yolks

½ cup (80 g /2.8 oz) powdered
  erythritol or Swerve

Optional: 15 to 20 drops liquid stevia

¾ cup (180 ml) fresh lemon juice
  (from about 4 lemons)

3 tablespoons (18 g/0.6 oz) fresh
  lemon zest (from about 3 lemons)

3.5 ounces (100 g) butter, ghee, or
  virgin coconut oil, cut into pieces

Combine the egg yolks with the powdered erythritol and stevia (if using) in a medium-size heatproof bowl. Add the lemon juice and lemon zest, and mix until well combined. Place the bowl over a saucepan filled with simmering water and stir constantly; make sure the water doesn't touch the bottom of the bowl. Keep stirring for 8 to 10 minutes, or until the custard starts to thicken. Then remove from the heat and add the butter. Place the bowl with the curd in a larger bowl filled with ice water and mix until cool. Pour into an airtight jar and keep refrigerated for up to 10 days.

NUTRITION FACTS PER SERVING (¼ CUP/60 ML):
Total carbs: 2.9 g / Fiber: 0.3 g / Net carbs: 2.6 g / Protein: 2.2 g / Fat: 39.5 g / Calories: 139 kcal
Macronutrient ratio: Calories from carbs (7%), protein (6%), fat (87%)

Pavlova Lemon Curd Sandwiches

MAKES: 8 servings
HANDS-ON TIME: 10 minutes
OVERALL TIME: 1 hour

British celebrity chef Mary Berry has a legendary recipe for a Pavlova roulade that's filled with cream and lemon curd. But in this low-carb version, I use the fluffy meringue base as a "sandwich" instead of rolling it up into a roulade: that way, I get to squeeze in even more of the lemony high-fat filling!

8 large egg whites

¼ teaspoon cream of tartar or apple cider vinegar

½ cup (80 g/2.8) powdered erythritol or Swerve

½ cup (45 g/1.6 oz) flaked almonds or coconut

1 cup (240 ml) heavy whipping cream or coconut cream (see page 73)

¾ cup (180 g/6.4 oz) Keto Lemon Curd (page 189), chilled

Preheat the oven to 350°F (175°C, or gas mark 4). Line a jelly roll pan with heavy-duty parchment paper. To prepare the meringue base, use an electric mixer to beat the egg whites and cream of tartar until stiff peaks form. Add the erythritol, a tablespoon (10 g) at a time, beating well on high speed. Spread the meringue evenly into the Swiss roll tray. Sprinkle with the flaked almonds or coconut. Place the tray on the middle or upper rack of the oven, and bake for 10 minutes. Then reduce the temperature to 300°F (150°C, or gas mark 2), and bake for another 20 to 25 minutes, or until firm to the touch.

Remove the meringue from the oven. Turn it upside down on a baking sheet lined with fresh parchment paper. Gently peel off the layer of parchment paper. Let cool completely and prepare the lemon-cream filling: simply whisk the cream in a medium bowl until it creates soft peaks, then gently fold in the lemon curd.

When the meringue is chilled, cut it in half down the middle. Spread the lemon-cream filling on top of one of the meringue halves (on the side with no almonds) and top with the other half (almond-side up). Chill for a few hours before slicing and serving. Store in the fridge for up to 5 days.

NUTRITION FACTS PER SERVING:
Total carbs: 3.7 g / Fiber: 0.8 g / Net carbs: 2.9 g / Protein: 6.4 g / Fat: 19.7 g / Calories: 217 kcal
Macronutrient ratio: Calories from carbs (5%), protein (12%), fat (83%)

Cheesecake Pockets Two Ways

MAKES: 3 servings
HANDS-ON TIME: 10 minutes
OVERALL TIME: 20 minutes

You might already have tried the Quick Tuna Melt Pockets on page 116, or the Mexican Pockets on page 117—but low-carb, high-fat "pockets" don't have to be savory. Stuffed with vanilla or chocolate filling, these keto treats are like individual handheld cheesecakes—and they're just as addictive!

Vanilla Cheesecake:

¾ cup (180 g/6.3 oz) cream cheese

1 egg yolk

2 tablespoons (20 g/0.7 oz) powdered erythritol or Swerve

½ teaspoon vanilla powder, or 1 to 2 teaspoons sugar-free vanilla extract

½ teaspoon fresh lemon zest

Optional: stevia drops to taste

Chocolate Cheesecake:

¾ cup (180 g/6.3 oz) cream cheese

1 egg yolk

2 tablespoons (11 g/0.4 oz) cacao powder or unsweetened cocoa powder (Dutch process)

¼ cup (40 g/1.4 oz) powdered erythritol or Swerve

½ teaspoon ground cinnamon

Optional: stevia drops to taste

Dough:

¾ cup (85 g/3 oz) shredded mozzarella

2 tablespoons (28 g/1 oz) cream cheese

3 tablespoons (24 g/0.8 oz) coconut flour

1 tablespoon (15 ml) melted ghee

TO MAKE THE CHEESECAKE: In a bowl, combine all the ingredients for the cheesecake filling of your choice. Add stevia to taste, if using. Set aside.

TO MAKE THE DOUGH: Melt the mozzarella and cream cheese in the microwave for 1 minute, checking halfway through. Alternatively, melt in the oven at 300°F (150°C, or gas mark 2) for 8 to 10 minutes. Mix and add the coconut flour. Stir until well combined.

Roll out the dough thinly between 2 sheets of parchment paper or use a nonstick mat and nonstick rolling pin. (When rolled out, the dough should be about 8 x 11 inches [20 x 30 cm].) Add the cheesecake filling to the center of the dough, then fold over like an envelope and seal the dough with your fingers. Do not press too hard or the filling will spill out. Using a sharp knife, poke some holes into the dough for releasing the steam while baking, and brush with the ghee. Bake at 360°F (180°C, or gas mark 4) for 18 to 20 minutes, or until golden brown and firm to the touch. Remove from the oven and let cool for a few minutes. Cut the pocket into 3 slices. Enjoy while still hot or let cool completely, then refrigerate in an airtight container for up to 5 days.

NUTRITION FACTS PER SERVING (VANILLA/CHOCOLATE SLICE):
Total carbs: 6.4/9 g / Fiber: 1.6/3 g / Net carbs: 4.8/6 g / Protein: 14.5/15.2 g / Fat: 32.8/33.3 g / Calories: 352/360 kcal / Macronutrient ratio: Calories from carbs (5/6%), protein (16/16%), fat (79/78%)

Paradise Squares

MAKES: 16 pieces
HANDS-ON TIME: 20 minutes
OVERALL TIME: 20 minutes + chilling

Skip the store-bought versions of these bars, and make your own instead! These Paradise Squares are flavored with fresh orange zest and turmeric—which lends them a striking golden color—plus warming spices such as cinnamon, cardamom, and vanilla.

5 ounces (142 g) 90% dark chocolate

1½ ounces (43 g) cacao butter or virgin coconut oil

1 cup (240 g/8.5 oz) coconut cream (see page 73)

3 cups (225 g/7.9 oz) unsweetened shredded coconut

¼ cup (55 g/1.9 oz) virgin coconut oil

¼ cup (40 g/1.4 oz) erythritol or Swerve

1 tablespoon (6 g/0.2 oz) fresh orange zest, or 1½ to 2 teaspoons sugar-free orange extract

1 teaspoon ground turmeric

½ teaspoon ground cinnamon

¼ teaspoon vanilla powder, or 1 teaspoon sugar-free vanilla extract

¼ teaspoon ground cardamom

⅛ teaspoon black pepper

Optional: few drops of liquid stevia to taste

Melt the dark chocolate and cacao butter in a double boiler or in a heatproof bowl placed over a small saucepan filled with 1 cup (240 ml) of water and placed over medium heat. Do not let the bowl touch the water. Stir constantly until combined and melted. Remove from the heat and set aside to cool slightly, about 5 minutes. Then pour half of the mixture evenly into an 8 x 8-inch (20 x 20-cm) parchment-lined pan or a silicone pan. Transfer to the fridge and chill for 10 to 15 minutes, or until set. Reserve the rest of the chocolate for topping.

In a mixing bowl, combine the coconut cream, shredded coconut, coconut oil, erythritol, orange zest, turmeric, cinnamon, vanilla, cardamom, and black pepper. For a sweeter taste, add the stevia and mix again.

Spoon the coconut mixture onto the chocolate "crust" and use a spatula to spread evenly. Drizzle with the remaining chocolate and refrigerate for 45 to 60 minutes to set before slicing. (If you use coconut oil to make the crust, it may be more likely to melt when held in your hands, so always store the bars in the fridge until ready to eat.)

NOTE: You can easily convert these squares into bars. To do that, use your hands to make 16 small 1.2-ounce (35 g) bars from the coconut mixture and refrigerate for 1 hour. Then, use a wooden skewer to hold each bar and use a spoon to cover in the room-temperature melted dark chocolate and cacao butter mixture. Unlike cacao butter, coconut oil melts at room temperature and is less suitable for the coating. Refrigerate until set.

NUTRITION FACTS PER SERVING (1 BAR):
Total carbs: 6.5 g / Fiber: 3.3 g / Net carbs: 3.2 g / Protein: 4.3 g / Fat: 18.1 g / Calories: 202 kcal
Macronutrient ratio: Calories from carbs (7%), protein (9%), fat (84%)

Czech Butter Cake

MAKES: 16 slices
HANDS-ON TIME: 15 minutes
OVERALL TIME: 1 hour

If you like pound cake, then you'll love this sugar-free butter cake, or Czech "babovka." It's very low in carbs, too. Protein powder stands in for the gluten in regular flour, ensuring that it's as light and springy as the traditional version.

1 tablespoon (15 g/0.5 oz) butter or ghee

2 cups (200 g/7.1 oz) almond flour

½ cup (60 g/2.1 oz) coconut flour

¼ cup (25 g/0.9 oz) unflavored whey protein powder (see page 31 for alternatives)

1 teaspoon vanilla powder, or 1 tablespoon (15 ml) sugar-free vanilla extract

1 teaspoon baking soda

¾ cup (150 g/5.3 oz) granulated erythritol or Swerve

6 large eggs

¼ teaspoon cream of tartar, or ½ teaspoon lemon juice

4½ ounces (128 g) butter or ghee, melted

1 cup (240 ml) lukewarm almond milk

¼ cup (60 ml) fresh lemon juice

1 tablespoon (6 g/0.2 oz) fresh lemon zest

¼ cup (22 g/0.8 oz) cacao powder

1 tablespoon (10 g/0.4 oz) powdered erythritol or Swerve

Grease a large Bundt cake tin with the butter. Preheat the oven to 300°F (150°C, or gas mark 2).

You will need three bowls: In the first bowl, combine the almond flour, coconut flour, protein powder, vanilla (unless using liquid extract), baking soda, and granulated erythritol.

Separate the egg whites from the egg yolks. In the second bowl, use an electric mixer to beat the egg whites with the cream of tartar (or lemon juice) until soft peaks form.

In the third bowl, whisk together the egg yolks, melted butter, almond milk, lemon juice, and lemon zest (and the vanilla, if using liquid extract).

To the bowl with the egg yolk mixture, slowly add the dry mixture. Stir until the batter is well combined. Mix in about one-third of the fluffy egg whites to make the batter lighter, then gently fold in the remaining egg whites.

Pour about two-thirds of the batter into the greased cake tin and use a spatula to spread evenly. Add the cacao powder to the remaining batter, and mix to combine. Spoon it into the tin and spread with a spatula. Transfer the tin to the oven and bake for about 45 minutes, until set, or until a toothpick inserted into the center of the cake comes out clean.

Remove from the oven and place on a cooling rack. Let cool completely. Place a large plate on top of the cake, then flip over to release the cake. Dust with the powdered erythritol, slice, and serve. Store at room temperature, covered with a kitchen towel, for up to 3 days; refrigerate for up to 5 days; or freeze for up to 6 months.

NUTRITION FACTS PER SERVING (1 SLICE):
Total carbs: 5.2 g / Fiber: 2.5 g / Net carbs: 2.7 g / Protein: 7.3 g / Fat: 15.8 g / Calories: 185 kcal
Macronutrient ratio: Calories from carbs (6%), protein (16%), fat (78%)

Tiramisu Crepe Cake

MAKES: 16 slices
HANDS-ON TIME: 45 minutes
OVERALL TIME: 60 minutes + chilling

This elaborately layered cake requires a little more effort, but it's worth every minute. It's just as indulgent as high-carb tiramisu, and its impressive presentation makes it perfect for any special occasion.

Crepes:

- **10 large eggs**
- **1 cup (240 g/8.5 oz) ricotta cheese**
- **¼ cup (30 g/1.1 oz) coconut flour**
- **1 teaspoon vanilla powder, or**
  1 tablespoon sugar-free vanilla
  extract
- **1 tablespoon (15 ml) sugar-free coffee**
  extract
- **1 teaspoon sugar-free almond extract**
- **¼ cup (40 g/1.4 oz) powdered**
  erythritol or Swerve
- **Pinch of salt**
- **12 teaspoons (60 ml) ghee or virgin**
  coconut oil for greasing, divided

Filling and Frosting:

- **3 cups (720 g/1.6 lb) mascarpone**
  cheese
- **3½ cups (830 ml) heavy whipping**
  cream
- **¾ cup (120 g/4.2 oz) powdered**
  erythritol or Swerve
- **1½ teaspoons vanilla powder, or**
  1½ tablespoons sugar-free vanilla
  extract
- **1½ teaspoons sugar-free almond**
  extract
- **1½ teaspoons sugar-free rum extract**

- **⅓ cup (29 g/1 oz) cacao powder**

TO MAKE THE CREPES: Combine all the ingredients for the crepes, except for the ghee, in a bowl. Heat a medium skillet greased with a teaspoon of ghee over medium heat. When the skillet is hot, use a ⅓ cup (80 ml) measuring cup to pour in the batter, creating a crepe about 8 inches (20 cm) in diameter. Swirl the pan to spread the batter into a thin layer. Cook for about a minute, or until the batter is set. Flip over using a spatula. Cook for another 30 seconds. Transfer to a plate and set aside. Repeat for the remaining 11 crepes, greasing the pan with a teaspoon of ghee between each of the crepes.

TO MAKE THE FILLING: Place all the ingredients in a large bowl. Process with an electric mixer until fluffy and well combined. You'll need about two-thirds of the mixture for the filling and one-third for the frosting.

To assemble the cake, line the bottom of a tall springform pan at least 4 inches (10 cm) tall and 8 inches (20 cm) in diameter with a piece of parchment paper. (If you don't have a tall springform pan, use heavy-duty parchment paper to create an 8-inch/10-cm ring and insert it in the bottom of your springform pan to make it "taller.")

Place one crepe inside the pan and top with ½ cup (80 g/2.8 oz) of the filling. Spread evenly and lightly dust with cacao powder (reserve some cacao powder for topping). Repeat for the remaining 11 crepes until the cake is complete. Then remove the cake from the springform pan, leaving the bottom of the pan intact to support the cake.

Decorate the cake with the remaining frosting. Spread some of the frosting on the top and sides of the cake. To decorate the top with the remaining frosting, use a piping bag with a round-tip attachment to create large droplets. Dust with the remaining cacao powder. Refrigerate for at least 2 hours before serving. Store in the fridge for up to 5 days.

NUTRITION FACTS PER SERVING (1 SLICE):
Total carbs: 5 g / Fiber: 0.9 g / Net carbs: 4.1 g / Protein: 9.9 g / Fat: 44.7 g / Calories: 470 kcal
Macronutrient ratio: Calories from carbs (4%), protein (9%), fat (87%)

Chocolate Cupcakes with German Buttercream

MAKES: 18 cupcakes
HANDS-ON TIME: 30 minutes
OVERALL TIME: 1 hour + chilling

Everyone needs a cupcake once in a while, even when you're eating keto. So treat yourself! These light, fluffy chocolate muffins are topped with custard buttercream frosting, and they're absolutely decadent—but completely sugar-free.

Vanilla Custard:

- 6 egg yolks
- 1 cup (240 ml) unsweetened almond or cashew milk, divided
- ½ cup (100 g/3.5 oz) granulated erythritol or Swerve
- ½ teaspoon vanilla powder, or 1 to 2 teaspoons sugar-free vanilla extract

Muffins:

- 1 tablespoon (15 ml) virgin coconut oil or ghee
- 6 large eggs, separated
- 1 cup (240 ml) unsweetened almond milk
- ½ cup (100 g/3.5 oz) granulated erythritol or Swerve
- 1 teaspoon vanilla powder, or 1 tablespoon sugar-free vanilla extract
- 1½ cups (150 g/5.3 oz) almond flour
- ½ cup (64 g/2.3 oz) ground chia seeds
- ¼ cup (25 g/0.9 oz) collagen powder (see page 31 for alternatives)
- ½ cup (43 g/1.5 oz) cacao powder
- ¾ teaspoon baking soda
- 1½ teaspoons cream of tartar or apple cider vinegar

TO MAKE THE CUSTARD: Place the egg yolks in a bowl and add ¼ cup (60 ml) of the almond milk and whisk until frothy. Pour the remaining ¾ cup (180 ml) almond milk into a saucepan and add the erythritol. Heat over medium heat, stirring until the sweetener has dissolved. Once boiling, slowly pour the hot milk into the egg yolks, whisking continuously to avoid scrambling (if you accidently scramble the eggs, process in a blender until smooth). Pour the mixture back into the saucepan and continue cooking over low heat, whisking continuously until the mixture thickens considerably. Remove from the heat, pour the custard into a bowl, and mix in the vanilla powder. Cover with plastic wrap, pressing it onto the surface of the custard to prevent a skin from forming on top. Let the custard cool completely.

TO MAKE THE MUFFINS: Preheat the oven to 300°F (150°C, or gas mark 2). Grease a muffin pan with the coconut oil. You will need three bowls. In the first bowl, combine the egg yolks, almond milk, erythritol, and vanilla (if using liquid extract). In the second bowl, combine the almond flour, ground chia seeds, collagen powder, cacao powder, vanilla (if using powder), and baking soda. In the third bowl, beat the egg whites with the cream of tartar until they form soft peaks. Add the dry ingredients to the egg yolk mixture, and combine well. Then stir about a third of the whipped egg whites into the batter to lighten it. Finally, gently fold in the remaining egg whites until well combined. Use a ⅓-cup (80 g) measuring cup to scoop the mixture into the muffin pan (you should end up with 18 muffins). Place in the oven and bake for 25 to 30 minutes until set. Let cool completely before decorating.

NUTRITION FACTS PER SERVING (CUPCAKE):
Total carbs: 5.5 g / Fiber: 2.9 g / Net carbs: 2.6 g / Protein: 7.5 g / Fat: 28 g / Calories: 293 kcal
Macronutrient ratio: Calories from carbs (4%), protein (10%), fat (86%)

Frosting:

1¾ cups (400 g/14.1 oz) unsalted
butter, softened at room
temperature
Pinch of salt
Optional: stevia drops or powdered
erythritol or Swerve

TO MAKE THE FROSTING: Use a hand mixer to beat the softened butter. Add the cooled custard, 1 tablespoon (15 ml) at a time, mixing constantly until smooth and creamy. Add a pinch of salt and sweetener if desired. Spoon the frosting into a piping bag and decorate each muffin with about 1.4 ounces (40 g) of the frosting. Refrigerate frosted cupcakes in an airtight container for up to 4 days. Both unfrosted cupcakes and the frosting can be refrigerated in separate airtight containers for up to 1 week, or frozen for up to 3 months. (Allow the buttercream to come to room temperature before frosting and serving.)

Halva Stacks

MAKES: 25 fat bombs
HANDS-ON TIME: 15 minutes
OVERALL TIME: 15 minutes + chilling

Halva is made from tahini, or sesame seed paste. I love it, but it's usually high in sugar. Not this keto version, though! These bite-size halva bars are sweet, nutty, and so easy to make—and, thanks to the added collagen, they'll curb your cravings and help you stay full for longer.

3 cups (750 g/1.65 lb) tahini (or use a cup each of each black, dark, and light tahini to create a layered effect)

1½ cups (150 g/5.3 oz) collagen powder (see page 31 for alternatives)

9 tablespoons (122 g/4.3 oz) virgin coconut oil

¾ cup (120 g/4.2 oz) powdered erythritol or Swerve

1½ teaspoons vanilla powder

1½ teaspoons ground cinnamon

Pinch of salt

Pour away any excess oil from the tahini (the oil would prevent the bars from solidifying). To create the three-layer effect, scoop the black, dark, and light tahini pastes into three separate bowls. Into each bowl, add a third of the remaining ingredients: ½ cup (50 g/1.8 oz) collagen powder, 3 tablespoons (45 ml) coconut oil, ¼ cup (40 g/1.4 oz) powdered erythritol, ½ teaspoon vanilla powder, ½ teaspoon cinnamon, and a pinch of salt. Mix until well combined. Transfer the black tahini "dough" to an 8 x 8-inch (20 x 20-cm) parchment-lined pan or a silicone pan. With a spatula, spread the dough evenly into the pan. Place in the freezer for 5 to 10 minutes to set, then top with the dark tahini dough, spread, and return to the freezer. Repeat for the light tahini layer, and place in the fridge for about an hour to set before slicing into 25 bites (5 rows by 5 columns) If you're using just one type of tahini, simply mix all the ingredients, spread evenly in the pan, and refrigerate before slicing. Keep refrigerated for up to 1 week, or freeze for up to 3 months.

NUTRITION FACTS PER SERVING (1 FAT BOMB):
Total carbs: 6.8 g / Fiber: 2.9 g / Net carbs: 3.9 g / Protein: 10.2 g / Fat: 21 g / Calories: 243 kcal
Macronutrient ratio: Calories from carbs (6%), protein (17%), fat (77%)

No-Churn Lemon & Raspberry Ice Cream

MAKES: 10 servings
HANDS-ON TIME: 10 minutes
OVERALL TIME: 4 to 5 hours

I'm a huge fan of no-fuss, no-churn ice cream, even though I have an ice cream maker. It's so much simpler, and you can use the base recipe to make almost any flavor you can think of. This summery lemon and raspberry variation is one of my favorites, but the options are endless!

Basic Ice Cream:

4 large eggs, separated

¼ teaspoon cream of tartar or apple cider vinegar

½ cup (80 g/2.8 oz) powdered erythritol or Swerve

1¼ cups (300 ml) heavy whipping cream or coconut cream (see page 73)

1 tablespoon (15 ml) sugar-free vanilla extract or 1 teaspoon vanilla powder

Topping:

1 cup (240 ml) Keto Lemon Curd (page 189), chilled

1¼ cups (154 g/5.4 oz) raspberries, fresh or frozen

TO MAKE THE ICE CREAM: Whisk the egg whites with the cream of tartar in a large bowl. As the egg whites thicken, slowly add the powdered erythritol. Continue to whisk until stiff peaks form.

In another bowl, whisk the cream until soft peaks form when the whisk is removed. (Be careful not to over-whisk the cream.) In a third bowl, mix the egg yolks with the vanilla extract or vanilla powder (or a combination of the two). Slowly fold the whisked egg whites into the whipped cream. Then add the egg yolk mixture, and gently fold in with a spatula until well combined.

TO MAKE THE TOPPING: Place the mixture in a freezer-safe container and use a spoon to swirl the lemon curd through it. Top with the raspberries, letting them sink into the mixture. Freeze for at least 3 to 4 hours, or until set. (For better portion control, divide the ice cream among eight 1-cup [240 ml] containers, filling them three-fourths of the way, and store in the freezer for up to 6 months.) Let the ice cream sit at room temperature for 10 to 15 minutes before serving.

NOTE: Create your own flavor variations by adding blackberries, blueberries, or strawberries to the Basic Ice Cream recipe. Or try making chocolate ice cream by gently folding in ⅓ cup (29 g/1 oz) cacao powder.

NUTRITION FACTS PER SERVING (ABOUT 1 CUP/100 G/3.5 OZ):
Total carbs: 4.4 g / Fiber: 1.2 g / Net carbs: 3.2 g / Protein: 4.2 g / Fat: 18.8 g / Calories: 207 kcal
Macronutrient ratio: Calories from carbs (7%), protein (8%), fat (85%)

Mexican Chocolate Fudgesicles

MAKES: 10 fudgesicles
HANDS-ON TIME: 20 minutes
OVERALL TIME: 4 to 5 hours

These rich, chocolaty, dairy-free popsicles are sure to slay even the most stubborn chocolate craving. They take just twenty minutes to whip up, but they're insanely delicious and so healthy: one popsicle covers almost a quarter of your daily magnesium and potassium needs.

Fudgesicles:

- 2 cans (800 ml/27 fl oz total) coconut milk
- 3 ounces (85 g) unsweetened chocolate, or dark chocolate with at least 85% cocoa solids
- ¼ cup (22 g/0.8 oz) cacao powder
- ¾ cup (120 g/4.2 oz) powdered erythritol or Swerve
- 1 teaspoon vanilla powder, or 2 to 3 teaspoons sugar-free vanilla extract
- 2 teaspoons (4 g/0.2 oz) ground cinnamon
- ½ teaspoon ground nutmeg
- ¼ teaspoon salt
- ⅛ teaspoon cayenne pepper
- Optional: liquid stevia to taste

Chocolate Drizzle:

- 2 ounces (57 g) 90% dark chocolate (or dark chocolate with at least 85% cocoa solids)
- 2 tablespoons (30 ml) melted virgin coconut oil
- Optional: unsweetened shredded coconut, or roughly chopped nuts such almonds, hazelnuts, or pecans

TO MAKE THE FUDGESICLES: Add the coconut milk to a saucepan. Bring to a simmer over medium heat. Remove from the heat, add the unsweetened chocolate, and let it melt. Add the cocoa powder, erythritol, vanilla, cinnamon, nutmeg, salt, and cayenne pepper. Mix until well combined. Set aside to cool to room temperature. When cool, taste and stir in liquid stevia if you prefer more sweetness. Pour into popsicle molds (about ⅓ cup/80 ml each). Add popsicle sticks and freeze for 3 to 4 hours.

TO MAKE THE DRIZZLE: When the popsicles are set, melt the dark chocolate and coconut oil in a saucepan or a microwave. Let it cool slightly (the drizzle shouldn't be too hot). To easily remove the popsicles from the molds, fill a saucepan as tall as the popsicles with warm (but not hot) water and dip the popsicle molds in for 15 to 20 seconds. Return the popsicles to the freezer for 5 to 10 minutes before drizzling. Optionally, sprinkle each with your preferred topping before the drizzle hardens. Serve immediately, or freeze for up to 6 months.

NOTE: Want to make these popsicles extra nutritious? Simply substitute 1 large (200 g/7.1 oz) avocado for ½ can (200 ml/6.7 fl oz) coconut milk and blend it with the cooled fudgesicle mixture before pouring it into the popsicle molds. Avocado, which is high in heart-healthy monounsaturated fats and potassium, pairs perfectly with chocolate. And it has a neutral taste, so it blends into the fudgesicle mixture seamlessly. You won't even know it's there—even if you're a picky eater!

NUTRITION FACTS PER SERVING (1 POPSICLE):
Total carbs: 7.8 g / Fiber: 2.6 g / Net carbs: 5.2 g / Protein: 3.8 g / Fat: 27.3 g / Calories: 273 kcal
Macronutrient ratio: Calories from carbs (7%), protein (5%), fat (88%)

References

Accurso, A., R. K. Bernstein, et al. "Dietary carbohydrate restriction in type 2 diabetes mellitus and metabolic syndrome: time for a critical appraisal." *Nutrition & Metabolism*, 2008. www.ncbi.nlm.nih.gov/pmc/articles/PMC1204764

Alirezaei, M., et al. "Short-term fasting induces profound neuronal autophagy." *Autophagy*, 2010. www.ncbi.nlm.nih.gov/pmc/articles/PMC3106288

Anderson, R. M., and R. Weindruch. "Metabolic reprogramming, caloric restriction and aging." *Trends in Endocrinology and Metabolism*, 2011. www.ncbi.nlm.nih.gov/pmc/articles/PMC2831168

Bisschop, P. H., et al. "The Effects of Carbohydrate Variation in Isocaloric Diets on Glycogenolysis and Gluconeogenesis in Healthy Men." *The Journal of Clinical Endocrinology & Metabolism*, 2000. academic.oup.com/jcem/article-lookup/doi/10.1210/jcem.85.5.6573

Bordoni, A., et al. "Dairy products and inflammation: A review of the clinical evidence." *Clinical Reviews in Food Science and Nutrition*, 2015. www.tandfonline.com/doi/full/10.1080/10408398.2014.967385

Boutcher, Stephen H. "High-intensity intermittent exercise and fat loss." *Journal of Obesity*, 2011. www.ncbi.nlm.nih.gov/pmc/articles/PMC2991639

Bronwen, M., et al. "Caloric restriction and intermittent fasting: Two potential diets for successful brain aging." *Aging Research Reviews*, 2006. www.sciencedirect.com/science/article/pii/S1568163706000523

Daley, C. A., et al. "A review of fatty acid profiles and antioxidant content in grass-fed and grain-fed beef." *Nutrition Journal*, 2010. nutritionj.biomedcentral.com/articles/10.1186/1475-2891-9-10

De Souza, Russell J., et al. "Intake of saturated and trans unsaturated fatty acids and risk of all cause mortality, cardiovascular disease, and type 2 diabetes: systematic review and meta-analysis of observational studies." *British Medical Journal*, 2015. https://www.ncbi.nlm.nih.gov/pmc/articles/PMC4532752

den Besten, Gijs, et al. "The role of short-chain fatty acids in the interplay between diet, gut microbiota, and host energy metabolism." *The Journal of Lipid Research*, 2013. www.ncbi.nlm.nih.gov/pmc/articles/PMC3735932

Flower, G., H. Fritz, et al. "Flax and Breast Cancer: A Systematic Review." *Integrative Cancer Therapies*, 2014. www.ncbi.nlm.nih.gov/pubmed/24013641

Foster, G. D., Ph.D., et al. "A Randomized Trial of a Low-Carbohydrate Diet for Obesity." *New England Journal of Medicine*, 2003. www.nejm.org/doi/full/10.1056/NEJMoa022207

Harvie, M. N., et al. "The effects of intermittent or continuous energy restriction on weight loss and metabolic disease risk markers: a randomized trial in young overweight women." *International Journal of Obesity*, 2011. www.ncbi.nlm.nih.gov/pubmed/20921964

Holt, S. H., et al. "An insulin index of foods: the insulin demand generated by 1000-kJ portions of common foods." *The American Journal of Clinical Nutrition*, 1997. ajcn.nutrition.org/content/66/5/1264.abstract

Kaplan, N. M. "The deadly quartet: upper-body obesity, glucose intolerance, hypertriglyceridemia, and hypertension." *Archives of Internal Medicine*, 1989. www.ncbi.nlm.nih.gov/pubmed/2662932

Kasubuchi, Mayu et al. "Dietary gut microbial metabolites, short-chain fatty acids, and host metabolic regulation." *Nutrients*, 2015. www.ncbi.nlm.nih.gov/pmc/articles/PMC4425176

Morrison, Douglas J., and Tom Preston. "Formation of short-chain fatty acids by the gut microbiota and their impact on human metabolism." *Gut Microbes*, 2016. www.ncbi.nlm.nih.gov/pmc/articles/PMC4939913

Mullington, J. M., et al. "Cardiovascular, inflammatory and metabolic consequences of sleep deprivation." *Progress in Cardiovascular Diseases*, 2012. www.ncbi.nlm.nih.gov/pmc/articles/PMC3403737

Reaven, G. M. "Relationships among insulin resistance, type 2 diabetes, essential hypertension, and cardiovascular disease: similarities and differences." *Journal of Clinical Hypertension*, 2011. www.ncbi.nlm.nih.gov/pubmed/21466618

Samaha, F. F., et al. "A low-carbohydrate as compared with a low-fat diet in severe obesity." *New England Journal of Medicine*, 2003. www.nejm.org/doi/full/10.1056/NEJMoa022207

Santos, F. L., et al. "Systematic review and meta-analysis of clinical trials of the effects of low carbohydrate diets on cardiovascular risk factors." *Obesity Reviews*, 2012. www.ncbi.nlm.nih.gov/pubmed/22905670

Thorning, T. K., A. Raben, et al. "Milk and dairy products: good or bad for human health? An assessment of the totality of scientific evidence." *Food & Nutrition Research*, 2016. www.ncbi.nlm.nih.gov/pubmed/27882862

USDA National Nutrient Database (ndb.nal.usda.gov)

Volek, Jeff and Stephen Phinney. *The Art and Science of Low Carbohydrate Living*. Beyond Obesity, 2011.

Volek, Jeff and Stephen Phinney. *The Art and Science of Low Carbohydrate Performance*. Beyond Obesity, 2012.

Volek, J. S., et al. "Comparison of a very low-carbohydrate and low-fat diet on fasting lipids, LDL subclasses, insulin resistance, and postprandial lipemic responses in overweight women." *Journal of the American College of Nutrition*, 2004. www.ncbi.nlm.nih.gov/pubmed/15047685

Whigham L. D., et al., "Efficacy of conjugated linoleic acid for reducing fat mass: a meta-analysis in humans." *The American Journal of Clinical Nutrition*, 2007. www.ncbi.nlm.nih.gov/pubmed/17490954

About the Author

Martina Slajerova is a health and food blogger living in the United Kingdom. She holds a degree in economics and worked in auditing, but has always been passionate about nutrition and healthy living. Martina loves food, science, photography, and creating new recipes. She is a firm believer in low-carb living and regular exercise. As a science geek, she bases her views on valid research and has firsthand experience of what it means to be on a low-carb diet. Both are reflected on her blog, in her KetoDiet apps, and in this book.

The KetoDiet is an ongoing project she started with her partner in 2012 and includes *The KetoDiet Cookbook*, *Sweet and Savory Fat Bombs*, *Quick Keto Meals in 30 Minutes or Less*, *Keto Slow Cooker & One-Pot Meals*, and the KetoDiet apps for the iPad and iPhone (www.ketodietapp.com). When creating recipes, she doesn't focus on just the carb content: you won't find any processed foods, unhealthy vegetable oils, or artificial sweeteners in her recipes.

This book and the KetoDiet apps are for people who follow a healthy low-carb lifestyle. Martina's mission is to help you reach your goals, whether it's your dream weight or simply eating healthy food. You can find even more low-carb recipes, diet plans, and information about the keto diet on her blog: www.ketodietapp.com/blog.

Acknowledgments

I'd like to thank the amazing team at Fair Winds Press who put so much hard work into my cookbooks. It's been an absolute pleasure working with you! Special thanks to Jill Alexander, Renae Haines, Heather Godin, Lydia Jopp, Jenna Patton, and Megan Buckley.

Index

almonds
    Keto Pad Thai, 163
    Mexican Chocolate Fudgesicles, 202
    Pavlova Lemon Curd Sandwiches, 190
arugula
    Avocado-Pesto Sauce, 135
    Mackerel Fat Stacks, 127
    Spicy Chorizo Cloud Eggs, 53
    Spicy Hollandaise Sauce, 67
    Spinach & Blue Cheese Roll-Ups, 78
    Summer Asparagus & Halloumi Salad, 104
    Tomato & Feta Bruschetta, 82
asparagus
    Crispy Five-Spice Duck Breasts, 156
    Pork Medallions with Asparagus and
        Hollandaise, 176
    Spicy Hollandaise Sauce, 67
avocados
    Abundance Breakfast Bowls, 69
    Avocado-Feta Salsa, 126
    Avocado-Pesto Sauce, 135
    Avocado Salsa Verde, 173
    Avocado-Stuffed Power Balls, 120
    Bacon-Wrapped Beef Patties with
        "Chimiole," 124
    Bacon-Wrapped Jalapeño Poppers
        (Guacamole Filling), 76
    California Sushi Wraps, 128
    Carne Asada Salad, 100
    Cheesy Spinach Pancakes, 52
    Cheesy Waffle Stacks, 59
    Chilled Avocado-Coconut Soup, 97
    Chimiole, 124
    The Easiest Cobb Salad, 107
    Egg-Avocado Salad Sandwich, 118
    Green Skillet Eggs, 60
    Green Smoothie, 187
    Guacamole Deviled Eggs, 77
    Mackerel Fat Stacks, 127
    Mexican Pockets, 117
    Old Bay Salad, 101
    Quick Guacamole, 59
    Salmon & Cream Cheese Unwich, 114
    Sausage & Brussels Sprout Hash, 63
    Spicy Chorizo Cloud Eggs, 53
    Spicy Hollandaise Sauce, 67
    Summer Asparagus & Halloumi Salad, 104

bacon
    Bacon & Cheese Butter, 44
    Bacon-Wrapped Beef Patties with
        "Chimiole," 124
    Bacon-Wrapped Jalapeño Poppers
        (Cheese Filling), 76
    Bacon-Wrapped Jalapeño Poppers
        (Guacamole Filling), 76
    Bacon-Wrapped Monkfish with Creamed
        Spinach, 144
    BLT Sandwich, 118
    Bubble & Squeak Breakfast Bake, 66
    Caesar Salad with Poached Egg, 103
    Cheesy Spinach Pancakes, 52
    Club Unwich, 114
    crisping methods, 41
    Crispy Cinnamon Waffles, 72
    The Easiest Cobb Salad, 107
    Induction Carbonara, 174
    Pork Medallions with Asparagus and
        Hollandaise, 176

Sausage & Brussels Sprout Hash, 63
Sautéed Chicken Livers with Creamy
    Mash, 160
Wedge Salad with Blue Cheese Dressing,
    109
beef chuck roast, for Thai Shredded Beef
    Bowls, 175
beef flank steak
    Carne Asada Salad, 100
    Steak Fajitas with Avocado Salsa Verde,
        173
beef, ground
    Avocado-Stuffed Power Balls, 120
    Bacon-Wrapped Beef Patties with
        "Chimiole," 124
    Breakfast Chili Bowls, 54
    Cheese-Stuffed Greek Bifteki, 182
    Induction Burger Stacks, 169
    Salisbury Steak with Quick Mash, 166
beef skirt steak
    Carne Asada Salad, 100
    The Perfect Skirt Steak, 170
    Steak Fajitas with Avocado Salsa Verde,
        173
blackberries, for PB & Jelly Chia Parfaits, 70
blue cheese
    Blue Cheese Dressing, 109
    Brie Egg Muffins, 57
    Buffalo Deviled Eggs, 77
    The Easiest Cobb Salad, 107
    Spinach & Blue Cheese Roll-Ups, 78
    Three-Cheese Crustless Mini Quiches, 119
    Walnut & Blue Cheese Butter, 44
    Wedge Salad with Blue Cheese Dressing,
        109
bok choy, for Salmon Ramen, 93
bone broth
    Bone Broth, 42
    Irish Pork Pie, 179
    Pork Chops with Mushroom & Mustard
        Sauce, 178
Brie cheese, for Brie Egg Muffins, 57
broccoli
    Easy Breakfast Italian Bake, 64
    Pork Chops with Mushroom & Mustard
        Sauce, 178
    Scandinavian Fish Tray Bake, 143
    Superfood Kale Slaw, 125
    Thai Shredded Beef Bowls, 175
broccolini
    Mediterranean Chicken Tray Bake, 154
    Thai Shredded Beef Bowls, 175
Brussels sprouts
    Bubble & Squeak Breakfast Bake, 66
    Sausage & Brussels Sprout Hash, 63
butters, savory, 44
butters, sweet, 47
cabbage
    Bubble & Squeak Breakfast Bake, 66
    Irish Pork Pie, 179
    Keto Pad Thai, 163
    Superfood Kale Slaw, 125
carbohydrates, 13–15
cauliflower
    Bubble & Squeak Breakfast Bake, 66
    Butter-Stuffed Spatchcock Chicken, 148
    Cream of Mushroom Soup, 90
    Harissa Skillet Chicken, 152
    Irish Pork Pie, 179

Pan-Fried Salmon with Superfood Mash,
    147
Salisbury Steak with Quick Mash, 166
Sautéed Chicken Livers with Creamy
    Mash, 160
cauliflower rice
    Bibimbap Veggie Bowl, 139
    Butter Chicken, 151
    Cauliflower-Chard Rice, 120
    Cauliflower Rice, 40–41
    Cheesy Waffle Stacks, 59
    Chicken Meatball Pho, 98
    Chicken Satay with Superfood Tabbouleh,
        164–165
    Lamb, Coconut, and Okra Curry, 183
    Masala Cauli-Rice with Grilled Halloumi,
        136
celery
    Nordic Salad, 108
    Old Bay Salad, 101
chard
    Bibimbap Veggie Bowl, 139
    Brie Egg Muffins, 57
Cheddar cheese
    Bacon & Cheese Butter, 44
    Bacon-Wrapped Jalapeño Poppers
        (Cheese Filling), 76
    Brie Egg Muffins, 57
    Carne Asada Salad, 100
    Ham & Cheese Sandwich, 118
    Induction Burger Stacks, 169
    Jalapeño & Cheese Muffins, 65
    Quick Tuna Melt Pockets, 116
    Spicy Chorizo Cloud Eggs, 53
chicken breasts
    Butter Chicken, 151
    Chicken Parmesan Casserole, 157
    Chicken Piccata, 159
    Chicken Satay with Superfood Tabbouleh,
        164–165
    The Easiest Cobb Salad, 107
    Mexican Chicken Bowls, 126
chicken, ground, for Chicken Meatball Pho, 98
chicken livers, for Sautéed Chicken Livers
    with Creamy Mash, 160
chicken thighs
    Caesar Salad with Poached Egg, 103
    Harissa Skillet Chicken, 152
    Keto Pad Thai, 163
    Mediterranean Chicken Tray Bake, 154
chicken, whole, for Butter-Stuffed
    Spatchcock Chicken, 148
chicken wings, for Crispy Ranch Chicken
    Wings, 81
chocolate
    Keto Power Bars, 129
    Mexican Chocolate Fudgesicles, 202
    Paradise Squares, 192
coconut
    Keto Pad Thai, 163
    Mexican Chocolate Fudgesicles, 202
    Paradise Squares, 192
    Pavlova Lemon Curd Sandwiches, 190
collard greens
    Anti-Inflammatory Egg Drop Soup, 94
    Green Skillet Eggs, 60
    Taverna-Style Greek Butterflied Sea Bass,
        140
constipation, 11

crabmeat
    California Crab Cakes, 67
    Old Bay Salad, 101
cream cheese
    Cheese-Stuffed Greek Bifteki, 182
    Chocolate Cheesecake, 191
    Horseradish & Pickle Roll-Ups, 79
    Quick Tuna Melt Pockets, 116
    Salmon & Cream Cheese Unwich, 114
    Spinach & Blue Cheese Roll-Ups, 78
    Vanilla Cheesecake, 191
cucumber
    Abundance Breakfast Bowls, 69
    California Sushi Wraps, 128
    Chicken Satay with Superfood Tabbouleh,
        164–165
    Chilled Avocado-Coconut Soup, 97
    Cucumber Salad, 181
    The Easiest Cobb Salad, 107
    Electrolyte Agua fresca, 186
    Golden Sardine & Caramelized Onion Dip,
        83
    Greek Keftedes Bowls, 123
    Mackerel Fat Stacks, 127
    Summer Asparagus & Halloumi Salad, 104
custard, for Chocolate Cupcakes with German
    Buttercream, 198–199

devilled eggs
    Buffalo Deviled Eggs, 77
    Guacamole Deviled Eggs, 77
duck breasts, for Crispy Five-Spice Duck
    Breasts, 156

eggplant
    Harissa Skillet Chicken, 152
    Vegetable Rose Pie, 130
eggs
    Abundance Breakfast Bowls, 69
    Anti-Inflammatory Egg Drop Soup, 94
    Bibimbap Veggie Bowl, 139
    boiling, 42
    Brie Egg Muffins, 57
    Bubble & Squeak Breakfast Bake, 66
    Buffalo Deviled Eggs, 77
    Caesar Salad with Poached Egg, 103
    California Crab Cakes, 67
    California Sushi Wraps, 128
    Cheese-Stuffed Greek Bifteki, 182
    Cheesy Spinach Pancakes, 52
    Cheesy Waffle Stacks, 59
    Chicken Meatball Pho, 98
    Chocolate Cheesecake, 191
    Chocolate Cupcakes with German
        Buttercream, 198–199
    Chocolate Soufflé Pancake with Pumpkin
        Pie Swirl, 73
    Club Unwich, 114
    Crispy Cinnamon Waffles, 72
    Czech Butter Cake, 195
    The Easiest Cobb Salad, 107
    Egg-Avocado Salad Sandwich, 118
    Garlic & Herb Focaccia, 48
    Greek Keftedes Bowls, 123
    Greek Omelet, 62
    Green Skillet Eggs, 60
    Gremolata Dressing, 153
    Guacamole Deviled Eggs, 77
    Induction Carbonara, 174
    Jalapeño & Cheese Muffins, 65
    Keto Lemon Curd, 189
    Keto Pad Thai, 163
    Mushroom Stroganoff, 134
    No-Churn Lemon & Raspberry Ice Cream,
        201

Pizza Dutch Baby, 56
poaching, 42
Pork Medallions with Asparagus and
    Hollandaise, 176
Salisbury Steak with Quick Mash, 166
Sausage & Brussels Sprout Hash, 63
Sausage-Zucchini Egg Muffins, 57
Sautéed Chicken Livers with Creamy Mash,
    160
Spicy Chorizo Cloud Eggs, 53
Spicy Hollandaise Sauce, 67
Summer Asparagus & Halloumi Salad, 104
Three-Cheese Crustless Mini Quiches, 119
Tiramisu Crepe Cake, 196
Vanilla Cheesecake, 191
Vegetable Rose Pie, 130
Zoodles & Eggs, 135
erythritol, 21

fats, 18, 19
feta cheese
    Avocado-Feta Salsa, 126
    Cheese-Stuffed Greek Bifteki, 182
    Chilled Avocado-Coconut Soup, 97
    Cucumber Salad, 181
    Greek Keftedes Bowls, 123
    Greek Omelet, 62
    Greek-Style Salad, 182
    Three-Cheese Crustless Mini Quiches, 119
    Tomato & Feta Bruschetta, 82
    Tyrokafteri (Spicy Greek Cheese & Pepper
        Dip), 87
fish, anchovies
    MCT Salad Dressing, 103
    Salty Anchovy Butter, 44
fish, herring, for Nordic Salad, 108
fish, mackerel
    Mackerel Fat Stacks, 127
    Nordic Salad, 108
fish, mahimahi, for Buttered Mahimahi with
    Green Beans, 142
fish, monkfish, for Bacon-Wrapped Monkfish
    with Creamed Spinach, 144
fish, salmon
    California Sushi Wraps, 128
    Nordic Salad, 108
    Pan-Fried Salmon with Superfood Mash, 147
    Salmon & Cream Cheese Unwich, 114
    Salmon Ramen, 93
    Scandinavian Fish Tray Bake, 143
fish, sardines
    Golden Sardine & Caramelized Onion Dip,
        160
    Nordic Salad, 108
fish sauce
    Keto Pad Thai, 163
    Thai Shredded Beef Bowls, 175
fish, sea bass, for Taverna-Style Greek
    Butterflied Sea Bass, 140
fish, tuna, for Quick Tuna Melt Pockets, 116
flax
    Garlic & Herb Focaccia, 48
    lignans, 23
    Mexican Pockets, 117
    Multiseed Keto Crackers, 84
focaccia
    BLT Sandwich, 118
    Caprese Sandwich, 118
    Chilled Avocado-Coconut Soup, 97
    Egg-Avocado Salad Sandwich, 118
    Garlic & Herb Focaccia, 48
    Golden Sardine & Caramelized Onion Dip,
        83
    Ham & Cheese Sandwich, 118
    Macadamia Cheese Dip, 86

Tomato & Feta Bruschetta, 82
Tyrokafteri (Spicy Greek Cheese & Pepper
    Dip), 87
fontina cheese, for Chicken Parmesan
    Casserole, 157

galangal, for Thai Shredded Beef Bowls, 175
garlic
    Anti-Inflammatory Egg Drop Soup, 94
    Avocado-Feta Salsa, 126
    Avocado-Pesto Sauce, 135
    Avocado-Stuffed Power Balls, 120
    Bacon-Wrapped Beef Patties with
        "Chimiole," 124
    Bacon-Wrapped Jalapeño Poppers
        (Guacamole Filling), 76
    Bibimbap Veggie Bowl, 139
    Blue Cheese Dressing, 109
    Breakfast Chili Bowls, 54
    Brie Egg Muffins, 57
    Bubble & Squeak Breakfast Bake, 66
    Buffalo Deviled Eggs, 77
    Butter Chicken, 151
    Cheese-Stuffed Greek Bifteki, 182
    Cheesy Waffle Stacks, 59
    Chicken Meatball Pho, 98
    Chicken Piccata, 159
    Chilled Avocado-Coconut Soup, 97
    Cream of Mushroom Soup, 90
    Crispy Five-Spice Duck Breasts, 156
    Garlic & Herb Butter, 44
    Garlic & Herb Focaccia, 48
    Greek Keftedes Bowls, 123
    Greek Omelet, 62
    Greek-Style Salad, 182
    Green Skillet Eggs, 60
    Gremolata Dressing, 153
    Irish Pork Pie, 179
    Keto Pad Thai, 163
    Lamb, Coconut, and Okra Curry, 183
    Lemon & Herb Butter, 44
    Macadamia Cheese Dip, 86
    Masala Cauli-Rice with Grilled Halloumi, 136
    MCT Salad Dressing, 103
    Mushroom Stroganoff, 134
    Pan-Fried Salmon with Superfood Mash, 147
    Pickled Red Onion, 181
    Quick Guacamole, 59
    Ranch Dressing, 81
    Salty Anchovy Butter, 44
    Satay Dip, 164–165
    Sautéed Chicken Livers with Creamy Mash,
        160
    Spicy Cilantro-Lime Vinaigrette, 100
    Steak Fajitas with Avocado Salsa Verde, 173
    Taverna-Style Greek Butterflied Sea Bass,
        140
    Thai Shredded Beef Bowls, 175
    Three-Cheese Crustless Mini Quiches, 119
    Turkey Meatballs with Sautéed Kale &
        Gremolata Dressing, 153
    Zingy Fennel & Squid Salad, 110
goat cheese, for Three-Cheese Crustless Mini
    Quiches, 119
Gouda cheese, for Chicken Parmesan
    Casserole, 157
green beans
    Buttered Mahimahi with Green Beans, 142
    Chicken Parmesan Casserole, 157
    Greek-Style Salad, 182

Halloumi cheese
    Bibimbap Veggie Bowl, 139
    Masala Cauli-Rice with Grilled Halloumi, 136
    Summer Asparagus & Halloumi Salad, 104

ham
Club Unwich, 114
Ham & Cheese Sandwich, 118
Mozzarella Roll-Ups, 79
Spinach & Blue Cheese Roll-Ups, 78
harissa paste, for Spicy Harissa Butter, 44
horseradish
Horseradish Dressing, 143
Horseradish & Pickle Roll-Ups, 79
Pork Chops with Mushroom & Mustard
Sauce, 178

jalapeño peppers
Bacon-Wrapped Jalapeño Poppers (Cheese
Filling), 76
Bacon-Wrapped Jalapeño Poppers
(Guacamole Filling), 76
Breakfast Chili Bowls, 54
Chilled Avocado-Coconut Soup, 97
Jalapeño & Cheese Muffins, 65
Jalapeño & Lime Butter, 44
Spicy Chorizo Cloud Eggs, 53
Spicy Cilantro-Lime Vinaigrette, 100
Tyrokafteri (Spicy Greek Cheese & Pepper
Dip), 87

kale
Brie Egg Muffins, 57
Cauliflower-Chard Rice, 120
Chicken Satay with Superfood Tabbouleh,
164–165
Pork Chops with Mushroom & Mustard
Sauce, 178
Superfood Kale Slaw, 125
Taverna-Style Greek Butterflied Sea Bass,
140
Turkey Meatballs with Sautéed Kale &
Gremolata Dressing, 153
kelp noodles
Chicken Meatball Pho, 98
Kelp Noodles, 41
Salmon Ramen, 93
ketoacidosis, 10
ketogenic diet
adaptation issues, 11–12
carbohydrates, 13–15
condiments, 20
constipation and, 11
cravings, 12
dairy and, 24
diarrhea and, 12
exercise, 36
fasting, 31–32
fats, 18, 19
fruits, 19
hypoglycemia, 12
induction phase, 9–10
insomnia, 12
introduction to, 8–9
keto adaptation phase, 10–11
keto breath, 12
keto flu, 27
ketone levels, 10, 33–34
legumes, 25
low-carb swaps, 26
maintenance phase, 12–13
nuts and seeds, 22–23, 35
protein, 16–17, 19
supplements, 27–31
sweeteners, 21–22
vegetables, 19
ketosis, 10
kimchi
Abundance Breakfast Bowls, 69
Bibimbap Veggie Bowl, 139

lamb, chopped, for Lamb, Coconut, and Okra
Curry, 183
lamb, ground
Cheese-Stuffed Greek Bifteki, 182
Greek Keftedes Bowls, 123
lamb steaks, for Lamb Steaks with Mint Pesto
and Pickled Onion, 181

macadamia nuts, for Macadamia Cheese
Dip, 86
maple extract
Keto Power Bars, 129
Maple & Pecan Pie Butter, 47
marinara sauce
Caprese Sandwich, 118
Chicken Parmesan Casserole, 157
Easy Breakfast Italian Bake, 64
Marinara Sauce, 43
Pizza Dutch Baby, 56
mascarpone cheese
Creamed Spinach, 144
Tiramisu Crepe Cake, 196
Vegetable Rose Pie, 130
Mexican chorizo
Avocado-Stuffed Power Balls, 120
Mexican Pockets, 117
monk fruit, 22
Monterey Jack cheese, for Club Unwich, 114
mozzarella cheese
Caprese Sandwich, 118
Cheesy Waffle Stacks, 59
Chicken Parmesan Casserole, 157
Chocolate Cheesecake, 191
Easy Breakfast Italian Bake, 64
Mozzarella Roll-Ups, 79
Pizza Dutch Baby, 56
Quick Tuna Melt Pockets, 116
Vanilla Cheesecake, 191
muffins
Brie Egg Muffins, 57
Jalapeño & Cheese Muffins, 65
Sausage-Zucchini Egg Muffins, 57
mushrooms, brown, for Anti-Inflammatory Egg
Drop Soup, 94
mushrooms, oyster, for Salmon Ramen, 93
mushrooms, porcini
Cream of Mushroom Soup, 90
Pork Chops with Mushroom & Mustard
Sauce, 178
mushrooms, portobello, for Mackerel Fat
Stacks, 127
mushrooms, shiitake, for Salmon Ramen, 93
mushrooms, white
Mushroom Stroganoff, 134
Sausage & Brussels Sprout Hash, 63
mushrooms, wild, for Brie Egg Muffins, 57

noodles, shirataki
Chicken Meatball Pho, 98
Keto Pad Thai, 163
Mushroom Stroganoff, 134
recipe, 41
nori sheets, for California Sushi Wraps, 128
nuts and seeds, activating, 42

okra, for Lamb, Coconut, and Okra Curry, 183
olives, black
The Easiest Cobb Salad, 107
Greek Omelet, 62
olives, green
The Easiest Cobb Salad, 107
Greek Omelet, 62
olives, sliced, for Spinach & Blue Cheese
Roll-Ups, 78

onions, red
Avocado-Feta Salsa, 126
Cheese-Stuffed Greek Bifteki, 182
Cucumber Salad, 181
Greek Keftedes Bowls, 123
Greek-Style Salad, 182
Mackerel Fat Stacks, 127
Pickled Red Onion, 181
Scandinavian Fish Tray Bake, 143
Superfood Kale Slaw, 125
Vegetable Salad, 169
Wedge Salad with Blue Cheese Dressing,
109
Zingy Fennel & Squid Salad, 110
onions, spring
Anti-Inflammatory Egg Drop Soup, 94
Bibimbap Veggie Bowl, 139
Buffalo Deviled Eggs, 77
Chicken Satay with Superfood Tabbouleh,
164–165
Chilled Avocado-Coconut Soup, 97
Irish Pork Pie, 179
Keto Pad Thai, 163
Mediterranean Chicken Tray Bake, 154
Old Bay Salad, 101
Quick Tuna Melt Pockets, 116
Ranch Dressing, 81
Salmon Ramen, 93
Thai Shredded Beef Bowls, 175
onions, yellow
Bacon-Wrapped Beef Patties with
"Chimiole," 124
Bacon-Wrapped Jalapeño Poppers
(Guacamole Filling), 76
Breakfast Chili Bowls, 54
Bubble & Squeak Breakfast Bake, 66
Butter Chicken, 151
Cheesy Waffle Stacks, 59
Chicken Meatball Pho, 98
Chicken Piccata, 159
Chilled Avocado-Coconut Soup, 97
Chimiole, 124
Cream of Mushroom Soup, 90
Golden Sardine & Caramelized Onion Dip,
83
Greek Keftedes Bowls, 123
Green Skillet Eggs, 60
Gremolata Dressing, 153
Irish Pork Pie, 179
Lamb, Coconut, and Okra Curry, 183
Masala Cauli-Rice with Grilled Halloumi, 136
Mushroom Stroganoff, 134
Onion Gravy, 166
Pan-Fried Salmon with Superfood Mash, 147
Pork Chops with Mushroom & Mustard
Sauce, 178
Quick Guacamole, 59
Sausage & Brussels Sprout Hash, 63
Sausage-Zucchini Egg Muffins, 57
Sautéed Chicken Livers with Creamy Mash,
160
Steak Fajitas with Avocado Salsa Verde, 173
Thai Shredded Beef Bowls, 175
Three-Cheese Crustless Mini Quiches, 119

Parmesan cheese
Caesar Salad with Poached Egg, 103
Cheesy Spinach Pancakes, 52
Cheesy Waffle Stacks, 59
Chicken Parmesan Casserole, 157
Creamed Spinach, 144
Easy Breakfast Italian Bake, 64
Induction Carbonara, 174
MCT Salad Dressing, 103
Pizza Dutch Baby, 56

Three-Cheese Crustless Mini Quiches, 119
Turkey Nuggets with Kale Slaw and Italian
  Dressing, 125
Vegetable Rose Pie, 130
pecans
  Keto Power Bars, 129
  Maple & Pecan Pie Butter, 47
  Mexican Chocolate Fudgesicles, 202
  Walnut & Blue Cheese Butter, 44
pepperoni, for Spicy Chorizo Cloud Eggs, 53
pickles
  Horseradish & Pickle Roll-Ups, 79
  Tyrokafteri (Spicy Greek Cheese & Pepper
    Dip), 87
pine nuts, for Avocado-Pesto Sauce, 135
poppers
  Bacon-Wrapped Jalapeño Poppers (Cheese
    Filling), 76
  Bacon-Wrapped Jalapeño Poppers
    (Guacamole Filling), 76
poppy seeds, for Multiseed Keto Crackers, 84
pork belly, for Irish Pork Pie, 179
pork chops, for Pork Chops with Mushroom &
    Mustard Sauce, 178
pork, ground, for Avocado-Stuffed Power
    Balls, 120
pork, ham
  Club Unwich, 114
  Ham & Cheese Sandwich, 118
  Mozzarella Roll-Ups, 79
  Spinach & Blue Cheese Roll-Ups, 78
pork loin, for Irish Pork Pie, 179
pork tenderloin, for Pork Medallions with
    Asparagus and Hollandaise, 176
prawns
  Old Bay Salad, 101
  Zingy Fennel & Squid Salad, 110
protein, 16–17, 19
provolone cheese
  Chicken Parmesan Casserole, 157
  Ham & Cheese Sandwich, 118
  Induction Burger Stacks, 169
  Quick Tuna Melt Pockets, 116
pumpkin, for Pumpkin Pie Butter, 47
pumpkin seeds, for Multiseed Keto Crackers,
    84

queso fresco, for Avocado-Feta Salsa, 126

radishes
  Bibimbap Veggie Bowl, 139
  Scandinavian Fish Tray Bake, 143
raspberries, for No-Churn Lemon & Raspberry
    Ice Cream, 201
ricotta cheese
  Bacon-Wrapped Jalapeño Poppers (Cheese
    Filling), 76
  Brie Egg Muffins, 57
  Three-Cheese Crustless Mini Quiches, 119
  Tiramisu Crepe Cake, 196
rutabaga, for Nordic Salad, 108

sauerkraut, for Abundance Breakfast Bowls,
    69
sausage, breakfast, for Abundance Breakfast
    Bowls, 69
sausage, Italian
  Easy Breakfast Italian Bake, 64
  Sausage & Brussels Sprout Hash, 63
sesame seeds
  Abundance Breakfast Bowls, 69
  Bibimbap Veggie Bowl, 139
  California Sushi Wraps, 128
  Multiseed Keto Crackers, 84
  Salmon Ramen, 93

shirataki noodles
  Chicken Meatball Pho, 98
  Induction Carbonara, 174
  Keto Pad Thai, 163
  recipe, 41
shirataki rice
  Butter Chicken, 151
  Lamb, Coconut, and Okra Curry, 183
Spanish chorizo
  Chilled Avocado-Coconut Soup, 97
  Spicy Chorizo Cloud Eggs, 53
spinach
  Abundance Breakfast Bowls, 69
  Anti-Inflammatory Egg Drop Soup, 94
  Avocado-Pesto Sauce, 135
  Bibimbap Veggie Bowl, 139
  Brie Egg Muffins, 57
  Cheesy Spinach Pancakes, 52
  Chicken Piccata, 159
  Chicken Satay with Superfood Tabbouleh,
    164–165
  Creamed Spinach, 144
  The Easiest Cobb Salad, 107
  Greek Omelet, 62
  Green Skillet Eggs, 60
  Green Smoothie, 187
  Mackerel Fat Stacks, 127
  Mushroom Stroganoff, 134
  Pan-Fried Salmon with Superfood Mash, 147
  Spicy Chorizo Cloud Eggs, 53
  Spinach & Blue Cheese Roll-Ups, 78
  Summer Asparagus & Halloumi Salad, 104
  Three-Cheese Crustless Mini Quiches, 119
  Tomato & Feta Bruschetta, 82
  Vegetable Salad, 169
  Zingy Fennel & Squid Salad, 110
squid, for Zingy Fennel & Squid Salad, 110
stevia, 21
strawberries, for Strawberry Cream Soda, 188
sunflower seeds
  Avocado-Pesto Sauce, 135
  Multiseed Keto Crackers, 84
supplements, 27–31
Swiss chard
  Anti-Inflammatory Egg Drop Soup, 94
  Cauliflower-Chard Rice, 120
  Green Skillet Eggs, 60
  Salmon Ramen, 93
  Taverna-Style Greek Butterflied Sea Bass,
    140
  Three-Cheese Crustless Mini Quiches, 119
  Zingy Fennel & Squid Salad, 110
Swiss cheese
  Bacon-Wrapped Jalapeño Poppers (Cheese
    Filling), 76
  Brie Egg Muffins, 57
  Club Unwich, 114
  Vegetable Rose Pie, 130

tahini
  Halva Stacks, 200
  Satay Dip, 164–165
Thai curry paste, for Thai Curry Butter, 44
tomatoes, canned, for Breakfast Chili Bowls,
    54
tomatoes, chopped
  Bacon-Wrapped Beef Patties with "Chimi-
    ole," 124
  Bacon-Wrapped Jalapeño Poppers
    (Guacamole Filling), 76
  Carne Asada Salad, 100
  Chicken Satay with Superfood Tabbouleh,
    164–165
  Chimiole, 124
  The Easiest Cobb Salad, 107

Greek Omelet, 62
Masala Cauli-Rice with Grilled Halloumi, 136
Quick Guacamole, 59
Summer Asparagus & Halloumi Salad, 104
Tomato & Feta Bruschetta, 82
Wedge Salad with Blue Cheese Dressing,
    109
tomatoes, halved
  Avocado-Feta Salsa, 126
  Greek Keftedes Bowls, 123
  Greek-Style Salad, 182
  Induction Burger Stacks, 169
  Mexican Chicken Bowls, 126
  Summer Asparagus & Halloumi Salad, 104
  Vegetable Salad, 169
tomatoes, sliced
  BLT Sandwich, 118
  Caprese Sandwich, 118
  Club Unwich, 114
tomatoes, sun-dried
  Cheesy Spinach Pancakes, 52
  Italian Dressing, 125
  Mozzarella Roll-Ups, 79
turkey, ground, for Gremolata Dressing, 153
turkey legs, for Turkey Nuggets with Kale Slaw
    and Italian Dressing, 125

vinaigrettes
  MCT Balsamic Vinaigrette, 78
  Spicy Cilantro-Lime Vinaigrette, 100

walnuts
  Walnut & Blue Cheese Butter, 44
  Wedge Salad with Blue Cheese Dressing,
    109
watercress
  Avocado-Pesto Sauce, 135
  Mackerel Fat Stacks, 127
  Pan-Fried Salmon with Superfood Mash, 147
  Spicy Chorizo Cloud Eggs, 53
  Summer Asparagus & Halloumi Salad, 104
  Tomato & Feta Bruschetta, 82
wine, for Chicken Piccata, 159

yacon syrup, 22
yogurt
  Butter Chicken, 151
  Greek Keftedes Bowls, 123
  Tyrokafteri (Spicy Greek Cheese & Pepper
    Dip), 87

zucchini
  Abundance Breakfast Bowls, 69
  Breakfast Chili Bowls, 54
  Golden Milk Smoothie, 187
  Green Skillet Eggs, 60
  Induction Carbonara, 174
  Jalapeño & Cheese Muffins, 65
  Mediterranean Chicken Tray Bake, 154
  The Perfect Skirt Steak, 170
  Sausage-Zucchini Egg Muffins, 57
  Scandinavian Fish Tray Bake, 143
  Vegetable Rose Pie, 130
  Zoodles & Eggs, 135
  Zucchini Noodles, 40